D1202863

PLEASE RETURN THIS TEXT TO:

_____

_____

_____

_____

_____

TIME IN

An Introduction to Therapeutic Activity Programming and Facilitation

AUTHOR: **MICHAEL BURNS**

EDITOR: **DENNIS MCDERMOTT**

ILLUSTRATOR: **KARIN BOSMA**

LAYOUT & DESIGN: **DANIELLE ADAMS**

COVER DESIGN: **MATT GARTON**

CHILD CARE PRESS

ISBN 978-0-9697302-1-7

childcarepress.net

Canadian Cataloguing in Publication Data

Burns, Michael, 1948 –

    Time In: An Introduction to Therapeutic Activity Programming and Facilitation
    ISBN 978-0-9697302-1-7
    425 pages
    8 1/2 x 11 inches

Book Design: Danielle Adams
Illustrations by: Karin-Ann Bosma
Cover Design: Matt Garton
Edited by: Dennis McDermott

Published in Canada by Child Care Press
    981 Pembridge Crescent
    Kingston, ON. K7P 1M8
    613·536·0367
    www.childcarepress.net

Printed and bound in Canada by Hignell Press, Winnipeg, Manitoba

THIS TEXT IS DEDICATED TO

DR. JEROME BEKER

(1933-2011)

Whose work in the field is an inspiration to all of us who engage with troubled children, youth, and young adults.

CONTENTS

ACKNOWLEDGEMENTS

First and foremost, this text, and I suspect all the ones that have followed it, would never have happened if it was not for the support and vision of two men—Gerry Fewster and Thom Garfat. Now legends in the field of child and youth care, these two not only supported the writing and completion of the text, they also supported its publication. Thank You Thom and Gerry!

I dedicated this text to the memory of Jerry Beker for many reasons and want to articulate a few. Jerry was always very supportive of my writing from the moment he knew that I had a passion for writing. He looked over most of my work offering suggestions and providing insight. I sent Jerry the original manuscript to Time In in 1993 and asked him to tell me what he thought. Jerry did more than that—he took the time to edit the entire text! Jerry demonstrated his dedication to the field in many ways and I am forever grateful for his contribution to my learning through his editorship of the first academic journal in the field of child and youth care, The Child Care Quarterly. Child and Youth Care has lost one of its founders and leaders, but his influence will continue through my writing and that of many others.

I would also like to acknowledge Dennis McDermott's influence and dedication to my writing and publishing. With this publication, Dennis will have edited and contributed to all my texts. He has been there for me during the struggles and the triumphs, and I suspect he will always be the one to encourage me to push it just a little bit further. I owe you big time Denny!

I am also indebted to all the professors and students who have used Time In over the past 20 years and supported its message. And to all those professionals who worked on its first publication—a big thank you.

This 20th anniversary edition has all new players except for Dennis and me. Danielle Adams, who did an amazing job on The Self in Child and Youth Care: A Celebration is back again with a clear, clean, and decisive style which she has chosen for the look of this text. Danielle also added the illustrations. Adding to her expertise is the major artist on this project, Karin Bosma, who you may remember did the layout and illustrating of Into the Dark Forest: Therapeutic Storytelling. Karin's beautiful style adds life and lyric to the text and makes the reader want to stop and just enjoy the artwork. I did use a couple of sketches from the earlier version of Time In and also one completed by my son, Dan, from my first book Stories in Child Care. The rest is all Karin.

A new contributing artist, Matt Garton designed the cover of the new edition to Time In. I am sure the professionals at the book displays will want to pick it up if only to get a closer look at Matt's illuminating design—Thanks Matt! Another important and recent addition to the team here at Child Care Press is Megan "Eagle Eye" Besner, who has a gift for being able to find a wealth of typos long after my eyes have lost their ability to focus. Megan has worked on my last two books, and her efforts have contributed immensely to the look and accuracy of this latest project.

Finally, I would like to thank my students and the faculty at St. Lawrence College for inspiring me to continue to strive for excellence in teaching and writing in this exciting field of child and youth care.

PREFACE

When we accepted an invitation to write a Preface for this new version of Time In we were immediately confronted with the problem of writing in the first-person plural. Rather than trying to negotiate a list of "we think" statements, we engaged an anonymous and unpaid editor to assume the role of narrator and, if necessary, mediator. As it happened, the secondary role turned out to be redundant. For professional reasons we instructed this mystery scribe to refer to us as 'Garfat' and "Fewster" rather than "Thom and Gerry."

Having had the privilege of providing the Preface for the first version of Time In, Fewster was quick to point out that this new publication is no simple update of the original. It is a comprehensive work in its own right that successfully incorporates the learning of both children and practitioners within the same conceptual and practical framework. Garfat agreed, pointing out that, apart from being an exemplary training manual, this book encourages us to think reflectively about pretty well everything we do in the name of Child and Youth Care.

The two old timers were equally impressed with how 'young' Michael Burns (they like to call him 'Mikey') manages to blend theory and practice without being pretentious or prescriptive. Drawing directly from his own extensive experience in the field, he brings life into the very heart of day-to-day professional practice. His style is sharp, uncluttered and, above all, personal. Unlike so many 'teach-yourself' texts, it's impossible to read this book without feeling a sense of connection with the author - an admirable achievement.

At it's core, the new Time In is still a first class practical training manual crammed with information, ideas and exercises for working with young people, regardless of the particular setting. But this is not just a collection of activities designed to fix or entertain kids. As Garfat said (or was it Fewster) "In Michael's book, kids are always subjects to be cherished and understood, not objects to be tagged and manipulated."

After so many years of practicing, teaching, writing and editing, Fewster and Garfat might be excused for being a little 'Ho-Hum' about new publications in Child and Youth Care - but not in this case. They're not even upset that the author abandoned them in favour of another publisher. On the contrary, they believe that everybody who lives or works with kids would benefit from what Michael Burns has to offer.

Garfat and Fewster have demanded a free copy each in return for not writing this Preface.

Confirmed, edited and approved by Gerry Fewster, Ph.D & Thom Garfat, Ph.D

INTRODUCTION

fun is laughter,
excitement, style
letting go
running wild.
fun is play and play is fun
individually it varies some.
fun is a healthy thing you see
it strengthens hearts
it's trouble free.
it can come out of nothing
that's for sure
fun recycles, fun endures.
take a daily dose of fun
spread it round to everyone
and if you've forgotten how to play
find a child and take a day
lift your heart up to the sun
mimic her
you'll have fun.

Therapeutic activity programming and facilitation is first and foremost about having fun. Therapeutic interventions with children, youth, and young adults need not be tedious, boring, painful, problem-focused, or intrusive. Time In provides another approach—one that focusses on the mentoring and nurturing of children from their earliest years to young adulthood by fun-loving and creative adults. The text refers to these adults as child and youth care professionals, which includes: child and youth workers, early childhood educators, elementary and secondary school teachers, therapeutic and recreational leaders, program coordinators, as well as leaders and volunteers providing activities and/or instruction to children, youth, and young adults.

Time In is a book that provides insight and instruction regarding the programming and facilitation of therapeutic activities in group settings. It is a book about creative play experiences, experiential learning encounters, and cooperative social interaction. Time In is an action-oriented text that allows the reader to participate actively in the learning process. It can be used as a vehicle to stimulate human interaction and as an instrument to promote awareness of the Self and of the other. It attempts to vitalize adults and children; its purpose is to help them to reclaim the vitality that they were born with. Many children and youth, because of the dysfunctional nature of many of our education and childcare practices, are stripped of their vitality and their joy of living. Time In and its facilitation of the play experience can help the child and the adult tap into this source of vitality through its open invitation to the participants to experience life in action. The text has no particular cultural bias in terms of children and youth. Many of the games and activities are from various cultures and their flexibility allows the leader to adapt them to the group's needs.

The games and experiences throughout the text encourage children and youth to value themselves and each other in the context of creative expression. Time In provides the therapeutic activity programmer and facilitator with opportunities to learn and teach healthy group interaction. Its diverse storehouse of games and activities provides experiences for individuals and groups who are at various levels of development and it suggests a wide variety of environments in which to play. It offers the student and the experienced child and youth care professional novel and creative methods to facilitate human interaction.

Children in Pain

Children labelled as atypical, troubled, emotionally disturbed, or psychiatrically disordered are often children that live in unhealthy circumstances that are either beyond their control or their ability to alter. However as a result of their victimization, it is often they who are labelled as having a disorder. The implication of this label or diagnosis places them at the centre or root of the problem. They have a disorder. This perception often leaves parents, educators, and other adults with the notion that the child is the problem. Anglin (2003), in his study of children in residential settings, states that many of these children are merely reacting to the pain in their lives—to the unhealthy, "disordered" circumstances from which they came. These children may be engaged in thinking, feeling, and behaving in a way that perpetuates or supports the unhealthy circumstance, but they are not the cause or the root. Steele and Raider (2009) remind us that traumatized children do not have "disorders," they have conditions as a result of terrifying experiences and/or life situations.

It is critical for the child and youth care professional to appreciate the child's perspective and make every attempt to empower children not "treat" them. Do children have psychiatric disorders? Yes there are such children, who often do require special psychiatric attention. However, they are victims as well—no child has ever asked for a psychiatric disorder. Therapeutic activity programming and facilitation is a child-centered attempt at assisting children who have been exposed to unhealthy circumstances to alter the effects of, and in many cases eliminate them from, their lives.

Therapeutic Activity Programming and Facilitation

Developing and facilitating therapeutic programs with groups of children, adolescents, or young adults is an intricate balance of recognizing and meeting the needs of the individual in conjunction with the needs of the group while focussing on a specific therapeutic theme.

The provision of such programs requires two complementary skills, programming and facilitating. This text differentiates between the programmer and the facilitator although in many cases they are the same person. However the skills are significantly different. Programmers design and develop the therapeutic program and modifying and adapting it to respond to evaluative data; they also coordinate their role with that of the facilitator. Facilitators are responsible for selecting group members, developing therapeutic relationships with each of the members, conducting group activities, performing ongoing evaluations of group interaction and response to the program, and are responsible for the level of safety and emotional wellbeing of each group member. The facilitator also coordinates his/her functioning with that of the programmer.

Therapeutic activity programmers and facilitators must also possess other skills in order to be effective with children, youth, and young adults in pain. They require a solid knowledge of typical and atypical human development, must be well trained in cultural and ethnic diversity, have a solid set of relational skills, and have a thorough appreciation of the therapeutic milieu and its effect on groups. Therapeutic activity programming is not just a pick up game of soccer with the boys in the group home, nor is it an experience that is forced or imposed on an individual or group as part of the "program." It is the careful planning, coordination, and facilitation of a series of activities, especially adapted to the individual participants, that has both pleasurable and therapeutic outcomes as its goal. The programmer must plan and coordinate the individual sessions, and in some cases a series of sessions, in turn the facilitator must be responsive and flexible enough to adapt, change, redirect, and refocus the activity, or series of activities, to meet the here-and-now needs of the participants. It calls upon practitioners to "know" their audience individually and collectively, and react efficiently to changes in this "knowing" over time.

The planning of the activity programs also needs to include the participants. What is therapeutic and pleasurable for one individual or group of individuals may not be for another. Participants assist the programmer in determining what is fun and what is therapeutic for them as individuals and as a group. Participant feedback is essential in developing effective therapeutic programs. Without participants' feedback, both verbal and non-verbal, the programmer is developing activities partially blind, working with only what he or she feels are in the best interests of the individuals and the group.

Finally the ultimate goal of all therapeutic activity programming is about interacting with children, youth, and young adults in a fashion that allows them to find their own rhythm, their point of balance, and their natural point of performance. The human being is constantly trying to achieve homeostasis or equilibrium both internally and externally. This sense of being balanced psychologically, and as a result physically, is sometimes referred to as a state of being centred or grounded. This is not a state of inactivity but a dynamic state that requires interaction and participation, whether internally in the individual or externally within the environment. It is a challenge to individual and group boundaries, encouraging and supporting an appreciation of the full range of experiences, but always returning the participants to that state of balance. This ability to self-regulate, to come back to centre, is critical for all children especially those who have had a life or life experiences that were chaotic, disruptive, traumatic, or unbalanced. Therapeutic activities can provide them with experiences that will assist them to learn how to create and maintain balance in their lives.

Overview of the Text

The text is divided into three sections: Theory, Resources, and Practice. Section A, "Theory," is intended to give the learner the basic theoretical framework for developing, designing, and implementing therapeutic activity play programs with groups of children. It begins by familiarizing the reader with play concepts and highlights the therapeutic benefits of play. Next the learner is introduced to the therapeutic value of the play environment (the therapeutic milieu) and provided with strategies to design an optimum therapeutic milieu as well as instruction on how to improve the existing environment. The third chapter in this section familiarizes the reader with basic therapeutic design methods using a developmental perspective. It lays out for the learner the specifics of planning, designing, sequencing, and evaluating therapeutic play programs. The next chapter introduces the reader to the group play experience; it highlights how group encounters can evolve and develop into healthy, dynamic, inclusive, and therapeutic play experiences. The non-competitive, cooperative play experience is used, in that chapter, as a catalyst to assist the student in developing fully functioning supportive groups. The discussion then moves to a focus on the role of leadership and play facilitation. It addresses leadership qualities and styles and requires the learner to assess their leadership potential. The final chapter in this first section emphasizes the importance of the therapeutic relationship. It asks the learner to examine their motivations for taking on the role of therapeutic facilitator and promotes a self-awareness focus. "Theory" gives the student and novice child and youth care professional the basic knowledge to begin to practice the role of therapeutic activity programmer and facilitator.

Section B, "Resources," contains over 150 games and activities that have been personally tried and tested with over 3,000 children, youth, and young adults. These provide an excellent source of activities to use during field placement practicum and internships. In this section, the first chapter specializes in activities that are bridges from one routine to another. These are the games played with groups while waiting for the bus, in between the last school lesson and recess, or just before mealtime. Bridging activities make transitions smoother—more pleasurable. This chapter also contains activities that anchor or ground children when they are feeling out-of-sorts, having a difficult time, or dealing with a stressful transition, and assists them to gain their equilibrium.

The following chapter in this section is a series of 30 activities that follow the stages of group development. Each activity reflects one of the developmental expectations of one of the four stages of group development. The third chapter in the series provides games for developing leadership within the group. It provides leader and leaderless games to assist the group in becoming more inclusive and adaptive to various environments and group situations. The next chapter focusses in on children who are challenged physically, environmentally, or are otherwise excluded from mainstream programs. These activities are easily adaptable to a wide variety of abilities and special needs. They provide opportunities for programmers and facilitators to "level the playing field" in order to include all participants. The final chapter in the section is specifically for older children, youth, and young adults. It caters specifically to their needs for "group-ness," challenge, teamwork, and the activities are more physically and intellectually sophisticated than some of the previous ones. The resources in this section contain all that is needed for the child and youth care professional to begin to, or continue to, facilitate therapeutic activities with groups of children.

The final section of the text, "Practice," presents the learner with advanced techniques in therapeutic activity programming and introduces the complex and powerful use of games and activities that have the potential to heal and to vitalize. These interventions are more complex and in-depth than the previous games and activities. Students and novice programmers and facilitators will need to have close supervision when initiating these interventions. The first chapter in this section provides the group learner with insight and techniques to assist children with expression of repressed emotions and difficult-to-manage feelings. Emotions that cannot be expressed are often energy consuming and they frequently handicap children in their ability to experience vitality. The next chapter introduces relaxation as a catalyst for emotional expression and, along with imagery and guided fantasy; this chapter offers the learner insight into the internal world of the child.

Storytelling is the topic of the next chapter in this section on therapeutic interventions, and here the learner is provided with the methods to achieve therapeutic goals with an intervention that is the least intrusive and perhaps the most powerful. The arts are discussed in the following chapter; art, drama, movement, and music are presented as effective mediums which allow children to express emotions, thoughts, and behaviors in order to encourage further their mastery of responsible and effective self-expression. The final chapter is a collection of four complete therapeutic activity programs that incorporate much of the theory and technique presented in the preceding chapters. It guides the facilitator from presenting basic education and skill development in feelings, thoughts, and behaviours to dealing with complex issues such as separation and divorce. This section on the practice of therapeutic activity programming provides the learner with over 80 interventions that can be utilized with children of all ages to assist them in dealing with the effects of trauma, abuse, neglect, and other life-altering experiences.

Time In is organized in such a way as to invite the reader to actively participate in the learning experience. Each teaching chapter begins with a metaphor and contains exercises that invite the reader to personally experience the topic discussed. These exercises are designed to allow the reader to reflect on their own experiences to make learning more meaningful. Self-awareness is essential to healthy interaction, and this text offers over 40 reflective exercises to heighten the reader's awareness in order to encourage personal growth and effectiveness. When these individual experiences are shared in a group or in a classroom setting, the reader is provided with accounts of several human reactions to the issues and the techniques discussed. Time In presents a unique opportunity for the reader and the classroom participants to integrate self-awareness and individual experiences into the learning process.

Throughout the text I use the term children to avoid the repetition of child, youth, and young adult. In most instances the games, activities, and interventions are written in the third person except where I felt the instructions to be critical, and in those cases I wrote in the first person. All instructions and dialogue with the group will need to be tailored to meet their developmental level, which will mean rewording some of the instructions and directions.

The text has been laid out with wide margins and spaces to allow the reader to make personal comments and add insights or instructors' notes. The exercises are presented in a workbook fashion to allow learners to complete them right in the text for convenience and future reference.

I tried wherever possible to provide a wide variety of references from the various disciplines that support healthy child development. I originally intended to keep the references specific to the field of child and youth care, but with the explosion of research and knowledge in neurology and trauma, I felt compelled to explore and add those references when appropriate.

Welcome to the text Time In: An Introduction to Therapeutic Activity Programming and Facilitation. I hope its pages inspire you to become the best child and youth care professional of all—the need for dedicated practitioners to carry this knowledge and practice to the children in our communities has never been greater.

"Child and youth work is not about changing or molding the child - it is about meeting the child in his world and allowing him to emerge from it and delve into it with his own ideas, interests, emotions, and associations. We are not here to make the child a better person but to allow him to become his person whether that supports our own vision of him or not.

– MICHAEL BURNS

THEORY

CHAPTER 1

Understanding Play As Therapy

My grandparents lived in a very scenic part of Southern Ontario where apple orchards and grape vineyards stretch across the countryside. They owned a tiny wood frame cottage on the edge of a small town. Their land was 12 acres of meadow, woods, pond, and barn. Grandpa was a seer, a gardener, and a musician. Grandma was a lover, a painter, and a seamstress. The gift they gave to us was the capacity to recognize the good and bad in everyone. They taught us to value our dark side and to befriend it. They believed in their grandchildren and they allowed us to grow with as little interference and with as much independence as possible. When we needed nurturing, they were there to care for us, and when we required disciplining, they were also available. Our mentors and at times our rivals, they always encouraged us to believe in what we felt was right. They taught us to live life, not to prepare to live it.

All their grandchildren spent time with them on their farm, and some of us spent most of our summers there. Our days were spent swimming in the pond, diving off the old maple tree swing, building tree forts and houses in the woods, laughing at Grandpa's jokes or trying to solve his riddles, riding Old Sam until Mel sent us home, and listening to Grandma tell stories of far-away places.

They presented to us many of life's mysteries and gave us the guidance and the opportunity to experience them on our own. Life with Grandma and Grandpa was an adventure—one as easy as child's play.

> **Play is an important survival skill for the human species: to play is not only to learn, but to learn to survive.**
>
> – OTTO WENINGER

This opening chapter orients the reader towards the use of play as a therapeutic tool. It outlines its therapeutic components and classifies therapeutic play into three categories. This chapter also discusses the benefits of directed and self-directed play and provides a brief introduction to the role of play facilitator. Play is presented as the central element in all therapeutic activity programs.

Play can be defined in many ways; each definition captures a part but not all of this unique experience. From our earliest records, in 380 BC Plato defined play as a preparation for a career in adulthood. He directed teachers "… to endeavour to direct children's inclinations and pleasures, by the help of amusements, to their final aim in life" (Morrow, 1960, p. 21-22). Freud (1922) felt it was a child's way to maintain equilibrium between the needs of the Self and the needs of society, and Montessori (1948) called it "child's work." Erikson (1950) saw play as a way to master the basic social skills of life: trust, autonomy, and initiative; and Piaget (1962) felt it was an act of assimilation. Much has been written about the importance of play and physical activity over this 21st century linking these activities to the development of self-esteem (Isenberg & Quisenberry, 2002), social/emotional development (Isenberg & Jalongo, 2006), healthy parent-child relationships (Ginsberg, 2007), brain development (McCain, Mustard, & Shankar, 2007), academic achievement (Hillman, Castelli, & Buck, 2005), and health (Lambourne & Donnelly, 2011).

Play is as natural as being oneself—beginning in infancy and continuing throughout the life span. Play is a universal method of attaining balance in one's life. It creates equilibrium for children and adults between the demands of living and those of being. When children are encouraged to play, to express their aliveness, they feel accepted and their existence validated. When children are stopped, discouraged, or stifled in their play, they feel rejected and wrong. They are put off balance, off centre, and require something to centre them again. Children at all stages of development learn through their play. They learn the art of being human in all of its complexities. The more they are encouraged to play and to express themselves through their play, the more they learn about who they are and how it is for them to be in the world.

Generally, children already know how to play and need very little supervision. They can, however, benefit from loving and healthy adults who can act as facilitators when they request one or when their safety needs require one. Child and youth care professionals can structure the child's environment to make learning opportunities more fruitful and pleasurable, with limited interference from adults. And even though play is a natural, instinctive activity, some severely traumatized children have to be taught how to play—a situation that requires a facilitator trained in therapeutic activities.

Therapeutic Play

Therapeutic play in this chapter will be divided into three classifications: play for pleasure or entertainment, play for awareness or skill development, and play for healing psychological wounds. All three contain therapeutic potential and qualities for assisting children in dealing with negative life circumstances.

PLAY FOR FUN: Entertainment and pleasure give play it's universal appeal and make it an extremely powerful motivator and stimulator for most children. Play as entertainment can alter a child's mood, reconfigure a social situation, and reward a child. Play for children that find themselves in difficult life circumstances can often be their only time to relax, feel safe, and be themselves. Play for pleasure and fun can have positive and therapeutic outcomes for all children.

Games for entertainment can be divided into three types: games of physical skill, strategy, and chance (Sutton-Smith, 1971). Games of physical skill are determined by the players' abilities in gross motor activities. The outcome is decided by who has the highest level of motor ability. Games of strategy are determined by the players' cognitive abilities. The player or team who has the highest level of cognitive ability decides the outcome. Games of chance are determined by luck. The outcome has no bearing on the players' abilities in the cognitive or physical areas. And games can also be just for the fun of it, with no other goal but to act as a release of the stress and pressure inherent in childhood.

PLAY TO LEARN: Play can also be used to provide learning opportunities and experiences that broaden the child's awareness. Structured and unstructured activities can be used to teach a new skill, to develop self-awareness, or to provide a forum for experimentation. Children can be taught mathematics by playing games that include numbers or taught the alphabet by learning a song. Youth can be made aware of emotions, thoughts, and behaviours by participating in a guided fantasy exercise. Young adults can be given opportunities to experiment with shape, colour, and design by participating in open-art exercises.

Play for awareness, such as cooperative games, activities of self-discovery and self-expression are an interesting bridge between play for fun and traditional win/lose games. The cooperative game has elements of physical skill, cognitive ability, and luck or chance. As well, it adds an emphasis on cooperation and a de-emphasis on competition. This allows more freedom of self-expression which allies cooperative games with play experiences. Activities of self-discovery and self-expression, in the same way, add structure to the child's ability to express the Self. Games and activities of this nature have both the elements of play and education. How and when to include competition in therapeutic games and activities will be discussed in Chapter 3, "Designing Therapeutic Programs".

Play teaches and enhances social development by allowing the child to practice various social skills in an imaginary context as a rehearsal for social life. Games allow children to exercise these skills in a more structured and sometimes more stressful situation as further preparation for the complexities of social living. Activities can directly prepare the child to deal with social situations. For example, children can role-play situations in order to gain insight into their behaviours and the behaviour of others. Social development is encouraged through play, games, and activities as the players interact with one another.

Play for teaching and awareness benefits emotional development through its interactive quality and its expressive nature. Players must both control and express emotions appropriately in order to be understood. This encourages children to befriend their emotions and to learn more about how they operate. Games require more control of emotion but at the same time allow children a vehicle through which to express their feelings. Activities can be structured so that children can directly experience emotion and can openly discuss its effect on them. Emotional development is fostered in play, game, and activity experiences by allowing children to express emotions and have them identified and discussed.

Intellectual development can be enhanced through play, game, and activity experiences by providing children with a context in which to explore, exercise, and express intelligence. Cognitive or intellectual development occurs during play as the child experiences and manipulates the environment. Play materials such as sand, water, and blocks provide the child with excellent learning experiences. Density, mass, volume, cause and effect, mathematics, the use of levers, structures, and force, for example, are all experienced in the free play situations of the preschool child. Games require the child to use the intellect to strategize, to problem-solve, to generate new and creative ideas, and to think abstractly. They also contribute and assist in language development. Activities can directly challenge the child's cognitive abilities by focussing on specific intellectual tasks (e.g., math games or problem-solving exercises). Games and activities make learning fun.

PLAY TO HEAL: Play is also used to assist a child to heal psychological wounding. Play therapy uses toys, props, and structured conversations to allow children to deal with and express grief. Sensory exercises allow a traumatized child to begin to repair the damage done to the sensory system. Art, drama, and music can assist children to make sense out of tragic events such as the loss of a loved one, a friend's suicide, or a family divorce. The play intervention in these situations is often structured and specific to the child's circumstances and life situation. These therapeutic interventions have well-defined goals and usually require a specific expertise such as formal play therapy or art therapy training.

> "Play is the only way the highest intelligence of humankind can unfold.
> – JOSEPH CHILTON PEARCE

Play therapy, pioneered by Melanie Klein (1932), Anna Freud (1946), and later Clark Moustakas (1953), is a free-play experience where the child acts out fears, anxieties, and negative experiences through play. A trained therapist watches and records the child's play to gain insight into the child's problems. At times this insight is shared with the child (if he or she is older) and/or passed on to parents and caregivers. Therapists and counsellors often use play, games, and activities as a way of building rapport with children in order to begin the healing process. Creative art therapists (see Chapter 15, "Art, Drama, Movement, and Music Therapy") use art, drama, music, movement, dance, and other mediums as a vehicle of self-expression for children who have been abused, traumatized, and victimized. These activities provide opportunities for self-expression and self-disclosure, which in turn benefit the healing process for the child. In short, play, games, and activities are therapeutic tools that provide the facilitator with a variety of opportunities to enhance the child's natural healing abilities (Levine & Kline, 2007).

Directed & Self-Directed Play

Therapeutic Play can be directed and controlled by facilitators and participants, or can contain little direction, or require no influence from others. Directed play such as games and structured activities are a form of play but are less of a free expression of the Self and more of an expression of the Self within the confines of rules. Conduct and roles in these play situations are more clearly defined and play more formalized. Games are generally introduced later in the child's development because of the demands that rules make on the younger child or on the child who is developmentally delayed. Games require impulse control, tolerance to frustration, acceptance of limits, and a high level of interpersonal interaction. When children have reached middle childhood, they are ready for the structure of games. Play for the child in middle or late childhood is almost always associated with rules and organization of thought and behaviour. Children in later childhood and teenage years thoroughly enjoy games of all complexities.

Some children, however, have not developed the abilities to function in highly structured games and activities and are much happier and better served developmentally when they are provided with less structure and direction in their play experiences. The degree of structure and level of facilitation of the child and youth care professional will be discussed throughout this text. Undirected play can be spontaneous in nature, or free-play opportunities can be provided that require little or no facilitation on the part of the adult. Huges (2003) states that free play must meet three criteria: the child has freedom of choice, the play activity is enjoyable, and the play is focussed on process not outcome. Play facilitators are encouraged to become involved in the undirected play experiences and play less of a spectator role. "Undirected play allows children to learn how to work in groups, to share, to negotiate, to resolve conflicts, and to learn self-advocacy skills" (Ginsberg, 2007, p. 183).

Free play in children appears to develop in stages, beginning with solitary play where the young child plays alone and does not include others in play. This solitary stage progresses to parallel play where the child plays alongside other children but does involve them in the play experience. The next stage is associative play where the child includes others in play, but there is no effort made to organize or cooperate with these others. The final stage is cooperative play that involves organized activities and games (Parten, 1932). These progressive steps in play can also be repeated at later stages in development. Traumatized, abused, and autistic children can be seen regressing and progressing through these stages, often as a result of their level of perceived safety within the play environment.

Play facilitation in both structured and unstructured environments will be the emphasis of this text and the successful play facilitator must have a child-centred focus in both environments.

The Role of Play Facilitator

Whether directing play or observing, the play facilitator can enhance or detract from the play, game, or group activity. This section points out specific areas of concentration for the student and the novice professional in an effort to mark out the importance of effective play facilitation. Safety, both physical and psychological, is at the core of all successful play experiences and should be the initial concern and a primary goal in group activity programming and facilitation.

The role of the facilitator in child-centred learning is a model of two-way communication. Children express an interest, a desire, or a question, and the activity program facilitator provides encouragement, motivation, and resources so that the individual or group might satisfy that curiosity, fulfill that desire, or answer that question. The child is able to express an interest in a particular area, and the play facilitator is capable of providing access to the necessary resources that are at an appropriate level for the individual or group. The facilitator can provide assistance and encouragement in order to motivate children to answer their own questions and fulfill their own desires. With this type of approach, the adult and child relationship is on more of an equal plane, giving the child control of the experience as well as the power to manipulate the environment in order to suit his/her individual needs.

By using the child as the focal point in play facilitation, and the environment and activity as the instrument with which to benefit the child, the therapeutic activity programmer and facilitator offers an experience that is truly child-centred. This focus on the child increases the level of therapeutic impact for all activities—it recognizes the child and not the program or activity as the key factor.

Personal Reflection – Your Play Experiences

1. List the play activities that you most enjoyed as a child.

_____

_____

_____

_____

2. Based on what you have read in this chapter, list the possible reasons as to why you enjoyed these activities.

_____

_____

_____

_____

3. List the play activities you enjoyed as an adolescent and pre-adolescent.

_____

_____

_____

_____

4. Why do you feel those activities were so meaningful—perhaps a need, want, or desire you feel these activities addressed?

_____

_____

_____

_____

5. List the play/leisure experiences that you enjoy in your life now.

_____

_____

_____

_____

6. Why do you feel those activities were so meaningful—perhaps a need, want, or desire you feel these activities addressed?

_____

_____

_____

_____

> You can discover more about a person in an hour of play than in a year of conversation.
>
> – PLATO

Review

• Play is what children and youth "do," and to play is to be "me" outside of all my other roles.

• Play can be entertaining, educational, and therapeutic.

• Play can be spontaneous, or planned, or can take on a structure and dimension of its own.

• Play can assist children and youth in all aspects of development.

• Play facilitators need to be child-and-youth-centred.

The therapeutic potential of play experiences can be greatly enhanced by the programmer and facilitator who pay close attention to the play milieu. Chapter 2, "Therapeutic Play Environments" continues the discussion concerning play as a therapeutic intervention by focussing the learner on how to create play environments that are safe, inclusive, and therapeutic.

Therapeutic Play Environments

Melinda's home and garden were always the main attraction for the kids in our neighbourhood. Whenever we walked on Melinda's property, either inside the home or outside in the gardens, we always were very close to nature. In one morning visit you could hear eight different song birds, sight a mother deer and fawn, pick armloads of vegetables, a basket of fruit, gather a magnificent bouquet of flowers, and enjoy a breakfast in the morning sun with any number of pets and animals.

Melinda's home was situated on a large piece of property on the edge of town and was an odd combination of flower shop, apothecary, and animal shelter. There was always an array of blooming plants no matter what time of the year. Max the St. Bernard and Chico the Chihuahua, along with a variety of transient mongrels (Melinda took care of strays until they were found a home), made up the outdoor canine corps. A menagerie of cats, both stray and domestic, roamed indoors. And a variety of ferrets, mice, and rabbits seemed to appear and then disappear throughout the day.

Melinda Woods was our friend and the neighbourhood sage. The folks in our town knew that visiting her meant they would always be welcomed by her friendly wave and that their concerns would matter to her. Melinda had a wealth of knowledge about herbs, plants, and natural medicines. Whenever we arrived, Melinda welcomed all of us with a big smile and an offer of something to eat and drink. We could sit anywhere, say anything, and always felt safe and sound. Melinda taught me about nature and how to learn from it.

> It is the child in man that is the source of his uniqueness and creativeness, and the playground is the optimal milieu for the unfolding of his capacities and talents.
>
> – ERIC HOFFER

The success of play as a therapeutic tool is dependant in part on how inviting the therapeutic space is to the children inhabiting it. Like Melinda's gardens, the therapeutic space needs to attract children and to provide safety for them to grow and develop. This chapter focusses on the therapeutic play environment or milieu and its effect on the play experiences of children. The value of outdoor play activities and their facilitation is emphasized, along with the various therapeutic elements in nature. Indoor play, its benefits, and the use of this type of milieu in providing therapeutic experiences provide the learner with ideas on how to make this environment therapeutic. Finally, the chapter discusses what to look for when evaluating play environments and suggests ways to convert the present milieu to one of increased therapeutic value.

The therapeutic milieu must be emotionally, socially, culturally, and ideologically safe in order to maximize normal development (Burns, 2006) and to increase the possibility of therapeutic outcomes (Levine & Kline, 2007). It needs to be inclusive in its design so that it meets a variety of needs for a diverse group of individuals. And there should be a component or element that addresses the individual child, giving them a sense of pride and ownership.

Independent of conscious awareness, children are constantly evaluating the level of safety and predictability of their surroundings and the individuals that occupy them (Porges, 2011). Porges coined the term for this ability "neuroception—how neural circuits distinguish whether situations or people are safe, dangerous, or life-threatening" (Porges, 2011, p. 11). When children believe their environments to be safe and the others within the milieu trustworthy, they are able to engage in socially appropriate behaviours and, in time, form positive social bonds. Safety is often a personal evaluation, and what may seem safe to the adult may not be so for the child. Levine and Kline (2007) remind us, "If it doesn't register in the body as something healing, comfortable or pleasurable, it is not a resource ..." (p. 135).

Physical safety requires equipment, playing surfaces, and the play area to be well maintained and all precautions taken to avoid any physical injury. This is not to say that the play environment is devoid of risk but that it has been evaluated and all possible safety hazards have been reduced or eliminated. Take the example of the climbing apparatus in an outdoor play area; there is the risk that children may fall off the equipment. However, the surface under the apparatus can be rendered safe enough to reduce any possible serious injury. The risk of injury is greatly reduced due to attention to, and maintenance of, the equipment, the play area, and any adjacent or surrounding areas.

Play environments need to be socially and emotionally safe—a place where emotions are welcomed and children are encouraged to express and act on their emotional and sensory experiences. This safety factor allows children to socialize more authentically and to be more successful in the social aspects of the play experience (Oatley, 2004; Rolls, 2005). Rules of conduct and behaviour need to be enforced so that all children feel a sense of safety and inclusiveness. Cultural (whether ethnic, racial, or social), and ideological safety is also essential in the play environment. Cultures should be respected and recognized within the play milieu by means of posters, literature, and music. It is useful to provide a variety of games and activities that reflect cultural diversity. The intention is that all children, regardless of race, religion, or cultural membership feel safe and valued and free to speak their mind within the play experience (Brascoupe, 2009; Hanley, 1999).

Children's play needs are simple; they can create their own play worlds out of nothing except their imaginations and their abilities to socialize. Elaborate equipment and over-supervision of play experiences make work out of, or interfere with, child's play. Children get frustrated, and adults feel unappreciated when good intentions turn sour. Whenever possible, the children who are using the play space should be involved in its planning, building, and maintenance. This allows children to feel a responsible part of their play area, and encourages them to express their wants and needs in order to make the play space more useful.

Children's developmental needs should always be considered when planning both outdoor and indoor play environments. Play environments have a critical role in normal child and youth development. Play and recreation areas can depress or stimulate activity, encourage or discourage creativity, limit or increase socialization, stifle or encourage self-expression, and can unite or divide the group. Careful consideration and manipulation of the play environment is a primary factor in group satisfaction with the play activity. The therapeutic milieu therefore often dictates the success or failure of an activity, game, or free-play experience. Play environments influence whether children will join in the play experience with wonder, or with some reservations, or even whether they will play at all.

> Environmental playgrounds, which encourage an active interaction with plants and animals, water and dirt, weather and the life cycle, offer children education at its most compelling.
>
> – JIM GREENMAN

Personal Reflection – Your Play Experiences

1. What play areas do you remember as a child?

_____
_____
_____
_____
_____
_____

2. After reading this chapter how would you assess the level of safety in your childhood play environments?

   a) Physical Safety

   _____
   _____
   _____

   b) Social/Emotional Safety

   _____
   _____
   _____

   c) Cultural/Ideological Safety

   _____
   _____
   _____

3. Evaluate the play environments and activities that you engaged in as a youth.

   d) Physical Safety

   _____
   _____
   _____

   e) Social/Emotional Safety

   _____
   _____
   _____

   f) Cultural/Ideological Safety

   _____
   _____
   _____

Outdoor Play Environments

Children are drawn to outdoor play areas, playgrounds, open fields, and wooded places in their environments. They come alive in the presence of nature, and they identify with it. Nature has a way of returning children to a state of homeostasis—a state of balance or equilibrium. The quiet, withdrawn child suddenly becomes noisy and adventurous when building a fort in the woods. The aggressive and overactive child softens and quiets as he/she cares for a pet rabbit. When the facilitator and programmer include the outdoors as part of their planning and presenting of activities, they find that their success increases significantly. Educators who include environmental learning as part of their curriculum have seen the dynamic role that the outdoors can play in the learning process (Knight, 2011; Rivkin, 1995). When children enter the forest, their whole psychology and physiology changes to accommodate to this different world. Playgrounds, woodlots, backyards, alleys or streets—the outdoors do make it all come alive.

ADVENTURE: Children prefer outdoor play environments (Chawla, 2007), possibly because of the greater variety of experiences and/or the increased mobility and behavioural independence (Kytta, 2002, 2004). Adventure playgrounds became very popular in Europe after World War II. They were filled with junk and debris left over from the bombings and staffed by adult play supervisors; children were allowed to use fire, earth, and water in order to create their own play worlds. Adventure playgrounds in the United States have proven to be highly popular too and have an excellent safety record for children (Greenman, 1988). They now exist in many metropolitan areas across Canada and the United States. Therapeutic activity programmers and facilitators, concerned parents, and local officials can easily provide similar types of experiences for children by using their existing facilities, and by making alterations that would make them more play-friendly. Trips to nearby nature trails, animal farms, wildlife areas, and outdoor events can supplement the play experiences of the neighbourhood playgroup. The first step in providing optimum play experiences for children outdoors is to take stock of what is needed, and what is readily available.

In addition to having a place for activity, children also need a place for quiet, rest, and less active play. A well-treed area, a shelter with tables, a tree fort, a cabin, a playhouse, a tent, a patio, or wooden boxes, all provide places for quiet reflection and less active play. Socialization and dramatic play often happen at quieter times in these places. Children find privacy and solace in their "cubbies," whatever they might be; tunnels and large sewer pipes provide interesting places to hide and play. Playground equipment that has moveable and changeable parts gives children freedom to change their environment and allows them to be more flexible in their play than permanent structures; for example, wooden boxes, canvas, and rope provide the potential for a wider variety of structures than a permanent lean-to. This allows children to create their own environments where they can be away from adults when the need arises.

CREATING AND DESTROYING: Children need to create as well as to destroy; they need to build and to take apart; they thrive on experiences that require them to use their imaginations and cognitive skills in order to interact with their play environment. Basic building tools such as a hammer, saw, drill, and screwdriver add a whole different dimension to children's play experiences. Lumber of all different sizes, wooden boxes, sawhorses, and planks provide children with opportunities to create a living and playing environment that is constantly changing as the imagination dictates. Buildings and boats, freight cars, and automobiles grow out of the interaction of children with these materials.

The basic elements of fire, earth, and water, coupled with basic building tools and supplies give children increased opportunities. Fire fascinates children for many reasons; it has power and destructive capabilities; it provides energy and warmth; and it has the ability to create and to destroy. Children in early childhood and middle childhood often are not given opportunities to experience fire because of its extreme danger. When activities and experiences are well supervised and developmentally appropriate, children can easily and safely experience this awesome element. Candles, a gas stove, a small-contained fire, or a large bonfire all carry this fascination. The building and use of

> **Play permits the child to resolve in symbolic form unsolved problems of the past and to cope directly or symbolically with present concerns.**
>
> **– BRUNO BETTELHEIM**

a fire should always be well supervised, and children should be well instructed in the identification of fire, fire hazards, prevention, first aid, and fire safety, but activities involving fire should not be overlooked when considering therapeutic activities.

Earth carries an equal fascination. Earth extinguishes fire; it is an element in the creation of plant life; and it too, is powerful and is part of the life cycle. These properties can best be seen in the garden plot, flower bed, stand of trees, nature trail, meadow, or forest area. The child can also create structures with the earth; sand castles, mud pies, hills, mountains, ditches, and caves are all possibilities. Digging tools and sand areas make the experience easier for younger children. Earth, like fire, provides a primary learning medium.

Water, the element that extinguishes fire, can also move the earth and make it change shape. Children's fascination with water exists because of its power and ability to create and to destroy. It, too, is primary in its ability to teach and to give exposure to many of the child's developmental needs. Water and earth provide ditches, ponds, oceans, and lakes, as well as that much coveted substance—mud. Water also gives life to the plants in the garden, the lawn, and the flowerbeds, as well as to the wild flowers and weeds in the ditches. Water can be frozen outside in the winter for skating and sliding. In the summer, it can be used for cooling, for quenching thirst, and it can be sprayed on plastic for a water slide. Children can be taught basic mathematics, physics, and science through witnessing water change in size, shape, and density. When the elements of fire, earth, and water are available for children, they continually find ways to interact and experiment with their basic properties.

PLANTS AND ANIMALS: When children are allowed to interact with the animal and vegetable worlds as part of their play experiences, their learning experiences are once again increased, and their humanity, as well as their position in the life cycle, can be realized. The act of digging up a small section of the playground and planting vegetables seems like a small task; yet, it carries with it a myriad of learning experiences. The entire life cycle of nature takes place in this special environment. Seeds are germinated into plants that grow from seedlings to adult plants and on to maturity; these plants produce seeds to complete the cycle and die in the process. When children take an active part in this process by preparing the soil, planting the seeds, watering and weeding the small plants, nourishing them to maturity, and harvesting them, they experience their life in harmony with their environment. A small garden plot can provide many lessons and experiences.

Animals, too, can be part of the play experience. Wild animals, birds, reptiles, fish, and insects often visit the playground areas. Feeding stations can be set up to encourage their presence; bushes, plant life, ponds, and shelters can be included in order to further attract them to the play area. Children can learn about the local wild animals and their habits by observing them firsthand. Some play areas have cages and shelters that allow children to view these animals and other domestic animals at a closer range. The process of caring for plants and animals, as part of the playground experience, makes the area even more special and exciting for the children (and adults).

NATURE WALKS AND DAY HIKES: The use of off-site areas for games and activities add variety and excitement to the experience. Hiking is an excellent way to enhance environmental awareness.

The first rule of hiking is to come prepared for any weather, and this involves clothing primarily. The first consideration is footwear. Nature walks, in most cases, require running shoes and socks; for longer hikes and backpacking trips, hiking boots with two pairs of socks are preferred. Clothing choices should always depend upon the climate of the region, and most climates fluctuate somewhat. When hiking, one should be prepared for wet weather and for cold weather. Each child can carry a small pack with the necessary gear and snacks inside. Hiking in marshlands obviously requires boots, and these can be packed as well. Headgear is a must for most hikers, sheltering them from the sun, the wind, and the rain. A pair of woolen mittens can come in handy for the cold days. Children should be given an appropriate clothing list in order to ensure that they are prepared; this also prevents them bringing too much gear.

The second rule of hiking is to know exactly where you are going, and to tell someone in authority where you will be. The best rule for the person who is organizing the hike is to be familiar with the trail beforehand. This allows for better planning on hike day so that the children will benefit most from the activity. Other precautions such as carrying a portable phone, trail maps, topographical maps and a compass, make getting there and coming home a simple process. A Global Positioning System (GPS) can be used for more adventurous hikes into the wilderness.

The third rule of hiking is to carry a first-aid kit and to bring someone who is trained in first aid. Anything can happen on even the most well planned hike, and when you are prepared, there will be no catastrophes. Young hikers can be taught basic first aid which increases the group's level of safety and encourages safety mindedness.

The fourth rule of hiking is to leave the environment intact. The cutting down of tree limbs and trees is inexcusable. Wild flowers and plants should be observed, drawn, or photographed, and not picked or trodden upon. All refuse should be taken back and disposed of, including that left by others. Collecting of insect and plant specimens to be studied at a later date should be kept to a minimum. Bird nesting areas, wildlife dens, and burrows should not be damaged or handled. Children can be taught at an early age to understand and to preserve our natural environment.

Good preparation makes for a good hike. Goals can be set by the therapeutic programmer and facilitator and by the children planning the outing in order to give it more direction. Experts in wildlife and nature can be brought along to point out some of nature's mysteries to the children.

Indoor Play Experiences

When you cannot be outside, there is lots of fun and excitement to be had inside. What the outdoor milieu does for the quality of the experience, the indoor environment makes up for in predictability and dependability. A comfortable indoor place, spacious enough to accommodate the group, provides a reliable and consistent space in which to play. The indoor play environment is also much easier to control and to manipulate. The temperature can be controlled, privacy can be maintained, safety is often more easily assured, and overall control of the group is much simpler. Furniture and equipment can be added, moved, or removed in order to give the indoor environment versatility. The ideal combination of both indoor and outdoor activities gives the programmer and facilitator environments suitable to any and all of the activities in this text.

Much of what can be played outdoors can be accomplished in many of the indoor settings frequented by children. The gymnasium is a very common setting for indoor play experiences and can provide a wide variety of large muscle activities in a safe, comfortable, and environmentally-controlled setting. Large-muscle activities such as running, jumping, rolling, kicking, throwing, hitting, bouncing, balancing, swinging, climbing, and sliding can all be provided in both structured and unstructured indoor play experiences.

Some cautions and concerns for running structured activities in the gym are space, noise level, and equipment. Children may have difficulties in large open spaces, and the gym can be a place where some children either regress and avoid large-muscle activity or become over-stimulated and find it difficult to control large-muscle behaviour. Painted boundaries and borders, partitions, pylons, and other physical structures can be used to reduce possible confusion and over-stimulation. Noise levels can be very high in the gym and are an important consideration when explaining safety rules, the rules to the game or activity, or when discussing the play experience with the children. Also, voices tend to echo in the gym, sometimes distorting or hampering communication. Whistles, gongs, chimes, or a good loud voice are very helpful in alerting the group. When discussing rules, safety measures, and the like, it is helpful to hold the discussion in a corner of the gymnasium. If the group is positioned with their backs to the wall and the speaker faces the group, then the acoustics are much better than in the open areas of the gym. It is also important to have the group members repeat and explain what was said to insure accurate communication.

This type of environment often includes large groups of participants, 20 or more, and they require at least a 10-1 ratio for adequate supervision. Providing proper equipment includes giving attention to floor surfaces, heating, and lighting as well as any equipment used for a game or activity. Safe gymnasiums are well lit, have well maintained surfaces, and are climate controlled (Evans, 2006). All equipment in safe gymnasiums are properly serviced, checked, and maintained at optimal levels.

The games room (sometimes known as the group room, craft room, etc.) is usually a smaller space than a gymnasium, and although it is appropriate for some large-muscle activities, it primarily involves fine-motor games as well as cognitive and language-based activities. These environments are often located in youth drop-in centres and group homes as well as recreational facilities. These spaces can be more easily changed and developed to suit the participants' and the activities' needs or restrictions. This environment usually services small groups of eight to 12 members. Safety and inclusiveness are very important considerations for this type of milieu.

Assessing the Play Environment

The first step in providing safe, inclusive, and successful group activity experiences, whether indoors or out-of-doors, is to assess the play area according to space, layout, surface, and equipment.

The amount of space in residential settings, foster homes, group homes, etc. is limited, and often the backyard or front yard space is a multi-purpose area. The major questions to be answered here are: How much of the backyard is available for children? Does the space have boundaries, for example, fences and hedges? Are there out-of-bounds areas? Are there any safety hazards to be aware of? Does anyone else require the use of the space? The answers to these questions provide the necessary data in order to assess the space available.

The best way to determine the layout is to make a map of the backyard. This map should include all aspects of the yard, such as the location of any trees, shrubs, storage areas, play equipment, and gardens. When mapping out the yard, try to include the measurements of these areas. This map should provide an overview of the area. When considering the layout of the yard, be aware of how traffic flow (the ability to move freely from one area to the other) in each area affects the entire play space; determine the direction of flow, and consider possible ways of improving the efficient use of the areas available by redirecting the traffic flow.

Indoors or outdoors, the surface, the parameters, and the equipment are all necessary considerations in the choice of play environments. Certain surfaces like wood, tile, concrete, sand, grass, clay, or pavement affect the quality of the activity. Boundaries or parameters insure structure and control of the activity. Walls, fences, hedges, hash marks, or painted lines provide boundaries with which to ensure order and contribute to the success of the activity. Equipment, from furniture to plastic hoops, adds versatility and variety to most activities. Grass, sand, humus, wood, cement, gravel, wood chips, asphalt, and outdoor carpeting provide unique play experiences for the child. Assessment of the potential types of playing surfaces available to the child in the planning of backyard play experiences allows for the efficient use of play space as well as diversity in play experiences. Swing sets, garden plots, bicycles, wagons, badminton nets, footballs, hoses, beams, building equipment, sand boxes, pools, trees for climbing, and a host of other equipment enhances the play experience. Make a complete assessment of play equipment by listing what is available and what is needed.

Proper and responsible attention to physical safety can prevent most, if not all, accidents with children and youth. An activity played on a sandy surface could be disastrous when played on a paved surface. An outdoor hike or canoe trip without proper training and experience can be a potential tragedy. Faulty and poorly maintained equipment can result in serious injury. Lack of attention to possible toxic or harmful aspects of the environment can also have very negative consequences. The programmer and facilitator should always be conscious of potential safety hazards or safety issues and should control the environment in order to maintain a high level of safety for the group experience. Emotional safety is also crucial; however, this is a more complex issue, which will be discussed in other parts of this book.

The indoor environment for the child is also important, for it is here that a large part of the day is spent. Indoor environments need to be stimulating and activity oriented. Like outdoor environments, space, layout, surface, and equipment are necessary considerations. The space considerations for indoors are similar to outside. Children function best in a space that has enough area for large-muscle activity and a quiet space that is away from the more active areas. The indoor environment can make good use of shelves, containers, and hangers to make a more easily organized play area.

The layout of the indoor space should insure a functional flow of traffic to each area, and ideally the different areas should be able to be accessed individually. Sometimes furniture can be positioned to set up boundaries to assist in creating useful play areas.

The surface of the indoor space is important in planning play experiences. It dictates whether water or sand can be used, whether the child can lie down on the surface, and the possible hazards for activity.

Board games, balls, hoops, and so on enhance the indoor environment by making it more activity oriented. Large pillows, puppet theatres, art easels, toys, and punching bags enhance play opportunities and provide opportunities for creative expression.

Attention to space, layout, and equipment can make therapeutic activities safe, inclusive, and affirming experiences.

Exercise 2:1

1. Draw a map or floor plan of a play environment in which group activities are held. You may wish to use an environment you are currently working in or a play environment from the past.

    • Colour in the areas that are out of bounds to all children, (i.e., for staff only).
    • With another colour, shade in the areas that are primarily for children.

Examine your map or floor plan, and answer the questions posed below.

i. Is there an imbalance in the environment, and if so describe?

_____
_____
_____
_____

ii. Would it be useful to have areas for children only? Detail your answer.

_____
_____
_____
_____

iii. Is there a private space for each individual? If not, how would you remedy this or do you feel this is not necessary and explain why?

_____
_____
_____
_____

iv. Does your environment make good use of the equipment and resources available? Detail your answer.

_____
_____
_____
_____

v. Is there easy access to all play areas? If not, how would you remedy this?

_____
_____
_____
_____

vi. Are there distinct boundaries? If not, do you feel they are necessary and if so, how would you remedy this?

_____

_____

_____

_____

vii. Are there any safety or health hazards? If so, explain.

_____

_____

_____

_____

2. Now draw an ideal map or floor plan of the existing play environment.

Review

• Safety is a primary concern for all therapeutic play environments.

• Outdoor environments offer unique opportunities for therapeutic value and influence.

• Indoor environments can provide participants with opportunities not offered in outdoor environments.

• Assessment of play environments should be held on an ongoing basis.

An enticing and well-managed play milieu opens the door for the next step in programming and facilitating therapeutic play programs. Chapter 3, "Designing Therapeutic Programs" provides an opportunity for the learner to utilize the information on play as therapy and the importance of the therapeutic milieu and apply that knowledge to the planning and development of therapeutic activity programs.

> A playground should be like a small-scale replica of the world, with as many as possible of the sensory experiences to be found in the world included in it.
> — RICHARD PATTNER

CHAPTER 3

Designing Therapeutic Programs

My Uncle Tom loved nursery rhymes and used to tell us stories with nursery rhyme characters in them using their characteristics and situations as examples of what he was trying to communicate. His favourite was the Three Little Pigs. Here is an example of one of his stories.

The three brother pigs decided to part ways and to explore a new environment, one of their own choice. Each decided to take his own path into the forest and set off to find a spot to build a home. The third little pig realized that safety in this new environment would be essential to his happiness. He decided that building his home focussing on this and a sense of belonging would be his next course of action. His "little voice" told him that, from past experiences, there was a "right time" for everything, and so he must be patient, plan, and wait for that moment. Sensing this, he set out to formulate a location, a design, and a building plan for his new home. He sat down under a sturdy oak tree situated by a stream in a quiet meadow and began to formulate his plan. Over the course of the day he built and rebuilt his domicile by forming pictures in his mind and by daydreaming about how it should look. The next day he talked to others in the area that had experience in building, and later on that evening consulted writings on the matter. The little pig considered angles, mass, and materials; he checked his ideas with how he felt about them, for verification and clarification.

After some time, he said to himself, "This is it—my best idea—a house of stone, positioned close to the trees, and on top of that hill!"

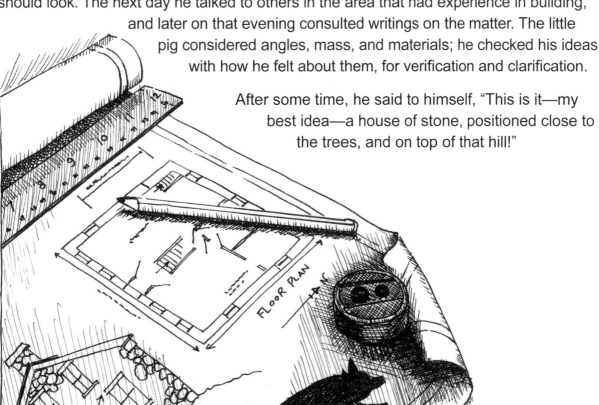

This chapter on program design outlines the developmental play needs of children, adolescents, and young adults. It discusses the importance of considering individual and group development when devising therapeutic programs. The need to sequence and time activities to complement individual group development is presented, and learners are provided with strategies to design programs that attract, engage, and assist children in healthy development. The need to evaluate programs is emphasized along with ideas on how to formulate questions and who to look to for the answers.

Program design is the careful planning, organizing, and sequencing of group activities for the purpose of insuring a positive and productive group experience. The process of program design considers the developmental and individual needs of each child in the group as well as the needs of the group as a whole. It addresses the sequencing of activities within the time frame of the program in order to maximize its benefits. It explores the elements of structure and spontaneity in the programming of activities, and it points out the need for goal-setting and program evaluation in successful program designs. The result of the third little pig's plan and process was a house that withstood the tests of time and the awesome power of the wolf.

Programming for Developmental Needs

The enhancement of the social, emotional, intellectual, spiritual, and physical lives of children is the overall goal of all interventions with children. An initial step towards this level of intervention begins with a solid understanding of development from infancy to young adulthood. Phelan (2008) writes, "Understanding a person's developmental stages is the key to creating useful growth and change," (p.77). Children's play activities can play a major role in this enhancement of personal growth. When designing children's play activities, their developmental levels and the developmental demands of the activity are of primary importance. This requires knowledge of normal and atypical growth and the developmental stages of the specific children within the target group, as well as knowledge of the developmental requirements of each activity presented in the program. Programming also needs to take into consideration normal group development when planning therapeutic activities. These stages of group development and suggestions for programming are discussed in Chapter 4, "The Therapeutic Group."

Achieving developmental levels, which are intended as one measure of wellness, are influenced by environmental factors and conditions such as: level of physical and emotional health, family dynamics, ideals held by the child or family, environmental stress, and one of the biggest factors in determining wellness—poverty. Impoverished, stressed, and in many cases traumatized children find themselves developmentally stuck. Even though their age reflects a certain developmental expectation, their experience finds them stuck and unable to advance into more sophisticated levels (Phelan, 2008). The therapeutic activity programmer will need to be aware of all factors influencing each individual child as well as those influencing the specific group of children involved in the programming.

The following are basic guidelines for six broad levels of development: Early Childhood (4-6), Middle Childhood (7-9), Late Childhood (10-12), Early Adolescence (13-15), Late Adolescence (16-19), and Young Adulthood (20-25). These are meant as guidelines for effective program planning and development, not as a way of solely determining developmental levels.

EARLY CHILDHOOD: Children in Early Childhood, 4-6 years of age, function best in self-directed play experiences and in programs where different activity centres are set up for them, and where they are allowed to explore these various play centres on their own. They are usually eager to learn, and therefore highly motivated to try new activities, provided that they can easily succeed and that they can receive immediate feedback for their efforts. Children in this age group are also highly imaginative; this makes art and drama excellent avenues for expression. They love story time, finger plays, and silly songs, provided that these are presented to them for short intervals that correspond to their attention spans. They typically have a short attention span and their abilities can vary from day to day. Repetition and routine allow this age group to practice their developmental strategies and tasks in order to develop competence. Art, dramatic play, music, sand, water, blocks, and large muscle centres provide children in this age group with the variety necessary to meet their varied developmental play needs. Children at this age are developing eye-hand coordination and they may not have established dominance, right or left-handedness. They often find it difficult when confronted with several choices and may require adult intervention and assistance.

Children in this age group have a variety of developmental abilities and challenges, and there can be a high incidence of developmental lags in this age group. Large group activities, highly structured activities, cooperative activities, team games, and activities that require accomplished motor skills are not particularly suitable. The game concept, which includes following rules and winning and losing, is not recommended for this age group. At times, these children can be antisocial, indulge in parallel play, or they may play cooperatively for short intervals in small groups. In general, play activities should be self-directed, varied, and reflective of a group of children who have a wide variance in abilities and interests.

Personal Reflection – Early Childhood

List the games, activities, and events that you enjoyed at this age.

_____

_____

_____

Do they reflect the developmental information listed above? If so, how, and if not, how would you explain this?

_____

_____

_____

_____

MIDDLE CHILDHOOD: Children in this age grouping are 7 – 9 years old. They are slowly increasing their attention spans, developing and mastering large and small muscle skills, and broadening their abilities to socialize and to cooperate. Programs that encourage further development in these areas are essential to the success of games and activities for this age group. Developmental levels of children in this age grouping are still quite diverse; therefore, the open-ended, free-flowing types of programs used for children in early childhood are also very successful.

Children in this developmental phase need help defining behavioural limits and boundaries, as they are prone to overestimating their abilities to manage tasks. Cooperative and well-structured activities can assist in these areas of development by providing the limits through the structure of the activity. The cooperative element allows children to make more accurate assessments of their abilities by comparing themselves to one another in a less stressful and non-competitive milieu. Children in this phase have a tendency to demand too much of themselves and can be quite impatient, impulsive, and sensitive to failure. Non-competitive games and the use of small groups of peers in each activity provide an experience that gives each individual child enough exposure to the skills required of the activity. This limits the numbers who witness the child's failure and impatience and provides a structure that promotes patience, cooperation, and success. Middle-childhood children have a need to be both an active and a passive participant in play. Small groupings allow the facilitator to give individual attention to the child who needs to withdraw as well as to the child who wishes to master the skill.

At their best, such children are active and energetic. They enjoy being challenged and tackling tests of strength and endurance. Through running, climbing, skipping, and jumping, those in middle childhood experience bursts of energy and often tire easily. The trampoline, large and small balls, ropes, ladders, climbing and balancing equipment, water play, tag, and wrestling allow the child to burn off these bursts of energy in an appropriate and self-developing way. Children in this age group are better equipped cognitively and emotionally to appreciate quiet games and activities. At the more mature end of middle childhood, children can attempt and be successful in team activities. Competition can also be introduced, but it should not be a focal point in overall programming.

At this age, the peer group is increasing in importance, and the dividing line between males and females is clearly drawn. Sometimes even antagonistic towards each other, boys and girls often do not want to be paired up with a member of the other sex. This sense of we-ness can be capitalized upon by giving children a part in developing programs and learning or teaching new games.

Personal Reflection – Middle Childhood

List the games, activities, and events you enjoyed at this age.

_____

_____

_____

Do they reflect the developmental information listed above? If so, how, and if not, how would you explain this?

_____

_____

_____

_____

LATE CHILDHOOD: Children in late childhood, from ages 10 through to 12, are generally more flexible, more predictable, and more accepting than any other age group. This is an age when children are very peer oriented; often, they form little cliques and speak in coded language. They are developing a strong sense of individuality; they are concerned with personal performance and with perfecting skills. As a result, they can often be moody, self-conscious, and argumentative. They have a healthy sense of fair play and honesty, which makes organized team sports and activities highly desirable at these ages. They are assertive, curious, accepting, and adventuresome.

Activity programming for this age group works well in large and small groups. They have the self-esteem, the power to concentrate, and the physical ability to play almost any game or activity. Most children in this age group are sociable and friendly, and if behaviour becomes a problem, the group usually knows how to deal with it.

Personal Reflection – Late Childhood

List the games, activities, and events you enjoyed at this age.

_____

_____

_____

Do they reflect the developmental information listed above? If so, how, and if not, how would you explain this?

_____

_____

_____

_____

EARLY ADOLESCENCE: This age group is from 12 to 15 years of age. The importance of the peer group is further heightened at this age. They are loyal to group principles and tend to be egocentric when comparing themselves to the out-group. Cliques are strong, and rebellion towards adults and authority intensifies in this age group. Programming for adolescents must include the group members in at least 50% of the decision-making. Creative problem-solving techniques, group discussions, and efficient use of group resources will assist this age group in developing their own activities, special events, and rules of conduct. The facilitator can play a role as a resource person, as a facilitator, and as someone able to assist in the efficient operation of the program. All group members should be encouraged to take an active role in programming.

Physically and emotionally, this is a time of constant change for the early adolescent. Growth spurts, hormone changes, and the emotional stress brought on by puberty are reflected in their somewhat unpredictable behaviour. The marginal feelings of no longer being a child, but not yet an adult, can cause frustration and confusion for this age group. Females mature faster than their male counterparts, and this can cause some difficulties in relationships. Social gatherings, parties, outings, and group projects are highly valued activities by this age group. Team sports and a wide variety of recreational activities occupy their leisure time. Games with risk, or simulated risk, allow this age group to satisfy their sense of adventure, to use their newly developed skills in abstract thought, and to exercise their problem-solving skills. The early adolescent is venturing out and exercising independence and autonomy. Facilitators will benefit by being more tolerant of individual behaviours and by tempering the need to control the group. The facilitator can withdraw somewhat from this age group by supervising the children through this developmental stage and by maintaining a positive influence through facilitation.

Personal Reflection – Early Adolescence

List the games, activities, and events you enjoyed at this age.

_____
_____
_____

Do they reflect the developmental information listed above? If so, how, and if not, how would you explain this?

_____
_____
_____
_____
_____

LATE ADOLESCENCE: This age group, 15 to 19 years of age, is seeking adult status, yet the abilities to achieve this vary with each individual. They are extremely loyal to their peer group and need that group's approval in order to feel a sense of belonging. This can be a very tumultuous time within the family. The adolescent is trying to break away from parental control and is developing new bonds outside of the family. This process of individuation causes the adolescent to become more self-reflective and to make attempts at becoming self-sufficient. Appearance is important, sex is important, and ideals are important. Discussion groups concerning these topics and others suggested by the group can serve as ways for teens to learn about and explore safely, with guidance, areas that are critical to their well-being.

This group loves team games and a wide variety of sport activities. They enjoy most of the games and activities used in the other age groups. The therapeutic activity programmer and facilitator can expect full involvement, planning, and execution of programming from the adolescent. They can take total responsibility for most of their games, activities, and special outings. The role of the adult is to facilitate the group experience and to assist in the efficient operation of the program.

Personal Reflections – Late Adolescence

List the games, activities, and events you enjoyed at this age.

_____

_____

_____

Do they reflect the developmental information listed above? If so, how, and if not, how would you explain this?

_____

_____

_____

_____

_____

YOUNG ADULTHOOD: Young adulthood (20-30 years of age) marks the peak of physical performance and biological functioning. It is also the time when individuals lay the foundation for the developmental changes of adulthood (Ateah, Kail, & Cavanaugh, 2009). This is a time of introspection, and some who have developed unhealthy habits may decide to adopt a healthier lifestyle. Feelings, thoughts, and behaviours are challenged, and individuals at this stage are open to new ideas, concepts, and ways of viewing the world. It is a time for developing intimacy (Erikson, 1950) and life-long relationships. Many are married, have children and are working on achieving career goals. This is also a time when many gay, lesbian, bi-sexual, transgender, or questioning adults feel freer to express their sexual identity and orientation. This is also a time when those who have experienced trauma, pain, violence, and the effects of poverty are more willing to seek out professionals in an effort to heal. However, they may still be hampered from healing due to poverty, lack of education, unemployment, young children to care for, and the effects of acute anxiety and depression.

Young adults thrive on team activities and competition but can also drop their competitive spirit and play just for the pleasure of adult contact. Discussion groups are usually lively and debate is welcomed. Individuals at this stage usually have a well-established ability to think abstractly and to engage in complex problem solving. At this stage most young adults are able to integrate emotion and logic and, with this the ability, to see and appreciate several points of view.

> It is becoming increasingly clear through research on the brain, as well as in other areas of study, that childhood needs play.
>
> – TINA BRUCE

Personal Reflections – Young Adulthood

List the games, activities, and events you enjoy/enjoyed at this age.

_____
_____
_____
_____
_____
_____
_____

Do they reflect the developmental information listed above? If so, how, and if not, how would you explain this?

_____
_____
_____
_____
_____
_____
_____

Read through the various lists of games, activities, and events over the course of your childhood and adolescence.

What patterns do you notice?

_____
_____
_____
_____
_____
_____

How did the meaning of "fun" evolve over your childhood and adolescence?

_____
_____
_____
_____
_____
_____
_____

Atypical Development

The above developmental classifications are meant to act as a guide to developmental norms, but many children of every age, for various reasons, have delays and disturbances in their growth and development. Some children are so seriously delayed or damaged emotionally that they have great difficulty functioning in a therapeutic group program. Children with physical, emotional, social, or intellectual delays require more planning and expertise than would otherwise be required. The group facilitator needs to observe and evaluate a child's behaviour (words and deeds) as a manifestation of his/her developmental phase and to learn to respond appropriately to developmental exceptionalities (Phelan, 2008). This observation and analysis of behaviour is critical when determining whether a child should be worked with individually before placing him/her into a group situation (see Chapter 4, "The Therapeutic Group").

Therapeutic activity programmers often deal with entire groups of children with exceptional needs and, in turn, must produce exceptional programs in order to be successful. Many, if not all, children with exceptional needs have met with failure and ridicule from other children as well as from adults. Their resistance to becoming involved in group activities that challenge their abilities is an obstacle to group satisfaction. Problems with attention span, frustration tolerance, impulse control, self-image, relationships, withdrawal, aggression, communication, and physical and mental ability are all major considerations in program planning for children with developmental delays. Expertise, careful planning, and realistic expectations are needed to make activities and experiences enjoyable and productive.

Programming Therapeutic Activities

The timing and ordering of activities is also essential to programming successful therapeutic play experiences. When the right activity is presented at the right time, the possibility for success and maximum benefit is greatly increased. This right time for the group is determined by the group's developmental level (see Chapter 4, "The Therapeutic Group") and by the pace of the program. The pace of the group, in most cases, is an abstract determination made by the facilitator on the basis of the leader's knowledge and experience with this particular group as well as on the social-emotional and environmental influences in place at the time of the activity. This is where the group leader's ability to be flexible helps to adjust the activity levels to suit the pace of the group.

The group leader must be able to anticipate shifts in the group pace and to respond to the change. The analyzing of the group's developmental stage and social-emotional tone is best done in the opening portion of the program. The pace of the group can often be anticipated by investigating what experience or experiences the group or its individuals have had just prior to the program. For example, the pace of a group just arriving after a long bus ride would be quite different from a group just being dismissed from recess or a gym class. The emotional level of a group that has just returned from a movie is quite different from one returning from a weekly home visit.

The facilitator who anticipates the pace and activity level of his/her group is more apt to program activities that meet the needs of the group as they arrive and to lead them to the desired level of performance and enjoyment. Having alternate plans provides the flexibility to the program that allows for changes in mood, weather, group composition, and any unforeseen developments. The program design must be flexible enough to meet the here-and-now needs of the group. The most creative and best-organized plan is doomed to failure unless there are alternatives to support it. The child care professional must be prepared at all times to go with the flow of the group and to change any and all activities if the group situation warrants it.

A useful way of sequencing a program is to divide it up into three basic parts: the warm-up, main theme, and cool-down. The warm-up, sometimes called the introduction, is intended to ease the transition from the state of "non-groupness" to a state of "groupness." This initial part of the program can also be the time for the facilitator to determine the group's mood and pace. It is also an excellent time to assess any possible problems

> One of the great mistakes is to judge policies and programs by their intentions rather than their results.
> — MILTON FRIEDMAN

with individuals in the group. The beginning activities should be a way of preparing the group physically and emotionally for the middle, or the body, of the program. This warm-up period does not necessarily need to reflect the main theme; it is simply a way to prepare the group for the main theme. Sometimes the warm-up exercises are focussed on having fun to allow the group time to reconnect, to burn off excess energy, or to relax and be calm. When the warm-up has achieved its aim, the body of the program can begin.

The main theme or body of the program is the activity, or series of activities, that give meaning and purpose to the group's getting together. The overall reason for the group being initially formed is reflected in the main theme. Perhaps the focus is on socialization, separation and divorce, or family. The body of the program is structured in such a way that it allows the free flow of activities to reach the intended goal, while maintaining a level of comfort and enjoyment for the group members. In addition, the facilitator must structure this time in order to be sure to leave enough time for the cool-down.

The ending or cool-down part of the program provides closure to the body of the program and prepares the group for the transition to leave-taking. For this, the facilitator needs to be aware of where the group members are going after the group ends. Do the group members need to leave in a calm relaxed state, do they need to leave energized and ready for action, or do they need to leave with something to think about for next session. This may mean slowing down the pace and consolidating lessons or themes so that members leave the group with a sense of completion. The seeds of new ideas, directions, or concepts can be planted at this time in order to give the group something to ponder until they meet again. This period is also an excellent opportunity for the facilitator to determine if there are some members who, based on their behaviour during the cool-down phase, need to stay behind for an extended cool-down period. Programs structured this way can provide optimum group experiences for its members.

Evaluating Programs

Another element in designing successful therapeutic play experiences is obtaining feedback from participants and others. The main question to address is: "Is there concrete evidence that the program is fun and has an effective therapeutic component?" This method of evaluation reflects which activities are successful with a specific group of individuals under specific circumstances. The value and importance of this method is that it is based on what works not on what is theorized to work. How success is determined is also an important consideration. Evaluating therapeutic programming and its effects on children requires ongoing assessment strategies. Evaluation also presents the child and youth care professional with the opportunity to grow and to advance his/her skills both as a programmer and as a facilitator.

The group members, the facilitator, as well as an outside professional observer or supervisor, are in ideal positions to evaluate individual program activities and the total program itself. Parents, caregivers, and other professionals involved with group participants can provide information on whether the problems experienced by the individual group members are becoming less of a concern. The group participants can give valuable information concerning the enjoyment and satisfaction quotient of the activity. They can also generate creative ideas to be used to enhance both of these factors. Facilitators can add personal observations and conclusions concerning group performance and adjustments to the activity. They can also comment on the amount of preparation and level of difficulty the activity demands and provide creative solutions and shortcuts to refurbish failing programs. Outside professionals can be most useful as observers and resource people for the group leader. They can provide ideas, suggestions, and criticisms to the group leader. The outside professional may take part in or observe the group, from time to time acting as a recorder of the group's level of functioning and how it responds to the facilitator.

Program evaluation must look at the developmental needs of each child and must reflect the intent or theme of the original program design. Programs are presented to the group in order to achieve a specific purpose. This purpose can be defined by a goal or series of goals that outline what it is the group is meant to accomplish. These goals can be broken down further into ways in which the goals will be reached, sometimes called objectives. The purpose, the goals, and the objectives can form the basis of an evaluation process that measures whether these have been accomplished.

A rudimentary evaluation process would require the group leader to determine the purpose or purposes of the group. For example, the purpose might be to provide early adolescent males with guidance in the practice of safe sex. The facilitator's next step would be to state more specific goals for the group so that the members have the opportunity to understand and agree that these are viable. Using the same example, the group goals might be: to create a safe atmosphere for the group members to speak openly and honestly about the topic; to include speakers or experts in the group sessions; and to explore other related issues like socialization, dating, and peer pressure.

The next step for the facilitator would be to make a list of objectives for each goal so progress (or lack of it) can be determined. As an example for the first goal, "to create a safe atmosphere for the group members to speak openly and honestly about the topic," the objectives might be: to speak with personnel in order to procure a quiet and comfortable room for the group meetings; to arrange the meeting room furniture to provide an atmosphere of equality; to form a set of standards and safety precautions that would insure confidentiality; and to discuss with group members at the first meeting any issues they may have with regards to group safety.

The purpose, goals, and objectives can be shared with the supervisor or consultant as well as the group members in order to insure that they are appropriate for the group. Once the purpose, goals, and objectives have been established, the degree to which they have been accomplished can be measured. When the program is in progress, ongoing evaluation can insure that the group is centred on its purpose. When the program is completed, the data can be gathered from all three sources (participant, facilitator, supervisor) and utilized to improve the program delivery.

Evaluation Methods

Successful and insightful evaluations depend on the methods used to obtain appropriate feedback, especially with children. There are many factors involved in asking a child to evaluate an adult. One such factor is that this does not occur regularly in children's experiences, so it is novel and can be threatening. Another is that children often want to please adults and want adults to like them. They may be concerned that a negative comment or evaluation may hurt or upset the adult. They may be worried about being punished or about appearing to think they know more than the adult. As children get older they often lose these concerns and can be more forthcoming in their evaluations. However many pre-teens and teenagers are reluctant to criticize adults, especially adults they like or wish to impress.

To increase the chances of getting useful feedback, here are some techniques that work well with children who have difficulty giving feedback. When there is time, individual sessions with children can decrease any peer pressure or discomfort in criticizing someone in public. Children can also be reassured that the facilitator welcomes the feedback and needs it in order to become a better facilitator. Questions should be worded so that children can give a varied response. Scales of 1 to 5 for young children and 1 to 10 for older children allow them to have more flexibility in answering. Open-ended questions (ones that require more than a yes or no answer) give more information than yes/no questions. The content of the questions, particularly for the young child, needs to be concrete (related to the five senses) and should not require too much reflection.

Feedback from children needs to be immediate, sometimes right after the session or series of activities and other times directly after the specific activity. The data can come as a result of the program planner asking the participants verbally or requesting their written responses. Direct fill-in-the-blanks questions such as "I did not like it when ….. "; "I felt uncomfortable when ……" ; "I did not feel safe when …." give children permission to be more forthcoming. Children can always respond contrarily if that was not their experience, but it does focus them on the task and gives them permission to relate possible emotional or sensory responses to the facilitator. Some questions will be aimed at exploring the pleasure, safety, and comfort factors while others will be to determine if the activity is providing the child with some skills, opportunities to express emotions, or develop awareness.

Many adolescents are less reluctant and uncomfortable giving adults feedback, and some welcome the opportunity. These situations can be very helpful and often result in the group assisting in the design of parts of the program and eventually entire sessions. Older teens can, with assistance from the facilitator, design total programs or major aspects of the program. Groups and individuals who can become involved at this level of evaluation can greatly assist the facilitator in the design of some very powerful and effective group programs. The adult continues to remain the primary programmer, but the children take on an increasingly more active role in the planning and development of their groups.

The evaluation methods used with youth are similar to those used with children, but adolescents can be asked more specific questions that require more reflection and contemplation. They can usually be asked abstract questions and ones that require problem solving and critical reflection.

Evaluation, both ongoing and at completion, can provide programmers and facilitators with the necessary information to upgrade their skills and to continually enhance the productivity and satisfaction level of the group.

Exercise 3:1

Develop five questions to ask a group of middle childhood participants who have completed a group on social skills.

_____
_____
_____
_____
_____
_____
_____
_____
_____
_____

Develop five questions to ask a group of adolescent participants who have completed a group on drug use.

_____
_____
_____
_____
_____
_____
_____
_____
_____
_____

Develop five questions to ask a group of young adult participants who have completed a group on death and loss.

_____
_____
_____
_____
_____
_____
_____
_____
_____
_____

> A man who works with his hands is a laborer; a man who works with his hands and his brain is a craftsman; but a man who works with his hands and his brain and his heart is an artist.
>
> – LOUIS NIZER

Review

- Knowledge of developmental stages are helpful when designing therapeutic activity programs.

- Considering individual needs and life situations of participants assists the program designer.

- Competition needs to be introduced slowly into therapeutic activity programs.

- Games and activities can be sequenced in such a way to maximize their influence and effect on group participants.

- Program elements need to be evaluated on an ongoing basis to insure that they are meeting group needs.

Now that the learner has a better appreciation of program design it is important to explore the dynamics of group development. Chapter 4, "The Therapeutic Group" provides essential information for both the facilitator and program planner. Group activities are the most popular form of therapeutic intervention, and therefore a general knowledge of how groups function is essential to the success of therapeutic activity programming.

CHAPTER 4

The Therapeutic Group

The life of the forest was changing drastically, and all its elements were worried and perplexed by the meaning of this change. It appears that a sickness was attacking and weakening the very life force. Plants, animals, and minerals were disappearing, leaving only deposits of a lifeless substance; the forest was dying. This day, a great assembly has gathered in the forest and many have spoken and listened to the problems they commonly face. A bear, known to many as Kamo, arises to speak.

"On behalf of Nature!" his eyes blood red from many sleepless nights, Kamo looked intently at his audience as he began to speak, "There is harmony in the forest when nature is allowed to prevail; there is purpose, there is cooperation, there is a healthy balance. The way of Nature is one of reliance; plant, animal, and minerals all act and react in relationship. We must help one another to regain what we have lost and communicate so we can adapt to each other's changes. Change, my friends, appears to be our only poem." The bear went on at some length expressing his fears and urging the group to unite. The union of the forest was in danger, and he feared that unless others were to agree to give as well as to receive, that he, and the generations after him, would be filled with the sickness.

They sat for many hours discussing ways to solve their dilemma. No answers came readily, but all were firm in their resolve to stay in the forest and work together.

> Norms of a group are constructed both from expectations of the members of their group and from the explicit and implicit directions of the leader and more influential members.
>
> – **IRVING YALOM**

Now that play and the milieu have been established as essential factors in the success of therapeutic programs and program planning as a tool to develop effective and attractive programs, group dynamics can offer vital information to the programmer and activity facilitator. Group dynamics, the nature of group life, is the study of groups of individuals in process—how they relate to each other, how they function as a unit, and how they react to their environment. The study of the complexity of life in the group requires a cognitive separation of it into parts without losing the gestalt of the experience. Each group is different with its own heart and soul. This chapter will point out specific areas, various dynamics, and predictable group behaviours. It asks the reader to take note that groups are dynamic. Life in the group, like life in the forest, is one of interdependence and change.

Knowledge of how groups form, and why groups develop, can assist the facilitator in effective group management. Insight into what behaviours are healthy and normal for groups can assist the leader in encouraging and/or discouraging certain behaviours and attitudes. An awareness of the forces that impact on group performance makes it easier for a group facilitator to provide a healthy and safe milieu. An understanding of group roles, and of how to encourage positive leading, provides the facilitator with strategies for encouraging healthy role development. The group facilitator, with an understanding of group dynamics, can more effectively guide the group towards its maximum potential.

Children are required to function in a wide variety of group situations that vary in complexity and importance. The demands and requirements placed upon a child as a member of a family are very different from those placed upon him/her as a member of a swim team. The importance of belonging and of feeling accepted in a peer group is much different than the child's relationship to the larger society, a more abstract group. If children are given a safe environment in which to explore as many types of relationships as they feel necessary, and if they are taught the values of group cooperation, they will be exposed to all of the skills that are necessary to live a socially healthy life. "Humans are highly social beings whose brains are designed to connect to others for a sense of belonging" (Brendtro & Mitchell, 2010, p.6).

The Importance of Group Work with Children

We are born in relationship, we develop in relationship, and we realize our self-worth in relationship. Socialization and functioning in groups has become more important as the world's population is growing at an alarming rate. Our cities and towns are growing and with this expansion, confederation and cooperation with one another is becoming more and more important. The very survival of the planet and its species is dependent upon how well we cooperate in dyads, triads, small groups, large groups, communities, countries, and as people of the world. The skills necessary to achieve the kind of harmony and cooperation needed are most easily taught to our young people as they grow and develop. We, as leaders of groups, must also model cooperation and compassion in order for these lessons to be integrated into action.

Jacobs, Masson, & Harvil, (2009) list a variety of ways that groups can be beneficial. Groups offer participants the experience of commonality, such as groups of bereaved children sharing their experiences. In this situation, just the fact that there are others who have experienced the same life event can be therapeutic. Groups can offer a wider variety of viewpoints, coping strategies, and insight than any one individual. Groups provide a space where members can practice skills, give each other feedback, and benefit from others' learning by witnessing their growth and development. Group experiences reflect the greater society and mirror real-life in a way that individual counselling cannot. Group members can also influence one another to stay committed to the group experience and the group task.

Group work also has a financial advantage. Group counselling is more cost-effective when compared to individual counselling. Human services budgets are being closely monitored and in many cases reduced each year. Groups become more attractive to administrators who are attempting to find ways to maximize funding.

When children are taught to satisfy their personal needs in conjunction with the needs of the group, they are able to learn a skill that will benefit their immediate world, and this will set precedence for their involvement in the larger environment. Cooperation and consideration of the group will once again become a focus of healthy living.

Group experiences for children and youth can be facilitated in such a way as to nurture and reward the types of skills and attitudes important to healthy group and community living.

Group Characteristics

Group work with children can be classified according to the reason for the group's involvement. Healthy groups are a balance of three main characteristics: task, maintenance, and dynamics. Some groups emphasize one of these over the others and other groups contain all three elements.

TASK GROUPS: The aspect of task refers to the goals and expectations of the group. The reason for the group's existence is usually reflected in its task aspects. A skill-building group is formed so that the group members might learn or improve upon a specific ability. The emphasis of this group is often upon the group leader who has mastered a specific talent. A group of children learning first aid is an example of a task-directed group. Another example of a task-oriented group is a planning group formed for the purpose of future action. A planning group often gathers in order to make recommendations or to prescribe a set of procedures in order to achieve a specific goal. A group formed to plan the Valentine's Day Dance would be considered a task group.

Personal Reflection – Group Experiences

Find a relaxing position and allow your thoughts to drift to the different groups you were involved with when you were in grade school, or in high school, or college. Allow your thoughts to pass freely from group to group. Give yourself a few minutes to recall these groups from the past. Now write down four groups that you found the most pleasurable, pointing out why.

Group #1

_____
_____
_____
_____
_____
_____

Group #2

_____
_____
_____
_____
_____
_____

Group #3

_____
_____
_____
_____
_____
_____

Group #4

_____
_____
_____
_____
_____
_____

Now write down four groups that you found the least pleasurable, pointing out why.

Group #1

_____
_____
_____
_____
_____
_____

Group #2

_____
_____
_____
_____
_____
_____

Group #3

_____
_____
_____
_____
_____
_____

Group #4

_____
_____
_____
_____
_____
_____

MAINTENANCE GROUPS: The maintenance aspects of a group concern the emotionality of the members and of the group as a whole. The reason for the group's success or failure largely has to do with how well the group members are maintained emotionally and how well they interact interpersonally. Do the group members feel satisfied and eager to participate in the group's task? Do they feel a sense of trust and safety within the group proportionate to the demands of the task? The maintenance aspects of the group can be identified in terms of three different areas: inclusion, control, and affection.

The individual group member must feel included in the group and needed by the group in order to be a productive and satisfied group member. Inclusion is vital to the group's ability to grow to its potential.

The issue of control also becomes a prime consideration for the group members. The healthy participation in the group activities requires the power and control of the activity to be shared among its members. The activity, game, or exercise that the group is participating in requires that the status and power of group individuals be fairly and evenly distributed.

The affection aspect of the group pertains to how the individual feels valued within the group. The feelings and the level of trust among group members are the major factors when considering the maintenance of the group. When feelings are considered important and worthy of consideration, children are able to respond with emotionally healthy behaviours, which insure satisfaction among group members. In this regard, facilitators need to adopt a sense of curiosity regarding feelings and refrain from judging them (see Chapter 12, "Dealing with Feelings).

Personal Reflection – Memorable Group Experiences

Refer to your list of positive group experiences made in the previous reflection. There is a good chance that the groups you listed, as the most pleasurable were the ones where the maintenance aspects of the group were considered and well maintained.

Relax yourself once again and conjure up four group experiences from the past that you found most memorable, perhaps group encounters where you learned something valuable about life. Give yourself 15 to 20 minutes to remember three to four instances. Briefly describe the impact these situations had on you and list the emotions and physical sensations you experienced.

Group #1

_____
_____
_____
_____
_____

Group #2

_____
_____
_____
_____
_____

Group #3

_____
_____
_____
_____
_____

Group #4

_____
_____
_____
_____
_____

Review your list again and note: what was the task; how important or unimportant were the maintenance aspects of the group?

DYNAMIC GROUPS: The dynamic quality of a healthy group allows it to grow, to change, and to develop as the challenges of the task and maintenance aspects evolve. Groups where creativity is valued, where power and control is shared, and where open communication is taught and respected, grow and develop towards their potential in time. In this type of group experience, group participants can all learn from each other's life situations and share a broader range of experiences with one another. The dynamic qualities of the group can be affected primarily through group process and the level of communication within group interactions.

Group process describes the way in which the group communicates. The participation, leadership, power, decision making, problem solving, conflict resolving, and morale of the group are the process elements. When the group interacts and communicates in a dynamic way, more possibilities can be realized through shared process.

The content of the messages, verbal as well as nonverbal, and the interpretation of the content also reflect the dynamic qualities of the group. When content of communication reflects flexibility and ownership in the group process, the individuals feel more connected and thus more able to risk the ups and downs of a dynamic relationship. Communication needs to be accurate and a feedback system that allows for validation is necessary. The content and meaning of group life is very important to its dynamics.

Nevertheless, the ability to be dynamic has a certain risk factor for the group members. Change always means loss, as well as gain. Change also involves moving from a familiar way of responding to a less familiar way, and this often results in anxiety or stress until equilibrium can be re-established. Trust in the group is a major factor in its ability to be dynamic. When the group members trust that they will be able to support each other through the pain of change, they will be more amenable to the dynamic forces.

Group Formation

Group characteristics lead to group formation—how are groups formed and what are the major elements in group formation? Groups can be programmed to meet for a series of sessions focussing on a specific topic. These groups usually have a consistent membership and meet only for the designated number of sessions. Such groups are commonly referred to as a closed group. On the other hand, an open-ended group is one that may address one topic or theme per session, or it may be a recreation group to keep youth off the streets. These groups are open-ended in that they do not run in a set series, they are simply ongoing, and regular attendance is not mandatory or as necessary as in a closed group.

Another important factor in group formation is determining whether or not to form a homogeneous or heterogeneous group. A homogeneous group is one in which the group members all have something in common. A group addressing masculine development for adolescent males would be a homogeneous group. A heterogeneous group is one where the group members have less in common than a homogeneous group or they are dissimilar in some aspects. A socialization group for school-aged children would be an example of a heterogeneous group.

There are distinct advantages and disadvantages to both types of groups. Groups for young drug users consisting of only current drug users often result in participants finding better contacts for drugs and more individuals to do drugs with. However, a group with non-users, active users, and reformed drug-users represents a broader scope on drug use. Alternatively, groups for children who have lost a parent or experienced divorce can be very powerful. Children who have experienced similar problems can often relate better to each other's situation. In these situations there is a feeling of not being alone—the only one who has experienced this. Members are often more empathetic towards one another and can often console each other more effectively than someone who has not experienced the problem.

A homogeneous group of children dealing with anxiety, with all very anxious participants, can often be very difficult to manage as participants may end up making each other more anxious. A heterogeneous group that addresses anxiety, on the other hand, might have participants who have had issues with anxiety and have begun to deal with them; there may be others who have recovered from serious anxiety, and still others who have not experienced issues with anxiety at all. In this type of group experience, group participants can all learn from each other's experiences and share a broad range of experiences with one another. It is very helpful for group participants to know that others are experiencing the same concerns, and still others who have learned to handle their anxiety. Individuals without anxiety issues can provide a calming effect on the group and often have much to contribute in ways to deal with anxiety.

The personality and social make-up of the group is an important factor in forming therapeutic activity groups. Some individuals are not ready for group interaction or are not ready to address the topic or issue addressed in the therapeutic group experience. Whenever there is the opportunity, the facilitator should screen prospective group members to determine their level of competency socially, as well as their readiness or interest in addressing the focus of the group. This screening will assist in preventing the excessive needs or complete disinterest of an individual member from interfering with the group's progress. It also insures that individual participants will not be placed in social situations where they cannot cope.

A simple screening method would be to conduct an open-ended group (a group that anyone can attend) that requires the group members to interact and participate in games and activities that test cooperation and individual participation. This group session will assist the facilitator to determining which individuals appear to be able to manage this particular social group situation. This group session can be followed up with individual interviews with potential group members. These interviews give the group facilitator an opportunity to strengthen rapport with the participant and to discuss with them the topic of the group session. Such meetings allow both facilitator and participant to make informed choices about group attendance.

Stages of Group Development

Once the groups are formed there are predictable stages that will cue the facilitator as to how the group is progressing at a developmental level. There are several theories regarding healthy group development; those by Corey (2012), Gladding (2011) and Yalom (2005) are a few of the more popular ones. Tuckman (1965) described the developmental stages of a group as forming, storming, and norming. Jacobs, Masson, & Harvil, (2009) refer to the stages as beginning, working, and closing. This text proposes a similar designation to that of Tuckman and Jacobs et al.

STAGE ONE | INTRODUCTORY STAGE: This is the "getting-to-know-you" stage of group development. In many cases the group members are meeting each other for the first time. It is useful to slowly build the group by using a number of pairing exercises where each member of the group has a one-on-one experience with all other group members. This type of beginning may last one or more sessions. The goal is to form a series of strong dyads—pairs of group members who have had some one-on-one interactions. Eventually activities can be included that require triads and then small groups of four. The idea is to slowly increase the size of the groups until the full complement of members are involved in the activity.

STAGE TWO | CONFLICT STAGE: This is the stage in group development when group members are beginning to become familiar with one another and personal issues and conflicts arise. This is a time also for group members to "act out" or "test" group facilitators. The personal conflicts and the testing are both opportunities for the facilitator to insure group safety. One of the reasons children test the rules is to find out if they will be enforced. If the facilitator enforces the rules, the group members will feel safer, and when they are consistently enforced, then most group members can relax and feel safe. This is an opportunity to ensure the group that no one will be allowed to purposely harm another group member either physically or emotionally. The conflicts that occur within the group also provide opportunities to group facilitators to teach and model healthy conflict-resolution strategies. Once the participants have tested the rules and resolved conflicts with one another, they are now able to work towards more satisfying task completion.

STAGE THREE | TASK AND PURPOSE STAGE: At this stage the group members are feeling safe with one another, have a trusting relationship with the facilitator, and are ready to address the task at hand. Up to this stage, facilitators have been dealing more with the maintenance aspects of the group than with the task at hand. Now energies can focus on the reason for the group's formation and work towards skill development, symptom reduction, or increased awareness.

STAGE FOUR | TERMINATION: The facilitator will have been preparing the group for some time now that the group does have an end. Termination is a very necessary stage of group development, and it prepares the participants to move on from the group. This is a time when group experiences are re-visited and shared among the group, a time to discuss skills developed and lessons learned within the group, and a time to say good-bye.

Healthy Groups

As the group progresses in its development the final goal is the formation of a healthy fully functioning group—one that can be defined as a collection of individuals who share feelings of belonging and share group pride. They feel that there is purpose and merit in the combining and coordinating of their collective talents and efforts. Group members communicate openly, value each other's opinions, and feel a sense of trust and safety in the group milieu. They are able to share roles and status in the group. Leadership responsibilities change to match the situation and the expertise of group members. They are able to confront problems and to see them as systemic issues and not as personality issues. When there is conflict within the group, group members have developed effective conflict resolution skills.

Exercise 4:1

Read over the definition of a healthy group in the last paragraph. Continue to read it until you are able to envision such a group. Remember this group does have weaknesses and problems; it usually begins fairly fragmented. Create in your mind an imaginary group of 10 children or youth.

Relax yourself and visualize such a group; imagine the dialogue and interactions among the group members, and try to get a feeling of what it must feel like to belong to such a group.

How would you see yourself in this picture as the adult leader/facilitator of this group? What would your behaviour be like?

_____
_____
_____
_____
_____
_____
_____
_____

What type of activities do you imagine this group to be involved in?

_____
_____
_____
_____
_____
_____
_____
_____

Describe your imaginary group's social interaction.

_____
_____
_____
_____
_____
_____
_____
_____

A healthy group has acquired a balance between its task, maintenance, and dynamic aspects. This type of group develops over time. When working in children's groups, realistic expectations and well-planned strategies allow the facilitator to assist in developing such a group but only if the children are capable of such an experience. The model for a healthy group allows the programmer and most importantly the facilitator to set a standard for group interaction.

How to Develop Healthy Groups

The first step is an obvious one, and that is to be a healthy person and to model appropriate behaviour consistently. The children in the group are constantly evaluating the facilitator's behaviour. The model for positive and healthy relationships for the group members is initially reflected in the behaviour of the group facilitator.

While the group facilitator models the appropriate relationship development skills he/she can be educating group members on appropriate relationship development and healthy group interaction (see Chapter 6, "Therapeutic Relationships"). When children understand what constitutes group health and can appreciate its worth, they will be more capable of working towards this goal. Effective communication skills such as assertive statements, open-ended communication, and active listening can be taught to children through group exercises and games. Preschoolers can understand the basic sharing rule that solves the problem of toy ownership. Children can be taught problem-solving techniques in varying stages of complexity that will give them skills to help them to deal with group and interpersonal problems. Conflict resolution is another important skill that children can learn in the group environment. They can learn to express their feelings, to empathize with others, and to comprise solutions that reflect the group's needs as well as theirs.

DEVELOPING GROUP RULES: The most effective way to set up enforceable rules within a group is to have the members take an active part in deciding on what they ought to be. A good rule of thumb is if you do not need a rule do not make one.

Here are some suggestions to assist the group in deciding group rules.

• When one person talks, the rest of the members agree to listen.

• Starting time, finishing time, and clean-up time is to be decided upon and enforced.

• Yes/ No to eating, drinking, etc.

• Personal issues discussed in the group are confidential.

• All members are to have an equal voice and vote.

• Decide whether consensus or the majority rule will be the deciding factor in problem resolution.

• Decide whether group membership will be limited or open to new members.

• How does someone become a member?

• Can anyone lose group status?

• No physical or emotional harm is allowed.

UNDERSTANDING GROUP ROLES: The final consideration in this chapter for effective group management is the awareness of the types of roles played by group members. An understanding of these roles, and their effect on the dynamics of the group, is a useful piece of knowledge for the facilitator. Various professionals from different disciplines working with groups have identified a number of roles played by group members. These roles, too numerous to mention, are present in one form or another in most groups. However, in this chapter we will concentrate on some key roles that are important for the facilitator to identify and work with: the clown, the scapegoat, the newcomer, the loner, and the bully.

The clown, joker, wise guy, wit, distracter, or whatever the label chosen to describe this group role, is the person in the group who can make others laugh. This ability, in and of itself, can be one of the greatest assets in the group. When the clown's behaviour is appropriate and the style of humour is healthy, the role provides a safety valve for all group members. Anxious or embarrassing situations handled with humour can allow individuals to save face. Laughter is a contagious and a healthy activity for all group members. However, when the clown's role is overplayed, it can be counterproductive to the group's health. It can slow down or even halt the progress of group tasks. The clown's need to make others laugh can be used by other group members to avoid uncomfortable situations that, if faced and dealt with, would move the group closer to its goal. The clown may resort to ridicule or put-downs to make the group laugh. Sometimes this character can act like a bully at times. As well, individuals finding themselves stuck in the role of the clown may often resent feeling that they always have to be funny. They may suffer when the group becomes more comfortable with each other and the need to relieve tension is not as great. Healthy clowning needs to be encouraged and to be fostered in all group members. Unhealthy clowning needs to be discussed, confronted, and shifted to a more productive form of interaction.

The scapegoat, doormat, or gopher is someone functioning in a very unhealthy role. These characters will do anything to receive approval which includes admitting to acts they did not commit, setting themselves up to be ridiculed by others, as well as engaging in other self-destructive behaviour. This group role can carry the negatives for the group and thus allow others to blame the scapegoat or use him/her to attempt to escape consequences. More than one member of the group can share this role, and it can be a very difficult role for the novice facilitator to deal with.

The facilitator will have to work extra hard in order to develop solid relationships with the group leaders and key members involved in the scapegoating. It is wise to maintain a non-judgmental attitude when dealing with this problem in order to model appropriate behaviour; however, the facilitator must have sufficient control of the situation in order to ensure group safety. If there is to be a confrontation, emphasis must be on a violation of the rule, rather than on the violation of another human being. A high degree of respect for human dignity must be maintained at all times, and this tactic of confronting or arguing about a rule, rather than denigrating a human being, gives the child an opportunity to sustain his dignity. In most instances, once a solid rapport is established, this method of confrontation when dealing with scapegoating is very effective.

The newcomer to a group situation, especially if the other group members have developed relationships with one another, is an outsider to the group and is trying to gain acceptance. This situation can be very stressful until this person feels accepted by the group. Entering into a new group can sometimes be very difficult. The facilitator needs to develop quick rapport with children who find themselves in this role in order to help the transition from outsider to insider. These children sometimes take on a negative role if they feel they will not be accepted any other way. Some children handle this transition well, and others, both members of the established group and newcomers, need to work at reaching out to each other. Sometimes the newcomer will decide to stay on the outside of the group and function as a loner.

The loner is a familiar role to most children, and it can be both satisfying and painful. Every man, woman, and child needs to have a certain portion of the day to be alone with their thoughts. Some children, especially those who have very little time alone, may choose the activity group as a time to be alone. More often, children who have had difficulty in the past socializing in peer groups will tend to place themselves apart from the group. A child with low self-esteem may not feel that he/she is worthy of acceptance into the group. Much like the newcomer, the loner is functioning outside or on the periphery of the group. The play facilitator can build a relationship with the loner and ease that person into other relationships by means of group games and activities.

The bully is a very complex and seductive role in that it reflects many of the social values encouraged in a capitalistic society—power, control, and the ability to maximize gain from effort. Bullies are reinforced for their behaviour and are able to control a group by the mere threat of their presence. This can be a very difficult role to give up due to its advantages for a fearful, resentful, or traumatized child. Initially bullies have no place in a group until their behaviour reaches a level of group acceptance. Before integrating children who bully into the group, they must have a solid relationship with the facilitator, therefore individual work with a bullying child is necessary before integration. This type of individual work usually begins in the form of recreational contact, sometimes with one or two peers involved, and sometimes with only the child and youth care professional. Once a relationship has developed between the child and the facilitator that is more positive than negative, the bully can often be slowly integrated into the therapeutic group setting. Without the relationship, facilitators often find themselves in a constant struggle to minimize the bully's effect on the group.

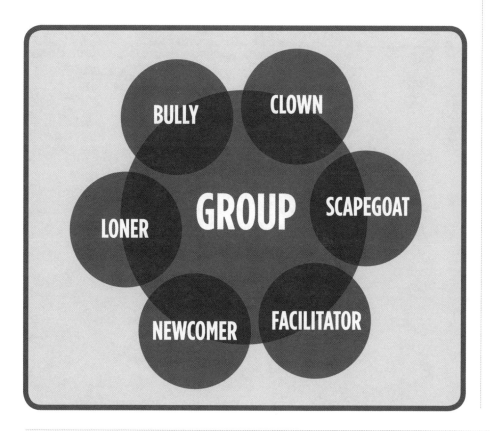

Personal Reflection – Group Roles

List the groups you belong to now, (e.g., family, classroom, teams, etc.), in a column along one side of the page.

Beside each group write down what you believe your various roles or role was in that group is, (e.g., leader, clown, initiator, spokesperson, etc.).

Beside each role listed, write descriptive adjectives that most reflect how you acted out this role (e.g., quiet leader, boisterous clown, etc.).

Throughout the week, share your list with the members of each group and get their reactions as to how they see you in the group.

GROUPS	ROLES	ADJECTIVES	REACTIONS

BRAINSTORMING TO RESOLVE CONFLICT: Brainstorming is a problem-solving technique that requires the participants to generate a variety of possible solutions to a problem. All suggestions are written down and are not judged until the process is completed. Sometimes within the less conventional, more bizarre solutions proposed, there are truly creative answers to the problem.

The most important step in brainstorming is to address the feelings and emotions connected to the incident, conflict, or problem. The emotional component to the problem can often prevent the members from resolving the conflict. For example, if Bob and Henry had a dispute about each others' behaviour, it would be important to discuss the incident to allow both of them to express their emotions towards one another or towards the situation. Once both of them have had a chance to express their emotions, they will be less likely to want revenge and more likely to cooperate to come to a mutually agreeable solution.

Here are 10 simple steps that make up the brainstorming process:

1. Identify the problem.

2. Address the feelings of the members concerning the problem.

3. List all possible solutions.

4. Review this list and exclude solutions that are impractical.

5. Prioritize all the possible solutions.

6. Select the top two solutions.

7. Discuss the solutions in terms of practicalities, money, time, and energy.

8. Decide on the best solution of the two chosen.

9. Make an action plan: Who will do what by when.

10. Set up a time when the solution can be evaluated by the group or a subcommittee.

Competition in Children's Groups

The successful management of conflict among group members can be one of the main considerations when deciding whether to introduce competition into the therapeutic play experience. The use of rivalry in team sports and in individual competitions is a well-known technique that can motivate and unite individuals in order for them to attain new levels of excellence. So, competition does have its place in children's activities; however, its use raises concerns among child and youth care professionals. There has been an over-emphasis on competition in children's activities for a very long time in our society. When it is used extensively, especially in social recreational activities, it runs the risk of instilling hostility, poor sportsmanship, and added pressure on the child to perform. As well, there are adverse effects on the individual group member's self-esteem and level of acceptance in the group. Programmers and facilitators must be ever cognizant of what effect added competition will have on group dynamics.

Competition can be successful in children's groups; however, certain procedures need to be followed, and certain questions need to be asked. Do all members feel comfortable with one another? Can group members make mistakes and still feel capable? Does the activity allow all members to compete evenly, or are there members much more skilled at the activity than others? If the activity allows for a handicap or advantage to be given to certain players, is it presented to, and dealt with by, the group appropriately? How is the competition to be presented to the group? Is it reflective of an attitude that fosters good sportsmanship and clean fair play? Does it promote respect for both teammate and opposing player? Are proficiency and increased ability recognized as primary goals in the activity? Are rewards primarily non-materialistic and viewed as secondary to the activity? Are activities presented in graduated degrees of competitiveness in order to allow monitoring of group reactions? Do the group members have fun and take pleasure in the activity?

On the other hand, non-competitive activities provide opportunities for children to enjoy the pleasure of skill attainment in an atmosphere of support and cooperation. They are structured in such a way that they enable children at various levels of developmental functioning to interact in a social play environment. Cooperative games teach socialization and goal attainment through interactions based on mutual respect and collaboration. There are no winners or losers, just participants; the enjoyment of interaction becomes the primary focus. The absence of competition reduces the threat of damage to self-esteem. Conflict is also minimized which lessens the incidence of behaviour problems among group members. As well, non-competitive, cooperative games are excellent for developing cohesion in a newly formed group. They can be used as bridges between activities, as warm-ups and cool-downs for program activities, and as ways to introduce a format for the discussion of feelings and attitudes. Their uses and strengths make them a must for all programmers.

Games and activities that require leadership to be shared among the group members help to promote the dynamic qualities of the group. Games that do not eliminate members or that count them "out" can help to build group trust and to lower the level of aggressiveness between members. Games that involve trust should not be introduced until members know each other, until they are able to communicate effectively, and until status is reasonably equal. The facilitation of appropriate and effective activities to promote group health requires careful planning on the part of the programmer.

The implications of group work for individuals from middle childhood and beyond are far reaching and each therapeutic facilitator and programmer needs to be constantly aware of the level of group functioning. Close supervision and proper evaluation of one's skill level in the process of group work with children and youth are necessary to optimally benefit each group member. The proper management of group behaviour through insight into group dynamics is the main focus of the group play facilitator.

Personal Reflection – Competition

What were your experiences with competition as a child?

_____
_____
_____
_____
_____
_____
_____
_____
_____

What were your experiences with competition as a teenager?

_____
_____
_____
_____
_____
_____
_____
_____
_____
_____

What is your philosophy regarding competition in children's therapy groups?

_____
_____
_____
_____
_____
_____
_____
_____

Review

- Group work is an important element of therapeutic programming.

- There are three characteristics of healthy groups: task, maintenance, and dynamic.

- Groups develop in predictable stages: introductory, conflict, task/purpose and termination.

- Non-competitive activities are preferred in the initial stages of group development.

- Group rules should be developed and maintained by the group.

- Group members often take on predictable roles.

- Conflict resolution is an important skill for all group members.

- Competition needs to be introduced slowly into the therapeutic group.

Now that the learner has developed a more acute awareness of group development the next step is to study and develop effective group facilitation skills. Chapter 5, "Facilitating Therapeutic Programs" addresses the importance of the leadership role both in relation to the program facilitator and the participants. Therapeutic activity programming can provide opportunities for empowerment of individuals participating in the group activity and skill development for potential youth leaders.

> Processing group experiences increases self-awareness, self-disclosure, healthy boundaries, and improved relationships.
>
> **– PAM THOMPSON & SAMANTHA WHITE**

CHAPTER 5

Facilitating Therapeutic Programs

My cousin Constance, an awkward adolescent, wanted desperately to become a juggler, and she could feel this need grow in her as each circus, carnival, and minstrel show passed through our town. The sight of the hoops and pins masterfully manipulated to suit the performer's fancy cast a spell over her. "What a spectacle!" she thought. The crowd would cheer xand whistle, and Constance could see that they were mesmerized by the jugglers' display of magic. She would come back after each event with such a strong desire to be a performer that she would talk and talk all night about the jugglers.

So Constance began to juggle with two tennis balls. Slowly, she began to feel and to listen to the experience, to watch and to concentrate on each small detail, and then she began to relax. Slowly, the objects and the person began to form the singular act of juggling. What she had learned through observation began to affect her performance.

While she was practicing, Constance would remember those impressive jugglers from her past, and with each memory her confidence and abilities grew. She increased her dexterity through imagery and rote. More and more hoops, balls, and pins were added to her repertoire. Her performances became more elaborate and her audiences grew larger and larger. One day, she found herself in the centre ring, and the audience was spellbound as the juggler performed her magic.

> To facilitate means, 'to make easy.' The group facilitator's job is to make it easier for the group to do its work.
>
> — **MICHEL AVERY**

Therapeutic play activities provide opportunities for facilitators to model effective and person-centred leadership so that participants can experience healthy group interaction and have a model for the future. Effective leadership is a lot like juggling, as it requires the coordination and implementation of a number of abilities, traits, and skills. This collaboration and integration must be balanced with the various needs and interests of a group of individuals. Therapeutic activity facilitators need to study and become competent in all the necessary abilities for effective leadership, develop the proper attitudes along with exceptional communication skills, and like that awkward teenage juggler, practice, practice, practice until they become an accomplished professional. This chapter will focus on leadership development, styles of leading, the qualities necessary for effective leadership, and strategies useful in developing leadership abilities in children and youth.

Skilled leaders play an important role in the overall development of children, and their influence allows children to grow and to develop physically, emotionally, socially, intellectually, and spiritually. Physically, through organized games and activities, the facilitator promotes the use of both large and small muscles. The skilled leader models the need for, and importance of, regular exercise and encourages appropriate physical activity and contact among peers.

Through the supervision of activities that encourage healthy expression of feelings, the facilitator creates an opportunity for emotional expression. Modelling empathy while handling the feelings of others provides direction for the child. Emotional development is further enhanced through the provision of opportunities for children and youth to become familiar with all of their feelings.

Socially, the skilled leader provides games and activities that encourage cooperation, stress healthy and constructive interaction, and emphasize appropriate social awareness and norms. Discussion of feelings, thoughts, and behaviours, and how these affect one another allow children to understand their social selves and to improve their social ability.

Intellectually, the facilitator along with the programmer of thera-peutic activities provides well-organized and stimulating pro-grams balanced with spontaneous and creative expression. The proper modelling of respect for both creative and pragmatic ideas and the presentation of games that challenge the intel-lectual capabilities of the group members are ways in which the skilled leader can enhance cognitive development.

Spiritually, the facilitator models a respect and reverence for all life. There is a tolerance and an understanding of the group's various religious beliefs by the adult leader that allows children to feel comfortable and accepted. The skilled facilitator provides activities that allow children and youth to discuss openly their spiritual feelings, beliefs, and experiences.

Leadership Styles

There are three basic leadership styles: authoritarian, demo-cratic, and laissez-faire. All three styles have their place in ef-fective group management and facilitation.

The authoritarian leader takes responsibility for the group's be-haviour and has final authority over the group. The authoritarian leadership style is one of power and control. The authoritarian is the dispenser of power in the group.

The democratic leader relies on group input before taking action or giving direction. The leader believes that all group members should have a part in decision-making. The democratic leader takes on the role of facilitator in the group. The term democratic leader was for a time changed by Baumrind (1978) and others to authoritative (vs. authoritarian) leadership. However this style reflected more of a "powerful-adult-in-control" style, which did not reflect that group members were "social equals" (Brendtro & Mitchell, 2010, p 5-6).

The laissez-faire leader is not about control, nor does he/she give much direction; this style is the polar opposite of the au-thoritarian. Remaining apart and often an onlooker in group activities, the laissez-faire leader will take no responsibility for decision-making but allows the group to decide. Laissez-faire leaders encourage and support, allow children to settle issues on their own, but are always present (Krueger, 1999), staying focussed on the children to gain knowledge, and remaining ever cognizant of group interaction to ensure safety.

The facilitator needs to acquire skills in all styles of leadership and to develop an awareness of when to use each style. Good leadership is reflected in the facilitator's ability to guide the group by whichever style the situation demands. Maintenance of the health and welfare of the group can be obtained auto-cratically or democratically from outside or inside the group. Limits that concern safety, once established by group consen-sus, need to be autocratically enforced. There is no discussion or exception about the limit; it is enforced consistently. All other rules and issues are best enforced through a democratically oriented strategy. Rules, be they from a game or from group norms, attitudes, and so on, are boundaries intended to assist the group in achieving optimum satisfaction and growth. Rules, and limits are meant for the betterment and enrichment of group life. Facilitators and group members need to be aware of when attitudes and behaviours impede the group and how to confront them head on if their existence is defeating the group's purpose.

Creativity and acceptance are desirable qualities and attitudes for group interactions. These qualities cannot be dictated; therefore a more laissez-faire or democratic style is most ad-vantageous in cultivating them in a group. Each group member requires the freedom to express his/her individuality as long as it does not impede the growth of the group. This tone of free expression allows group members to act freely and spontane-ously, without fear of jeopardizing the group or the child's posi-tion in the group.

Personal Reflection – Leaders

Take a moment to relax and search back in your mind to recall memories concerning the leaders that you have known in your lifetime. Close your eyes and think back to those influential leaders in your life. There were some you admired, and perhaps there were some you did not. Each one of those people taught you something, or many things, about how to be a good leader. Allow yourself to remember, as clearly as possible, how they looked, how they sounded, and how you felt about them. Make a list of these leaders, and be sure to list any particular lesson or ability they contributed to your leadership style.

Leadership Qualities

The importance of leadership styles necessitates a discussion of leadership qualities. Effective leaders are individuals who have skills that allow them to excel as mentors, teachers, and facilitators. Therapeutic activity programmers and facilitators must take stock of their qualities and skills and pledge to improve on them and to develop new talents that will make them more effective. Facilitators must have a positive attitude, be dependable, and responsible. Skilled leaders are well-organized, flexible, observant, and effective communicators. They must be able to be directive, nondirective, and democratic as the situation demands. They are also facilitators of the wisdom of everyday life—how to be and function in the minutiae of life.

POSITIVE ATTITUDE: A positive attitude needs to be projected in all areas towards the children as a group and as individuals, towards the environment and the activities, as well as towards co-workers and other professionals involved in the children's lives. Group leaders are role models for the children in their group, therefore they need to project a warm, friendly, and compassionate Self that instills confidence and trust in the group members.

DEPENDABLE: A facilitator upon whom the children can rely provides an element of personal safety and trust. A dependable leader will provide consistent limits and interventions necessary to make play safe and enjoyable. When the facilitator can be depended upon to follow through, children are able to relax and to trust that what is communicated has meaning. Dependability and trust are interdependent, and without trust, children's behaviour and level of enjoyment are seriously affected.

RESPONSIBLE: Facilitators have the responsibility to reflect the image of someone who takes responsibility for all aspects of themselves. They are outwardly and inwardly responsible for their feelings, thoughts, and behaviours. They are responsible for the fulfillment of their wants and needs. They must be effective in conflict resolution and openly accept the consequences, both positive and negative, for their behaviour. Responsible leaders are those who constantly strive towards self-awareness, self-fulfillment, and self-responsibility.

Personal Reflection – Responsible Living

Answer the following questions and provide examples that support your answers.

When I express feelings and opinions, do I speak in general terms, or do I speak specifically about my experience?

_____
_____
_____
_____
_____
_____

Do I satisfy my wants and needs by actively pursuing and achieving my goals, or, do I wait passively to have my needs met?

_____
_____
_____
_____
_____
_____

When faced with a problem, do I confront the issues and try to come to an appropriate resolution, or, do I not act and hope it will resolve itself?

_____
_____
_____
_____
_____
_____

Do I find myself blaming others or events for my misfortunes, or, do I take responsibility for my own choices?

_____
_____
_____
_____
_____
_____

Do I check out my behaviour by asking for feedback and clarification?

_____
_____
_____
_____
_____
_____

Am I able to accept the positive strokes that others give to me?

_____
_____
_____
_____
_____
_____

Do I find myself rescuing others when they get into trouble, or, do I support that person's efforts to solve their own problems?

_____
_____
_____
_____
_____
_____

ORGANIZED AND FLEXIBLE: Programmers of therapeutic activities need to have activities and games well planned and organized. However, this organization should also allow for some flexibility and creative expression. The programmer and facilitator should have clear goals and objectives in mind. Difficult tasks should be broken down into easy steps. The well-organized leader also knows how to access necessary resources and knows where these resources are at all times.

SKILLED OBSERVER: Children are constantly communicating to each other nonverbally. They also send messages to the observer about their emotional states. A skilled observer with a sound knowledge of child development can interpret nonverbal messages and is mindful of "clue behaviour." Clue behaviour is a behaviour pattern or a single behaviour that is common to the child and reflects his/her emotional state. It is not difficult to read but is idiosyncratic and requires knowledge of, and a solid relationship with, each child. The facilitator who is able to decode these messages by watching and obtaining verbal feedback from the child can anticipate problems and put interventions in place that will remedy the situation.

EFFECTIVE COMMUNICATOR: The facilitator requires skill in both listening and communicating. Language needs to be clearly articulated and appropriate to the age of the group participants. Language needs to be congruent in that the verbal portion of the message needs to coincide with the nonverbal portion of the message. Language should reflect the three main sensory modalities. The use of visual, auditory, and kinesthetic (tactile/ emotional) language increases the chances that all participants will appreciate the message communicated.

Communication should not be judgmental, analytical, or critical. It should reflect an accepting attitude. Instructions, praise, and other important communications can be repeated to insure clear understanding. The onus is on the facilitator to insure that all group members have heard and understood the communication.

Positive listening requires the group leader to listen intently to the communicator when appropriate; the communication can be paraphrased to gain clarification. Feedback to the communicator in the form of nonverbal and verbal communication will assist the sender in feeling understood. Verbal feedback, like asking for clarification or verbalizing that you understand, and nonverbal feedback, like nodding your head, smiling, and making eye contact, can assist the communicator in feeling understood.

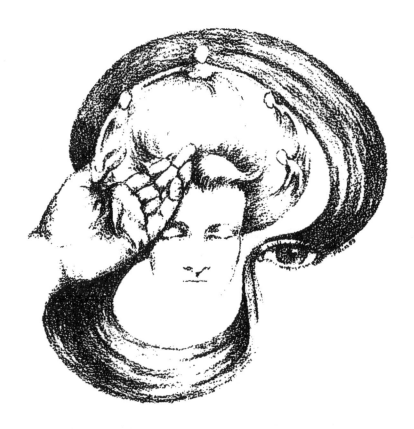

"Coming from your center, being there, teaming up, meeting them where they're at, interacting together, counseling on-the-go, creating circles of care, discovering and using self, and caring for one another.

– MARK KRUEGER"

Personal Reflection – Communication

Read through the following list of suggestions that concern positive communication styles. Note the areas that you feel confident in and comment as to why. Also, note the areas that you feel you need to improve upon and make suggestions as to how you would go about improving that skill.

Quality of Language: Choose your words carefully; say what you really mean. Do not use slang. Do not talk down to, or over the heads of, listeners, but do use words and terminology appropriate to the level of the listeners.

_____

_____

_____

_____

_____

_____

_____

Clear Expression of Ideas: Organize your ideas beforehand. Express your ideas in a logical sequence. Use complete sentences with one idea per sentence. Stick to your purpose (don't ramble or get off topic).

_____

_____

_____

_____

_____

_____

_____

Voice Production: Vary the tone of your voice (avoid using a monotone). Speak with an adequate amount of volume. Vary the pace at which you speak, but guard against speaking too slowly or too quickly (most of us speak faster than we realize). Open your mouth; avoid mumbling.

_____

_____

_____

_____

_____

_____

_____

Body Language: Project an "open" appearance (arms and legs uncrossed, relaxed). Watch what you do with your hands; are they covering your mouth or playing nervously with a pen or coins in your pocket? Make eye contact with your listeners. Does your body language match what you are saying? Try not to send conflicting messages.

_____

_____

_____

_____

_____

_____

_____

_____

Courtesy: Phrase your ideas, questions, answers, etc. as politely as you can. Be careful not to interrupt others. Be a good listener as well as a good speaker.

_____

_____

_____

_____

_____

_____

_____

_____

BEHAVIOURAL MANAGER: Facilitators must continually refine and test their behaviour management skills, and all of the qualities mentioned above are helpful in this regard. When each child is recognized and encouraged both as an individual and as a group member by the group facilitator, behaviour management becomes much easier. When a child needs to be reminded of the rules or needs to take a time-out, this is not a punishment; this should be presented as a positive strategy out of concern for the individual.

Behaviour management should not be intrusive, and this requires a sound knowledge of appropriate behaviour and a solid relationship with the child. Managing children's behaviour is a balancing of the needs of the group, the needs of the child, and the level of relationship. As the group becomes more familiar and the child feels more a part of the group, the need for behaviour management is usually lessened. Similarly, as the relationship between facilitator and child grows, the need to manage behaviour decreases. If the game or activity being presented to the children requires a lot of behavioural intervention, likely the group is not ready for that activity or game. The facilitator needs to be aware that punishment serves the adult's need to control but, in most cases, does not serve the needs of the child.

Managing children's behaviour is an art, and one that the practitioner and the field are constantly developing. Therefore, it is essential that facilitators continually upgrade their skills as behavioural managers and stay current with the literature.

Personal Reflection – Negative Leaders

Refer back to the list of leaders in your life. Think back on those leaders and answer these questions. When did you feel that they were being too punitive, too restrictive, or too "old-fashioned" in their approach? If you are having trouble remembering the past, think of the leaders that you have in your life in the present and ask the same question.

_____
_____
_____
_____
_____
_____
_____
_____
_____
_____
_____
_____

In most cases, your feelings were probably correct because many adults were raised in punitive systems where most behaviour was punished, and rules for conduct were strict and not child oriented. Go back now to the situations that you recalled, and decide how it could have been handled to your satisfaction.

_____
_____
_____
_____
_____
_____
_____
_____
_____
_____
_____
_____

FACILITATOR: When given a leadership role, we often do just that, lead. Leading is important; however, often children need the adult to step back from the group and to facilitate. This means changing from the person who controls the activity to someone who has initiated it and now watches, or who has merely suggested that play is appropriate now and then sits back and observes. A facilitator allows the children to lead and is present to insure emotional and physical safety. The leader becomes observer and is no longer part of the group.

This facilitation sets the stage for spontaneity, creativity, shared leadership, and social learning. This facilitation role is the final evolution of the adult group leader. When the facilitator can allow the group to function on its own with very little intervention, then the task as group facilitator is complete. This stage does not come without a lot of hard work and a great deal of practicing the aforementioned skills as well as having a solid understanding of child development and group behaviour. Phelan (1990) writes about the developmental levels or stages of facilitators and maintains that child and youth care professionals, with experience and solid supervision, develop from being concerned with their own safety through predictable stages to become a creative, free-thinking professional.

Developing Leaders in Children's Groups

Once the facilitator has established his/her role as adult group leader, the ultimate aim should be to evolve out of this role. The evolution allows for natural leaders to emerge as well as the leadership potential in all children. The group's evolution to the ideal of shared leadership and this transfer of power shapes cooperation. The facilitator not only needs to become a skilled leader but also needs to be able to develop this quality in others. Recognition of emerging leaders in the group is the first step in the transfer of power. Through keen observation, these leaders can be identified. Group members will often maintain more eye contact with these children in order to pick up non-verbal cues from them. Natural leaders often initiate free play activities, settle disputes among members, speak first or last in group discussions, and provide solutions to group problems.

> The great leaders are like the best conductors— they reach beyond the notes to reach the magic in the players.
>
> – BLAINE LEE

Once these leaders begin to appear, they need to be given leadership roles and responsibilities as early as possible. By singling these children out, their leadership is recognized and affirmed by the facilitator. In well-established groups, recognizing the leader(s) is the course of least resistance since they already have leadership status. During group activities, existing or natural leaders can be asked to pass out equipment, to choose teams, to invent or teach a new game to the group, to help set up for the game, and to assist with any other means of leading. Once their leadership is recognized or established, these natural leaders will feel more comfortable when other group members take on leadership roles. Also, the group members will feel less anxious with having to compete with these sometimes very powerful leaders in order to develop their own leadership skills. Once the atmosphere is established and the group feels safe, appropriate leadership skills can be practiced and enjoyed by all group members. For examples of activities focused on developing leaders in the group see Chapter 9, "Leader and Leaderless Games".

Some children are better leaders than others and some, perhaps, are not meant to be leaders. Nevertheless, all children can learn from the experience and can develop an appreciation for what it is like to lead as well as to follow. The most effective way to develop positive leadership abilities is to model those desirable qualities for all members to observe. McWhirter et al. (McWhirter, McWhirter, McWhirter, & McWhirter, 2010) add that shared leadership within groups can lead to empowerment of group members and in time motivate members to exercise choice, confront adversity, and develop purpose in their lives.

Leaders often emerge from games that challenge the group's ability to work together. These types of leaders are usually good problem-solvers and efficient organizers. Their skills can be singled out and recognized during feedback sessions or during group discussions. They also emerge on the playground when everyone is bored. These leaders are usually the creative group members who have unique ideas and ways of presenting them that spark the group's imagination.

Leaders emerge during times of stress to comfort and to soften the emotional burdens of the group. These are the humanitarians of the group who are in touch with their emotional selves. Their contribution also needs to be recognized by facilitators, and in time, they need to be appreciated by the group members. Leaders can also emerge when group morale is low and when motivation levels and energy levels are spent. They are often comical leaders and, in some cases, charismatic leaders who help the group rise above its depression. Their skills are very valuable to the group at both a task and maintenance level.

Other leaders appear when their talents and abilities are well suited for the activity, for example, athletic ability in team sports. These children can show leadership and instill confidence in team members. Once again, their talents should be recognized and valued by the facilitator and the group.

Negative Leading

Successful child group leaders may need guidance in order to enhance their skills and lead appropriately. When children in the group try to influence the other members to be uncooperative or to be physically or emotionally hurtful to the leader or others in the group, they are endangering themselves and the other members. They are leading, or are attempting to lead, the group in a negative direction. This type of leading is not to be tolerated and must be stopped quickly. The group needs to know that this type of interaction is not healthy and will not be encouraged or fostered in the group setting.

There are often some negative interactions that are borderline, that is, they are not destructive enough to be overtly harmful, yet they are not positive either. These behaviours are best dealt with outside the larger group and discussed with the child after the group has finished. An explanation of the facilitators concerns along with suggestions as to how the child can support the group and the facilitator usually results in a decrease in negative leading. The facilitator should keep in mind to reinforce children when they do lead in a positive manner. Also developing techniques and interventions to redirect any negative leading can be discussed with potential leaders both inside and outside the group experience.

The incidents of negative leading can primarily be dealt with by a word or two to the offender and then, some positive feedback or encouragement given shortly after. If the behaviour continues, a mild confrontation as to why the child is continuing the behaviour is required. Stay away from judging the child and from using putdowns. Body contact, for example, a hand on the shoulder, can be beneficial. "Signal interference" (Redl, 1952), a predetermined signal to alert the child that he/she is leading negatively, is another effective way to reduce negative leading. The strongest deterrent to negative leading is the relationship between facilitator and child—the child complies not based on the consequence but based on the mutual respect between him/her and the facilitator. Finally, if the behaviour continues, the child must be timed out or asked to leave until he/she is able to establish the necessary controls in order to behave appropriately in the group.

Group facilitation is another key element in the profession of child and youth care, and the ongoing enhancement of these skills is of primary importance in the delivery of optimum care and education.

Exercise 5:1

Leadership can be used to empower youth and can lead to activism. Make a list of three issues facing youth today and comment on what youth could do as a group to address each concern.

Issue #1

_____
_____
_____
_____
_____
_____
_____
_____
_____

Issue #2

_____
_____
_____
_____
_____
_____
_____
_____
_____

Issue #3

_____
_____
_____
_____
_____
_____
_____
_____
_____

> The provision of limits and structure are vital in creating a framework for freedom.
> – JUDITH RUBIN

Review

• Using various leadership styles is useful in responding appropriately to group needs.

• Leadership qualities and skills need to be continuously evaluated and further developed.

• Developing and recognizing natural leaders is important to group safety and level of comfort.

• Negative leading needs to be stopped or redirected.

Healthy, effective leadership by the child and youth care professional is an important catalyst for the development of therapeutic relationships within and among group members. Chapter 6, "Therapeutic Relationships" investigates the profound effect that therapeutic relationships can have on children and youth. It highlights the importance of developing and maintaining relationships that have the child as the focus and the facilitator as the initiator and agent of the relationship.

Therapeutic Relationships

When I was a young man, I had the privilege to work at a native education centre and to listen to Alice Steiner tell the ancient story of the sacred tree. "A seed appeared for all the peoples of the planet," she began. "Rich soil from the earth, water from the heavens, energy from the sun, and life's breath from the winds caused it to grow into a strong, healthy, beautiful creation—a Sacred Tree. Over time it became a gathering place where others could find shelter, healing, balance, and security. Its roots grew deep into the soil—deep into the soul of the earth—into the legends and myths buried underneath. Its branches stretched out over the years to embrace all in its path while leaves protected it from the harshness of weather. Birds, small animals, insects, and humans made it their home, sleeping under its crown, nesting in its foliage, burrowing into its bark, protected and included.

"'The life of a sacred tree,' say our elders, 'is one of constant change from stage to stage.' Its influence grows stronger as birds, animals, and insects living under and on its branches raise and nurture their young. In time, these creatures whisper their wisdom to be caught and stored by the tree's thick roots. Humans come and go, and their stories become carved beneath its branches and within its rings.

The heart and soul of the tree will grow in chorus with its connection to the earth and its communion with those around. Year after year its flowers appear, brightening the sky, and then wilting to become seeds that are blown and spread by the wind to appear and reappear once again before all the peoples of the earth."

> Relationship formation actually entails one of the most basic interpersonal human strivings—the salutary *experience of interconnectedness* where each person lends energy and rootedness to the other.
>
> — HENRY MAIER

Rapport and relationship development are the basis of child and youth care; without a trusting relationship between child and adult, no real healing can be accomplished (Brendtro, 1969; Burns, 1984; Fewster, 1987; & Maier, 1979). This chapter will focus on strategies conducive to developing rapport and cultivating healthy relationships with children, youth, and adults. It begins by asking the reader to explore the Self as a way of preparing for effective relationship development. The importance of verbal and nonverbal communication in rapport development and an awareness of self-esteem and its impact are discussed. This chapter emphasizes the importance of physical touch in the practice of child and youth care, while at the same time maintaining appropriate physical boundaries. And finally, the concept of sensory modalities is introduced and how this information can be employed in developing quick rapport and establishing effective therapeutic relationships.

Rapport, that first feeling of trust and respect, like a tiny seed when its environment nurtures it, gives birth to a healthy relationship. That relationship, in turn, provides the individuals involved with opportunities to grow and to flourish. Quick and efficient rapport-building strategies, as well as the skills necessary for the development of solid relationships, are the necessary elements that nourish all children, even those whose environments and life experiences have made it difficult for them to grow (Garfat, 2008). Phelan (2008) describes three levels of therapeutic relationship development. Level one—a safe and trusting connection with the child, which evolves into level two, a mentor-mentee relationship in which the facilitator acts as a resource and guide; this, in turn, evolves into level three, which Krueger (1995) termed "nexus" or intimate relationship with the child. The ultimate therapeutic relationship, or level three, is the final goal of each therapeutic activity facilitator. This nexus with the child is a continuous series of verbal and nonverbal modelling situations. Thus, if the goal is to be a life-model for the child, the facilitator will need to investigate what kind of model he/she is presenting.

Personal Awareness

In order to begin the process of effective rapport building and relationship development, an awareness of the Self is crucial (Brendtro, 1969; Burns, 2012; Fewster, 2001; Garfat, McElwee, & Charles, 2005; Krueger, 2007; Ricks, 2003; Stuart, 2009). Self-awareness, for both programmers and facilitators, is basic to their ability to form meaningful relationships with children in their care. They should have a sound knowledge of their individual strengths and weaknesses and an awareness of their behaviour patterns and behavioural strategies. It is also important that they have an understanding of how they were nurtured as children in order to work through roadblocks that hamper effective rapport building. Attitudes toward helping and the need to help children must be explored in order to ensure that a healthy focus is maintained (Fewster, 1990). Effective caregivers must maintain an air of genuineness that can only come from a great deal of personal awareness.

Discovering who you are (the Self) and how to develop into a skilled facilitator of therapeutic activities does not happen in a vacuum; it requires interaction with a group of individuals also seeking awareness or with a reputable counsellor, therapist, or life coach. Some awareness can be attained though journaling, reading, the arts, and self-help workbooks, but in the end, it comes from getting feedback from others. Most of the exercises in this text ask the reader to apply what has been written to their own experience. Delving into the Self and individual experiences is a good beginning and a way to stay focussed on self-awareness. When these awarenesses are shared and discussed with a group, further awareness is often attained.

Learning about the Self can be a difficult experience at times, and a support system of friends with whom to discuss personal problems and from whom to receive emotional support is helpful. Providing support and receiving it from others is an experience that can also be "Self- revealing."

Discipline is an important factor in developing self-awareness. Time can be set aside for regular alone-time to reflect on the Self, for one-to-one time to participate in meaningful relationships with significant others, and also cumulative time—enjoying everyday social life, the carrying out of day-to-day routines and role functions. The minutiae of life can be a profound teacher and test for the evolving self-aware professional. Maier (1971, 1987) believed that tending to it with the child was the essence of child and youth care practice. He also wrote, "… it is within the minutiae of life and not in the big events that one's personal pursuits and direction are determined" (1987, p. 67).

To begin to explore the concept of Self and to further increase your self-awareness, complete the reflective exercises provided throughout this chapter. If you wish to explore the concept of Self in detail, please see The Self in Child and Youth Care: A Celebration (Burns, 2012).

> The self is often seen as a singular noun, whereas it may be better considered as a "plural verb".
>
> – DANIEL SIEGEL

Personal Reflection – The Self

Please note each "[pause]" is approximately three seconds.

Make yourself as comfortable as you can, set down your book, and let your mind drift for 30 seconds. … Allow yourself to feel more relaxed with the passing of each second.

First of all, visualize your present Self [pause], your physical Self [pause], your emotional Self [pause], your social Self [pause], and your intellectual Self [pause].

Try to get a clear representation of these images in your mind [pause]. Take all the time you need to develop a clear image of your physical, emotional, social, and intellectual Selves; **make a quick sketch of each image.**

PHYSICAL ME

EMOTIONAL ME

SOCIAL ME

INTELLECTUAL ME

Now visualize in your mind these parts of your Self again, and imagine it is three years from now. What changes, adaptations, and improvements would you like to see over the next two to three years?

Now sketch those images.

PHYSICAL ME

EMOTIONAL ME

SOCIAL ME

INTELLECTUAL ME

Self-Esteem

Once the facilitator has spent time getting to know him/herself, it is also important to assist children with their feelings of Self. When developing relationships with children, the individual child's feelings of self-worth must always be kept at the forefront of any strategy. A clear message of total acceptance needs to be projected by the facilitator at all times. This total acceptance, however, does not mean tolerance of negative behaviour. When the child's behaviour is unacceptable or even inappropriate, this needs to be communicated. But, every attempt should be made to make the distinction between unacceptable behaviour (what the child does) and the value of an individual (who the child is). The behaviour may be unacceptable but the child remains lovable and capable. Punishment, ridicule, and other forms of negative discipline should not be used; the negative effect of these methods on the child's self-esteem and on relationships within the group can be devastating. Positive reinforcement through praise and the redirection of negative behaviour provides the child with the necessary elements to control individual behaviour. Construction of appropriate environments and activities that promote positive behaviour should be routine considerations when working with children in a group or individually. When the child feels valued by the facilitator and when the child is able to trust that professional, self-esteem will grow. This elevated feeling of self-importance will usually provide the child with the strength necessary to follow rules and to interact positively in relationships with others.

Remember, however, that self-esteem is not something that changes quickly—it develops over time and is usually best developed through skill development and acquiring more effective social skills. Children will feel more self-confident when they realize or discover that they are "good" at something—"I am a good speller!" "I make awesome models!" "I made the basketball team!" When you teach children skills, their sense of accomplishment increases, as does their sense of self-worth. Also, if you assist them in being more social, they begin to appreciate that they are liked by the group and therefore must be "a good person," "a valuable person." Self-esteem is developed through skill acquisition and enhanced through self-awareness.

Simon (1988) presented six conditions for facilitators to develop within their relationship with the child as a way of nurturing and maintaining self-esteem. The first condition is belonging; children need to feel connected to at least one significant adult as well as a peer group. The second condition is advocacy; children need at least one adult to advocate for them when they are unable to advocate for themselves. Third is risk management; children need support and encouragement to take risks and then assistance during any crisis periods that should arise as a result. The fourth condition is empowerment; children need opportunities to make their own decisions and choices. Fifth is uniqueness; someone needs to assist children to realize and appreciate their own unique abilities and qualities. The final condition is productivity; children need to be encouraged and supported to be productive and have purpose in life.

> It's not enough for adults to contend that they care; the task is to convincingly demonstrate caring to youth who have not always found adults deserving of their trust.
>
> – ERIK LAURSEN

Personal Reflection – Strengths and Weaknesses

Take a minute to quiet yourself, relax, close your eyes, and regulate your breathing. I want you to focus on your strengths for a minute and take a personal inventory. Think of all your abilities, positive aspects of your character, and your particular talents—your strengths. Once you have discovered as many of your strengths as you can right now, open your eyes and refocus back on the room. Now list below your top five strengths, abilities, talents, or traits using one or two words to describe them.

Strength #1

_____

_____

Strength #2

_____

_____

Strength #3

_____

_____

Strength #4

_____

_____

Strength #5

_____

_____

Take each of your strengths one at a time and list any activities and behaviours that promote or interfere with this strength. Also note if there are situations where you could apply this strength more effectively.

Strength #1

_____

_____

Strength #2

_____

_____

Strength #3

_____

_____

Strength #4

_____

_____

Strength #5

_____

_____

Take a moment to relax yourself again, regulate your breathing, and let go of any tension in your body/mind. Now think about areas in your life or aspects of your Self that are weak or cause you distress [pause, pause]. Now make a list of your three biggest weaknesses. If you want to keep it confidential, give them code names. Next to them, answer these three questions:

When does this weakness occur most often?
Where (place, situation) does this most often occur?
With whom does this happen most often?

#1

_____

_____

_____

_____

_____

#2

_____

_____

_____

_____

_____

#3

_____

_____

_____

_____

_____

Communication

Communication is a vital part of self-esteem and relationship development and is a complex operation that is affected by how, what, when, where, and why something is said. It is also heavily dependent on the nature of the past and present experiences of the sender and the receiver of the communication. Factors such as voice tone, tempo, diction, hand gestures, body position, eye contact, emotional status, social status, sex, age, and the maturity of the speakers, all make up the complex process of verbal and nonverbal communication; as well, there are the words themselves, their syntax, semantics, and their understood meanings. Communication, both verbal and nonverbal, is emphasized throughout this text. When facilitators take time to analyze and improve their communication skills, their effectiveness and their influence with children increases. The messages we send verbally and nonverbally form the basis of all social relationships. The importance of language cannot be stressed enough. Its implications and various levels of complexity need to be seriously considered.

Nonverbal communications carry four times the conversational weight of verbal messages when both are used in language. Therefore, it is most useful to consider what is being communicated nonverbally to children. Facilitators should be aware of how they communicate nonverbally and an appreciation of what constitutes nonverbal language. Children's communication is often highly nonverbal and, in many cases, messages and even whole conversations can be had nonverbally, particularly with children who are closely linked with one another—siblings, close friends, even bitter rivals. Some children use nonverbal communication to communicate unconscious reactions to situations and experiences. A physical reaction to a stranger entering the room, or a physical reaction that is out of the ordinary for the child, could be an important message for the facilitator. Facilitators need to become adept at not only interpreting the obvious body language of children but also at interpreting the nuances in their communications.

Personal Reflection – Preparation

The following is a useful exercise that will help facilitators to appreciate the factors that influence nonverbal communication. You are encouraged to try it now, and most importantly, to try it just before coming into contact with the children in your care.

Ask yourself the following:

• "How am I feeling about myself, mentally, physically, spiritually, and emotionally, today?"

• "What are my relationships like with my significant others?"

• "What are my feelings about the children, collectively and individually?"

• "How do I feel about my co-workers, supervisors, and/or administrators?"

• "Do I need to communicate any of my feelings to the children or staff members?"

• "Am I prepared to work in the present today, or will the past or future be foremost in my mind?"

Once dressed and ready for work, find a full-length mirror. Stand in front of the mirror and ask yourself:

• "What messages am I communicating through my appearance, my hairstyle, clothing, shoes, etc.? "

• "Do I like what I see? Can I say to myself, 'I love you'"?

• "What changes, additions, or subtractions can I make right now to make a difference?"

This exercise can be performed every day. It only takes a few minutes, and it contains very important information to be aware of when working towards therapeutic relationships with children and youth.

Touch

The power of touch is exemplified with this example of what became termed as "hospitalism." In the 1930s, infants in orphanages, hospitals, and long-term care institutions were diagnosed with a condition, fatal for some, that was a literal wasting away due to lack of physical contact. Hospitalism (anaclitic depression) was marked by severe developmental delays and the infants' failure to thrive. Children need to be touched, stroked, cuddled, and held. Without this tactile stimulation, children do not thrive. Their emotional Selves grow gnarled, crooked, bent, and deformed. They can be smoothed, straightened, and supported by appropriate physical touch (Montague, 1986).

Children who are kinesthetic in orientation (see "Sensory Modalities" on the next page) understand their worlds through the sense of touch. Their brain is most interested in what they touch, feel, and sense—this information is essential to them in all primary functions. Without the sense of touch, they are handicapped and forced to understand the experience through their non-dominant modalities. Kinesthetic children who have been traumatized, abused, living in stressful conditions, or have learning disabilities often require additional sensory stimulation in order to thrive.

The culture's ever-increasing realization of the extent of physical and sexual abuse has thrown many child and youth agencies and professionals into a panic. Lawsuits and allegations have marred the reputations of workers and agencies. Some institutions, especially those servicing the adolescent and pre-adolescent population, have passed sanctions against child and youth care professionals hugging and holding the youth in their care. The tragic irony of this situation is that children and youth in care need touch to get well, yet their healers have their hands tied. McElwee, McKenna-McElwee and Phelan (2002) address the issue of touching and hugging and urge professionals to "risk" touching children appropriately and "risk" assisting them to learn to deal with their own personal needs for touch.

Children, with few exceptions, have a strong need for physical contact and, for some, this is their primary mode of learning. They need to touch and to be touched in order to understand.

Children under stress require more physical contact than usual. The facilitator's task is to guide the child towards what are appropriate and inappropriate ways of fulfilling this sometimes-ravenous need. Once a positive relationship has been established, all children benefit from appropriate physical contact, though perhaps in varying degrees. This is especially true for those children who are hypersensitive to touch; physical contact should be initiated slowly and monitored until the child is comfortable with being touched. Such cases of hypersensitivity in children should always be treated under the care of a team of professionals.

Among different cultures, families, groups, and pairs, physical contact is enjoyed and transmitted in a wide variety of healthy and wholesome ways. This text contains several activities that provide opportunities for children to engage in appropriate touch (see for example, Chapter 11, "Teen and Young Adult Play" – Contact Exercises). Programmers and facilitators can include sensory needs (see for example, Chapter 12, "Dealing with Feelings" – Sensory Experiences). An environment where open and honest physical contact is provided allows each child to fulfill his/her needs from whomever or whatever is appropriate.

Physical Boundaries

Physical contact is a necessary part of communicating with children, but it is also important to determine and respect their physical boundaries. Most humans have an imaginary boundary around their person known as their personal space. This space is the distance or proximity between one person and the other and measures the level of comfort between the two participants. In some cultures, personal space is large, and in other cultures, only a small personal space is preferred. There is a distance that is maintained when speaking with casual acquaintances, but that is quite different from the distance maintained when we are speaking with intimate friends. The level of comfort that proximity provides is dependent on the relationship.

Children are sometimes not given proper respect in terms of their personal boundaries. Facilitators need to be aware of this need within children and quickly identify those boundaries. A respect for boundaries can also be discussed and pointed out to the group. Facilitators and group members need to respect any members need to put limitations on others concerning their personal space. Through discussion, observation, and staying "present" (Krueger, 1999) or focussed, the adult honours personal space—knowing when to move closer and when to retreat. Usually permission to cross this boundary is given nonverbally, however, when in doubt, it is best to ask for permission. Children, in turn, can be taught to set boundaries and limits for their physical selves. They can be taught to pay attention to the sensations and emotions that help inform them of their personal space (Artz, 1993).

Sensory Modalities

Sensory modalities like physical boundaries are specific to the child. An awareness of sensory modalities can therefore be useful when attempting to develop rapport, enhance self-awareness, and strengthen relationships with children. All experience, past or present, internal or external, can be categorized as primarily involving seeing, hearing, touching, tasting, or smelling. Children, like all humans, have a stronger or more dominate sense, that which they use and rely upon more frequently. This is their preferred modality (Dilts, Bandler, Bandler-Cameron, DeLozier, & Grinder, 1980; Bandler, 2008; Gibson, 2011).

Some children rely more heavily on their visual modality to make sense of their worlds. This can mean they are more affected by, or concerned with, what they see, both internally in the mind's eye and externally. Other children rely more heavily on what they hear; they use their auditory modality more frequently. As a way to best understand their worlds, some children may rely on their kinesthetic modality, feeling externally by using their sense of touch or feeling internally by experiencing and re-experiencing their emotions. The sense of smell and the sense of taste are extremely powerful and useful in the early stages of development but, as the child gets older, they are not as frequently used as the auditory, kinesthetic, and visual modalities. This preferred modality can be identified in a number of ways and by various techniques (Dilts, Bandler, Bandler-Cameron, DeLozier, & Grinder, 1980; Bandler, 2008; Gibson, 2011).

Personal Reflection – Preferred Modality

Take a moment to relax, regulate your breathing, let go of any tension in your body/mind, and respond to the following questions:

Do you prefer to be given directions to a friend's house orally or to have a map drawn on a piece of paper? Someone who prefers to have the directions told to them is more apt to rely on their auditory system. If the preference is for the map, the person is likely more visually oriented.

_____

_____

_____

When learning a new skill, do you benefit from trial-and-error experimental learning? Those of us who prefer trial-and-error learning may rely more heavily on the kinesthetic modality—touch and emotion.

_____

_____

_____

When meeting people for the first time, do you attend more to what the person says and the sound of their voice, or how they look, or how they make you feel (e.g., your "gut feeling" about them)?

_____

_____

_____

Think about the words you use to describe your experiences; are they visual, auditory, or kinesthetically oriented?

_____

_____

_____

What about your interests and favourite pastimes are they kinesthetically, visually, or auditory oriented?

_____

_____

_____

Identifying the Preferred Modality

Children display characteristics that make their preferred sensory modality identifiable (Barbe, 1982; Gibson, 2011)). Visual children organize their world by means of what they see and what they perceive visually. They tend to speak using predominantly visual words (Bandler & Grinder, 1976; Gibson, 2011). For example, take note of the words in italics, *"Look, you can see the sailboats really clearly now, Dad. Notice all the coloured angles near the bow. What a sight!"* These children are often more concerned with their appearance. They also tend to do well in mathematics. Visual imagery is often more easily attainable for these children, and they frequently have vivid and colourful dreams. A visual child often needs to see something before believing it to be true, and therefore, understands best when shown how to accomplish particular tasks. Visual children tend to look at the person who is speaking and to pay attention to visual cues more often than other children.

Auditory children, on the other hand, will speak using words that predominantly relate to sound (Bandler & Grinder, 1976; Gibson, 2011). For example, take note of the words in italics, *"It sounds to me like she won't listen to what you're saying to her. I think she has turned you off."* These children are real "talkers" and tend to speak early in their development. Their voice tone is apt to give indications of their moods. Their tempo when speaking is often very rhythmic. Reading and spelling are favourite subjects in school, and auditory children may do poorly in math except when learning times tables. Auditory children learn best when given verbal instructions and can often listen very well when they appear to be inattentive.

Kinesthetic children learn best through their sense of touch and their emotions. They speak most often in feeling words (Bandler & Grinder, 1976; Gibson, 2011). For example, take note of the words in italics: *"I have a feeling that if he does not get in touch with what's bugging him, we are all in for a rough time."* These children may be labelled "clingers" or "huggers" due to their strong need for physical contact. They are often considered "sloppy" since they pay more attention to how their clothes feel than how they look. Their voice pitch is slightly lower than visual and auditory children. A kinesthetic child is often the child who is labelled "emotional." They use a lot of hand gestures when speaking and often count on their fingers. Kinesthetic children usually enjoy crafts and body contact sports.

It is important to note that the above profiles of visual, auditory, and kinesthetic children are not foolproof and, like all categories and stages, the facilitator must be aware of the child's individual style. However, children presenting profiles similar to the ones outlined above can be hypothesized as being either visual, auditory, or kinesthetic.

Developing Rapport through the Preferred Modality

Here are a few approaches and techniques to assist you in using the child's preferred modality as a way of enhancing rapport.

VISUAL CHILDREN: Speak to this child using visual language. Whenever possible, include a visual representation of what you are communicating. Be aware of your physical appearance and how you appear to this child. Be very careful of incongruent messages (e.g., when your words and body posture do not match). Painting, drawing, picture books, photography, television, and computers are some of the activities preferred by visual children.

AUDITORY CHILDREN: These children like to be spoken to and to be permitted to talk things out. They respond best to spoken (vs. written) language. Voice tone and tempo, as well as inflection, can be very important when trying to effectively communicate with auditory children. Listening to music, singing songs, and talking on the cell phone are some of the activities enjoyed by the auditory child.

KINESTHETIC CHILDREN: The sense of touch and physical closeness are very often important to these types of children. Handshakes, a pat on the back, or a hug are effective ways of communicating acceptance to kinesthetic children. When communicating verbally, use feeling and tactile words; some type of physical contact while communicating is helpful as well. Back rubs, wrestling, clay, and drama are some very effective ways to encourage and stimulate kinesthetically oriented children.

Exercise 6:1

Bandler & Grinder (1976) describe reflecting as a form of "pacing" or "mirroring"; it is simply imitating or mimicking the child's behaviour. This technique is probably the most effective way of establishing quick rapport, and it is the one used either consciously or unconsciously by most competent facilitators. Try this technique on a child or unsuspecting friend.

• Observe the child, paying particular attention to the child's posture and facial expression.

• Recreate or imitate the child's posture and expression.

• Take on the mirror image of the child, and visualize the child in your mind. Clues and symbols abound in using visualization.

• When the child moves, changing posture and expression, you follow, mirroring the child.

• As this mirroring is taking place, be aware of any emotions or physical sensations (e.g., feeling of anger, muscle tension) that you experience.

• Having successfully mirrored the child's posture and expression, begin to use word phrases similar to those used by the child.

• Match the child's language by responding with visual words when the child uses visual language; use auditory words when the child uses auditory language; and similarly, employ kinesthetic, olfactory, and gustatory language when the child does.

• When you have successfully mirrored and feel comfortable with mirroring the child's language, observe some of the child's more subtle nonverbal behaviours, (e.g., breathing depth and rate, gestures and mannerisms, eye and head movements, etc.).

• You can then mirror one or more of these subtle behaviours.

• As the child changes behaviours, follow by matching them.

• Become aware of emotions and physical sensations taking place in your body as you mirror the child.

• Having successfully mirrored the more subtle nonverbal behaviours, you can now mirror the more subtle verbal behaviours, (e.g., voice tone and tempo, inflections, pronunciations, etc.).

These steps may be repeated several times during an interaction with a child. It is important not to mimic the child in an obvious way, which might make the child feel self-conscious or agitated. A more subtle and unobtrusive style of mirroring is most effective. It is through this process that the facilitator can begin to appreciate more fully the child's experience. The child feels a sense of comfort by experiencing, consciously and unconsciously, this mirroring process and thus more relaxed, validated, and understood.

Review

- Personal self-awareness is a key element in the development of therapeutic relationships with children, youth, and young adults.

- Self-esteem takes a long time to change and develop.

- Self-esteem develops through acquiring skills.

- Nonverbal communication is critical to the development of rapport.

- Touch is an essential component in rapport and relationships.

- Personal boundaries are important to honour.

- Identifying and utilizing sensory modality information is a powerful way of developing rapport and maintaining therapeutic relationships.

This chapter completes the first section of the text "Theory." Section Two, "Resources" (Chapters 7 through to 11), provide learners with 150 activities to use in developing and strengthening their abilities as therapeutic activity programmers and facilitators. The first chapter in Section Two, Chapter 7, "Bridges and Anchor Points," addresses the importance of transitional periods in therapeutic programming and the use of activities to relax and centre children by providing, for the reader, 35 games and activities focussed on these two goals.

> Personal relationships are the fertile soil from which all advancement, all success, all achievement in real life grows.
> — **MAX STEINGART**

RESOURCES

CHAPTER 7

Bridges and Anchor Points

Bridges are games, songs, or activities that make transitional periods (times when a child is between routines or changing from one environment to another) easier to cope with for both the child and the adult. Sometimes children need just a little adult assistance to make transitions and moments of stress easier to manage. Fritz Redl (1952) called this "hurdle help." Bridges span the gap between one situation and another or from one emotional state to another. Bridges can also be used in unstructured play situations. When the facilitator senses that "trouble" is about to materialize in the play situation, a bridge activity can often redirect the group or adjust the mood of the group. When children are waiting in line for tickets, travelling in the car, between homework and supper, or when they have 10 minutes before recess, bridges help children to settle themselves emotionally and to occupy themselves cognitively and behaviourally through these transitional times.

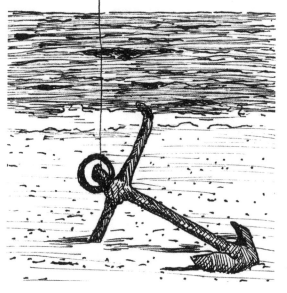

Anchor points are games, techniques, or activities that relax and centre the child or youth in order for them to regain equilibrium. Anchor points can also be used to expel excess anxious energy. Sometimes an anchor point is a one-to-one activity, sometimes it is forming a circle, sometimes it is playing the group's favourite game; all of the time, it is familiar, comforting, and positive. When youth are waiting to speak with their lawyer, feeling distraught or unsettled over a relationship, behaving negatively or becoming withdrawn, anchor points can lift their spirits, change their behaviour, or adjust their thinking to allow them to cope more effectively with their here-and-now experience.

> We build too many walls and not enough bridges.
>
> — ISAAC NEWTON

Activities

Bridges

TABOO

Taboo is a word game that asks the players to carry on a conversation about a certain person, place or thing; however, they are not allowed to say the person's name or the name of the place or thing. They must replace the name with the word taboo. This activity can be expanded to using more than one word, with children developing their own vocabulary.

NOT A WORD

Not a Word is a game of silence, and about who can stay quiet the longest. Hand signals can be used during the game so that the players can still communicate. The first person to speak gains one point but can have the point removed if he/she can remain silent for one minute.

EAGLE EYE

This is a game for travellers. It will need to be preplanned by someone who knows the journey well. Several landmarks that are on the route are selected, listed, and given different point values, depending on how difficult they are to see. Other more common persons, places, or things can also be included in the game, and they would be given a lesser point value. The player who sees the landmark first scores the appropriate point value.

TIME QUIZZES

These can take many forms, but there are two major ideas involved. One is guessing when certain time intervals occur (e.g., clap when 30 seconds is up); the other is guessing how many times something will occur in a designated span (e.g., how many green cars will pass by in the next three minutes).

I'M THINKING

I'm Thinking is a guessing game much like I Spy. "I'm thinking of an animal that rhymes with now." "I'm thinking of a person that rhymes with pill." "I'm thinking of a show that rhymes with granny."

I'VE GOT A SECRET

I've Got a Secret is a guessing game where a player thinks of a famous person, place, or thing. The group can ask the person questions and he/she must answer with either a yes or no. The group must guess the secret.

NAME THAT TUNE

Name That Tune requires a source of music. The game starts when the first three to five seconds of the song or musical composition is played. After the five seconds has passed, the music is stopped and players must guess the song title or ask a question that requires a yes or no answer (e.g., "Is this a Rock and Roll song?"). If the group is unsuccessful, a few more seconds of the composition can be played as a further clue.

THE LETTER GUESSING GAME

The player who starts has 60 seconds to think of as many words that start with a certain letter of the alphabet. The word must be found in the dictionary to qualify.

CARTOON TRIVIA

Each player thinks of a favourite cartoon character. One player is designated to lead. The leader begins by concentrating on his/her cartoon character while the rest of the group tries to guess who the character is. The group must ask questions that require a yes or no answer. The leader responds to each question by either nodding "yes" or by shaking his/her head "no". The leader receives one point for each incorrect question (no). Once the character is guessed or the group concedes, the player whose cartoon character receives the most incorrect guesses wins.

RADAR EARS

This game is played with paper and pens about half way into a road trip or when the group is listening to the radio, or playing music. Ask the group to make a list of all the songs, including songwriters and recording artists, which have been played on the radio during the trip or time together. They might also list the commercials and news items that have been broadcast.

HULL GULL

This is a game for pairs. One of the pair has an object that will fit easily in one hand (button or coin). The player puts his/her hands behind the back and moves the object to one hand or the other. The player then extends his/her hands out in front, and the opponent must guess which hand has the object. If he/she is correct, the coin or a point goes to the opponent. If incorrect, the other player scores a point, and another round begins.

TRAVELLING ALPHABET

Players must follow the sequence of the alphabet and locate signs that begin with each letter of the alphabet, starting with the letter A and then B and so on, until the whole alphabet is run through. The first player to notice the sign and call out the letter scores the point. Only one letter per sign is allowed. This game can also be played by calling out the first number of a vehicle license plate that begins with the number one up to zero.

HIGH FIVE

When someone in the group says something positive then anyone can yell out "High Five!" and everyone in the group high fives each other (raising one hand up over the shoulder with palm facing out and slapping another player's upheld palm) and yells out with much enthusiasm "High Five!"

LOW FIVE

If someone in the group says something negative then anyone in the group can whisper or speak softly "low five" and the group low fives one another (dropping one arm down with palm facing outward and gently slapping another player's palm) and with very little enthusiasm says "low five"

MIND READING

This game is played with small groups of three to four players, same format as "One, Two, Three" except the three or more players are trying to read each other's minds so that they will all put out the same number of fingers, all ones or all twos. When they succeed, they all receive a point. Teams can be challenged to try it with three or four fingers.

I SPY

This is an old favourite and can be used for colours, sounds, the beginning letter of a word, etc. "I spy with my little eye something that is red." "I hear with my little ear something that sounds like hiss." "I spy with my little eye something that begins with a.

LICENSE PLATES

Paper and pencils are required for this activity. Participants are asked to collect as many different state and provincial license plates including the plate numbers and/or letters, or to find the alphabet in order (A-Z), or to find the highest number on a plate. Collecting the names or phrases on personal license plates can be another way to play this game.

ROCK, PAPER, SCISSORS

This hand game is played in dyads. Players begin by clenching their fists, holding them out in front of themselves, and then shaking their fists in an up and down motion three times. On the count of three, players hold out a clenched fist, two fingers, or an open hand. A clenched fist signifies a rock, two fingers signify scissors, and an open hand signifies paper. The game centres on the concept that a rock smashes scissors, scissors cut paper, and paper wraps around rock. For example, if one player holds out an open palm (paper) and the other holds out two fingers (scissors), the player holding out the two fingers wins.

ONE, TWO, THREE

This is a game played in triads and as in "Rock, Paper, Scissors" the players move their fists up and down and on the count of three hold out one finger or two. The player who is odd person out—the player who does not match up with the other two—scores the point.

GAMES FOR WAITING

Players are asked to close their eyes, relax, and pick out 10 different sounds in the environment. Instruct the players to count the sounds, one on each finger, one at a time until completed. When the group is finished, they compare sounds.

"Look around you and find 10 different signs. Count them on your fingers, one at a time. When you are finished, close your eyes. When everyone is finished, the group can compare the different signs."

"Get in touch with your environment, and feel the different textures or sensations. Count them on your fingers, one at a time, and when you are finished, put your hands on your hips. Discuss the different tactile experiences."

Anchor Points

BREATHE

This exercise works best if you use the following instructions:

"Close your eyes, take a deep breath and while breathing in, count 1,…2,…3,…, and now let it out, counting 1,…2,…3,…4,…. Now breathe in again, counting 1,…2,…3,…4,…, and let it out, counting 1,…2,…3,…4,…5,…. In again one more time, count 1,…2,…3,…4,…5,…, now let it out, counting 1,…2,…3,…4,…5,…6,…."

CENTRING

Ask the group to sit in a circle. Once seated, ask them to place their palms on their abdomen. Instruct the group to imagine that their hand is on the centre of their Self like the centre of a circle. Tell the group to imagine that when they breathe in, they are breathing in energy from the earth. When they breathe out, they are sending that energy back into the universe. Have the group members practice this exercise until they are all breathing in a relaxed manner.

MENTORS

Ask the group to close their eyes and try to imagine someone who they feel is _____ (here the facilitator names a quality or attribute such as strong, patient, wise). When they have a picture of that person, ask them to be aware of how that person looks, then to imagine that they can hear this person's voice. And then ask them to imagine that they have become that person. The group can share their choices with one another.

MOVEMENT TO CENTRE

Ask the group members to begin to move around the play area. Direct them to move a little bit faster, and then faster, and so on, until they are all moving quickly around the play space. Now ask them to slow down just a bit, and then slower, until the group is walking very slowly around the play space.

THOUGHT LABELLING

Explain that thoughts can be memories from the past, ideas about the future, or can be about the here and now. Instruct the group to close their eyes, let their minds drift, and begin to label their thoughts. If they are remembering the past, they are to label that thought as "past"; if they are thinking about what might happen later on, label it "future." And if they are thinking about what is happening right now, label that "present." Group members can share their thoughts with one another.

Variation: Thoughts may appear as pictures, sounds, or sensations. Ask the group to close their eyes and label their thoughts. If they are thinking in pictures, they are to label them "visual," in sounds "auditory," in sensations or emotions "kinesthetic."

SHAKE

Ask the group to begin by letting their arms fall down to their sides then gently starting to shake their hands in a back and forth motion (like they were shaking water off their hands). Once they all have begun to shake their hands, ask them to allow the shaking to travel up their arms so that they are now shaking their arms in a back and forth motion. Once accomplished, ask the group to have the shaking travel down from their shoulders right down to their waist so that now their whole upper body is shaking. Once completed, ask them to let the shaking travel down their legs to the soles of their feet. Now their whole bodies are shaking. Finally ask the group to move their feet up and down while shaking their entire bodies.

> Every now and then go away, have a little relaxation, for when you come back to your work your judgment will be surer.
> – LEONARDO DA VINCI

STANDING OVATION

This is a spontaneous game that can be initiated by anyone in the group, or a group member may ask for an ovation for him/herself. It begins by someone in the group shouting out, "I want a standing ovation!" This is a cue for the rest of the group to stand up and clap and cheer for the group member. The game can also be directed to someone other than the player. This begins with, "I want to give Jack a standing ovation!"

LAY STILL

Ask the group to lie down and to make sure they have enough space around them so that they are not touching each other. Pick the person who seems the most relaxed to be the leader. Instruct the leader to stand. Group members lying down are asked to be as still as possible; if they move and the leader sees them, then they are a leader as well. The game proceeds until one member is left lying.

GROUP HUG

Ask the group to form a circle. The whole group scrunches up and tightens the circle, and members place their arms around one another in an embrace. Ask the group to close their eyes and feel the energy of the group. Sometimes there is a group member who needs a hug more than the rest, and that player can start out in the centre of the circle.

CHUCKLE BELLY

Ask the group to stand and form a single line. The player at the beginning of the line is asked to lie down. The next player is asked to lie down so that his/her head is resting on the first player's abdomen. The group is then instructed, one at a time, to lie down so that their head is resting on the abdomen of the player next to them. When the group is finished they should all be lying down connected and forming one line. This exercise can also be played with group members in a circle such that the first person's head is on the abdomen of the last person.

Now ask player number one to begin to laugh, or you may want to tell a joke or sing a silly song to get the group laughing. Once someone starts, the rest of the group usually follows suit until the whole line is laughing.

EVERY PICTURE TELLS A STORY

Cut out interesting, provocative, and positive pictures from magazines, or collect a series of pictures involving the group, and back each of them with light cardboard or construction paper. These pictures can be a way to introduce discussion using a theme or subject. Ask the children to write or tell a short story about each photograph. The group can be asked questions regarding the picture (e.g., What do you think the characters in this picture are thinking or feeling?")

AFFIRMATIONS

Please note, each "[pause]" is approximately three seconds.

This exercise uses courage as the desired attribute; however, any feeling, talent, or attribute can be inserted to replace the word COURAGE. Use the following dialogue.

"Imagine a person whom you believe to be COURAGEOUS and be aware of any similarities between you and that person. Say to yourself, 'I am strong and courageous just like _____.' See yourself and this person in your mind's eye, hear the person's voice, and imagine you feel some of his/her COURAGE.

"Now allow your mind to drift to a time when you felt COURAGEOUS. Be aware of how you looked [pause], how you sounded [pause], and how your body felt. As you are experiencing this feeling, say to yourself, 'I am strong and courageous and can handle any situation.'"

CAR WASH

Instruct the group to stand and form two lines with the players facing one another. This line is the car-washing line. Instruct players one at a time to walk down between the two lines. The players in the car washing line reach out and rub, stroke, and "wash" the player going through the line.

FANTASY TRIP

This activity is meant as a quick way to focus or relax children. Ask the group to find a comfortable spot where they feel safe. When they are ready, ask them to close their eyes and get ready for a fantasy trip (see Chapter 13, "Relaxation, Imagery, and Guided Fantasy"). Suggest that they travel in their minds to a far away place. Ask them to look around to see where they are and what they are doing. Instruct them to notice any pictures, sounds, smells, tastes, and feelings as they explore this place.

Once they appear settled, ask them to get ready to come back to the here and now. Ask that they come back slowly, and when they return, to slowly open their eyes.

THE DREAM ARM

This activity works best with a demonstration. Ask for a volunteer, or select a person and demonstrate for the group. The person can either stand or sit. Ask the player selected to think of a favourite television show, preferably a half-hour program. Some children prefer a cartoon. When the player has chosen, ask him/her to close his/her eyes, raise an arm up over the head, and pretend to be watching the program. Instruct the player to slowly lower his/her arm, and suggest that as the arm is lowering, the show is progressing. When the player's arm reaches his/her side, the program should be completed. As the player lowers his/her arm, stop it with your hand at intervals and say, "It is time for a commercial." While holding the players arm up, make a positive comment (affirmation, see "Affirmations") such as, "Won't you be surprised when you wake up tomorrow and feel rested and alert," or "Today is going to be a good day for you," or "You are going to be happy when you leave here today." Continue until the player's arm is resting by his/her side.

Now ask the group to pair-up and take turns with the dream arm. Players may need suggestions for appropriate affirmations.

Chapter 8, "Games for the Developing Group" provides the facilitator with a series of activities paced to reflect the four different phases of group development discussed in Chapter 4, "The Therapeutic Group." The facilitator can use the series with newly formed groups or can adapt it to fit groups that are already familiar with one another.

> Play allows us to develop alternatives to violence and despair; it helps us learn perseverance and gain optimism.
> – STUART BROWN

CHAPTER 8

Games for the Developing Group

This chapter focusses on the use of games and activities to direct and enhance group development. It provides a series of games and activities for the facilitator to introduce to groups at the various levels of development. Groups need to grow and mature at their own pace; certain activities can enhance this development, and others can be counter-productive and even threatening if introduced too early in the developmental process. Groups begin as a collection of individuals, and if allowed to progress under controlled circumstances and with the guidance of a professionally trained facilitator, they can develop over time into harmonious cooperative units.

The following series of activities is meant to take the newly formed group through a collection of group experiences that will provide them with opportunities to grow and to develop. They are a series of group activities that follow normal group developmental phases (see Chapter 4, "The Therapeutic Group"). They can, however, be utilized for groups that are already in the various phases of development. The initial phase of getting to know one another is important for the development of safety, which should always be the primary consideration of group facilitators. This phase allows children to slowly get to know one another in a safe and controlled setting. The second phase is one of experimentation and begins to ask participants to cooperate to achieve a common goal. In this phase, participants learn more information about one another and begin to form personal bonds. The third phase challenges the group to make decisions and to problem-solve using consensus as the ideal. This phase asks group members to begin to trust each other and to care for and treat one another with respect. The final stage, termination, contains activities for group members to say good-bye to one another and to comment on the overall group experience.

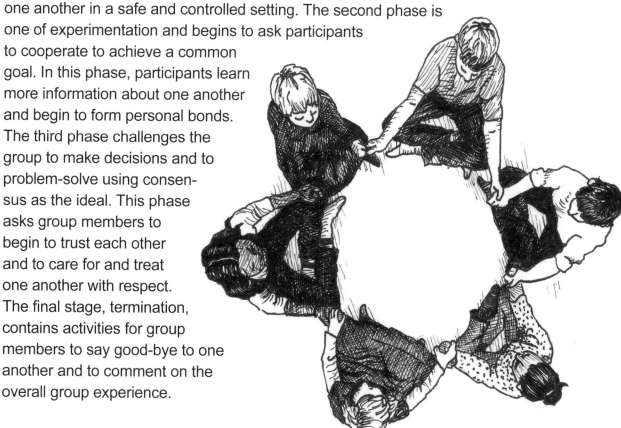

> A small group of thoughtful people could change the world. Indeed, it's the only thing that ever has.
>
> — MARGARET MEAD

Activities

Group Development: Stage One

WHO IS ON MY BACK?

Even before children are formally introduced to one another, they can interact in this humorous and non-threatening activity.

Cut out pictures of characters that are well known to the group members, for example, cartoon characters, movie stars, famous people, and famous places. The names can also be printed on a piece of construction paper. The activity requires a character for each participant and a safety pin so that the picture can be pinned on the back of each child's shirt.

As each member enters the room, the picture or name of the famous character is pinned on the back of his/her shirt. The participant is then told that they may only ask questions that require yes or no answers. Their task is to try and figure out who the character is. The participant is also instructed to answer questions from other group members with a yes or no. All players remain active until the last character is guessed.

This activity may not work well with preschoolers. Take care when selecting the characters so that the group members know who they are and will be able to guess them fairly easily. If you are playing this game with a group that already has rapport with one another, you can increase the amount of interaction by choosing more obscure characters or by allowing only one question for each group member.

I AM ... THIS IS

Names are very important when developing rapport and building self-esteem. Also, knowing someone's name makes interactions with that person more comfortable. This exercise gives the children an opportunity to hear the names of the group members frequently in a short space of time. The variations of this game may give the group facilitator some insights into the children's interests, feelings, and self-image. This works well as an opening exercise.

Call the group together and ask them to form a circle. Explain to them that you are going to play a game for them to learn each other's names. Start with the person on your left; that person is to say, "I am (child's name)," for example, "I am Bill." The person on Bill's left is to say, "I am Ann, and this is Bill." The person on Ann's left is to say, "I am Mary, this is Ann, and this is Bill." This process continues until the last person (the group facilitator) repeats everyone's name until the whole group has been named. You might wish to repeat the game going in the opposite direction.

Variations: Use the same format as above, only ask group members to introduce themselves and add something that they enjoy doing (e.g., "I am baseball-playing Bill, and this is bike-riding Ann.").

Use the same format as above, but this time group members introduce themselves by describing how they feel (e.g., "I am curious Bill, and this is happy Ann.").

This can be a difficult game for young children or for children with memory problems, so smaller groups may need to be formed. Another way to overcome the problem of too many names to remember is to divide the circle into quarters and to play the game with only one quarter of the names at a time. The rest of the group listens and learns the names as well. If a group member has trouble remembering, give the person sufficient time to remember; otherwise, other group members can provide clues or can simply mime the name. In the variations, some children may have difficulty thinking of an appropriate adjective. Before starting the activity, children can be provided with a variety of examples to help them make a selection.

I'D LIKE YOU TO MEET MY NEW FRIEND
This exercise is a pairing exercise, and it provides the group members with their first opportunity to communicate on a one-to-one basis. It also allows the group to learn more about each of its members on a personal level.

Call the group together and ask them to pick a partner, someone whom they do not know very well. Tell the group that they have three to five minutes to talk to their partner in order to find out at least three different things about them (e.g., age, grade, family members, pets, hobbies, etc.). Suggest that they take turns, and tell them that you will signal them when half of their time is up so that both get a chance to speak. When the time is up, ask the group to form a circle; then, ask the group, one by one, to introduce their partner to the group and to include the information that they just gathered from their partners.

This is often the children's first time speaking for any length of time in the group, and it may be difficult for them to remember all the information. During the introduction to the group, allow partners to confer with one another in order to ensure that the information is correct and complete. As each member finishes, ask the partner being introduced if there is anything they wish to add to what has already been said.

PAPER BAG INTRODUCTIONS

Lunch-sized paper bags are required for this activity, one for each player. Instruct the players to place the bag over their right hand. The object is to wear out the paper bag. Players are required to continue to introduce themselves, by shaking hands, to the group members until their bag will no longer stay on their hand. If members know each other, they must introduce themselves as a different fictitious character with each handshake.

MIRRORING

This nonverbal exercise allows children to imitate one another and to communicate nonverbally.

Instruct the group to form dyads. Ask each pair to decide who will be A and who will be B. Player A is to take on a series of three poses. After each pose, player B is to imitate it. When all three poses have been mimed, player B takes on a series of three poses for player A to mime.

Next, A is asked to take on three poses that depict three different emotions. After each pose, B is to take on that pose and guess which emotion it is depicting. Player B then takes a turn with three emotions. A is asked to take on each pose and guess which emotion it represents.

FIND YOUR PARTNER

Making contact with members of the group, and forming connections with one another, is important to a newly formed group. In this game, children are provided with an opportunity to make these very important contacts.

This activity requires the facilitator to create puzzles out of construction paper or out of pictures from a magazine. To make the puzzles, cut the construction paper or picture in a haphazard way to form two pieces.

Each puzzle will require two people to solve it. Mix puzzle pieces together, distribute them, and ask group members to pair up with the person in the group who has the other piece of the puzzle. The game can be played several times or can be used as a way to form dyads out of the group.

Puzzles can also be cut into more than two pieces to make the activity more difficult or to form triads or small groups.

SPECIAL SOUNDS

This is a fun activity that can be useful to begin a longer pairing exercise. Children can use their imaginations to come up with their own unique sound. The variation can be used as a creative way to form dyads, triads, or small groupings.

Ask the group to pair up with someone they have not paired with before or someone they do not normally pair up with. Have each pair decide on a sound that they will use to identify each other. Spread the pairs around the room and ask them to close their eyes and locate their partner using only their special sound to locate one another.

Variations: On small strips of paper, print the names of farmyard animals. Each type of animal will have two strips of paper with its name on it. The papers are passed out, one to each participant. Children are told to read the name on the paper silently to themselves. They are not to tell anyone what their animal is.

Ask the group members to spread out around the room. Instruct them to close their eyes and make the sound of their animal.

When they hear another animal sound that is the same as their own, the participants are told to try to make their way around the room with the purpose of pairing up with the person making the same animal sound. This exercise can be used for forming groups of any number of individuals by varying the number of strips for each animal.

NOTICING OTHERS

This game of observation allows group members to make more contact in a nonverbal fashion. Children are given the opportunity to observe each other at close range.

Ask the group members to pair up and sit down facing one another. Instruct the pairs to spend two minutes noticing what their partners are wearing, the way they are sitting, and everything about them. Suggest to them that this game will challenge their visual memory. When the two minutes have elapsed, ask the pairs to sit back to back. Instruct each player to change three things about themselves (e.g., remove a piece of clothing or jewelry, undo a button, roll down a sock, etc.). When each player has completed this task, they are asked to turn around and face one another. Now they are to guess which three things are different.

1, 2, 3 - SHAKE

Each person, without talking, decides on the number 1, 2, or 3 for him/herself. Instruct the players that if a player chooses the number one, he/she shakes the other players' hands once; if he/she chooses two, he/she shakes players' hands twice; and three, he/she shakes three times. Players begin by facing one another and take turns shaking each other's hands. Once members discover others with the same number, they stick together and mingle to discover others, until there are three groups. This game is to be done in absolute silence.

SEVEN-UP

This is a good activity for newly formed groups and well established groups alike. It reinforces the first names of group members and allows for casual, non-threatening competition.

Ask the group to sit down together facing the front of the play space. Ask the group for seven participants to volunteer to be the leaders. The leaders will stand up in front of the group. If the group is less than 15, it is beneficial to lessen the number of children designated as leaders in the game. All other players are to close their eyes until they are told to open them. The leaders will quietly walk up behind players who have their eyes closed and gently tag them on the shoulder. Once each leader has tagged a member, he/she is to return to the front of the group. The group is then asked to open their eyes. Those who were tagged have one guess to choose which leader tagged them. Players who guess correctly get to replace the leader, and those who guessed incorrectly remain seated.

Group Development: Stage Two

DIFFERENCES

This activity allows group members to share some personal information in a small group setting. This activity requires pencils and paper for each member.

If the group has over eight members, divide it into smaller groups. Post the list below for all group members, or make up individual lists.

• What is your full name?

• What day, month, and year were you born?

• What city/town were you born in?

• How tall are you?

• What is the colour of your eyes?

• What is the colour of your hair?

• What is your ancestry?

• Do you belong to a specific religious group?

• Who is your best friend?

• How many people are in your family, and what are their names?

Ask each of the group members to gather the information requested and to write it down on the sheet provided. When lists are completed, information can be shared with the small group and then with the entire group if time allows.

PERSONAL SPACE

This activity is an excellent way to help group members define their personal space before continuing on to more challenging forms of group interaction. When the results are shared in the group, members have a good understanding of each other's personal boundaries.

Ask the group members to form pairs. Request that one member of the pair be A and the other be B. A is to stand in front of B, approximately six feet away. When B is ready, A is to slowly walk toward B but must stop when B signals him/her to stop. B is to stop A when he/she is as close as B would like that person to come. Repeat this procedure with A standing six feet away on B's left and moving towards B until he/she signals him/her to stop. Continue with A standing on B's right, and then standing behind B and moving forward until B signals A to stop. Repeat the exercise with A and B switching places. Sometimes it is useful to then draw a circle around B to indicate his/her personal space.

Once completed, ask the group to discuss their experiences one dyad at a time so that group members witness where each other's personal space and boundaries are. Discuss within the group how each member felt about the process. This can lead to a discussion about the importance of personal space. Focus questions might be: Do personal boundaries vary with different group members? Is it important to respect one another's personal space?

CONTACT EXERCISE

This exercise allows group members to gradually begin to make contact with each other. If it is done in a fun-loving, non-threatening way, it allows group members to slowly enter into each other's personal space.

Ask the group members to begin walking around the room helter-skelter with their eyes down, noticing no one but themselves and remaining silent. After a few minutes, ask the group to continue moving, but to make eye contact with each group member as they pass by. In time, ask them to move faster, but to avoid bumping. Next, ask them to slow down and then to speed up. When the group seems to be warming up, ask them to continue moving slowly and to shake hands with each other without talking. Next, to shake left hands, then elbows, then knees, then backs, feet, etc.

ART CHARADES

To play this game the facilitator prepares a list of movies or famous names. The participants will also need paper and pencils. The group is divided into teams of no less than five players for each team.

Ask the teams to form along a predetermined starting line and to leave space between the groups. The game begins by each team sending one member to act as leader to the facilitator. The facilitator is positioned about 10 metres from the starting line. Once all the leaders are present, the facilitator quietly tells the leaders the movie or the famous name. The leaders then race back to their teams and attempt to communicate the name to their members by drawing pictures or symbols, trying to get their teams to correctly guess the movie or famous person. Once the team has guessed correctly, the leader must then race to and tag the facilitator. The first team to guess correctly wins that round. The teams select new leaders and the game continues.

GRANDMOTHER'S TRUNK

This is a good circle activity that exercises the group's memory and sequencing abilities. The exercise serves as another reminder for names and assists the memory process by word association. The members' names, now that they are better acquainted, take on a new meaning when used in activities. These names are now a source of memories and, when spoken aloud, often trigger pleasant thoughts.

Ask the group to form a circle. Tell the group that you want them all to think of something to put into grandmother's trunk. Instruct them that the object they place in the trunk must start with the same letter as in their first name, for example, "My name is Larry, and I put a laptop in grandmother's trunk." The next player repeats the statement and adds their item, for example, "His name is Larry, and he put in a laptop, and my name is Jasmine, and I put in a Jeep." Each player in turn repeats the objects already in the trunk and then adds another to the growing list. If the players have difficulty remembering, allow them extra time, or they may ask someone in the group for help.

Variations: Tell the group that they are going on a trip and they must put something into grandmother's trunk in order to go along. Explain that you will decide if they can come or not. Do not tell players that the item has to have the same initial as their first name, or you may decide to have a different condition, for example, it has to rhyme with the player's first name—Tom can bring a bomb. Whatever the condition is to get to go on the trip, it is kept from the group, and they are expected to figure it out on their own. In the original example, if Larry decides to put a football in grandmother's trunk, he is not allowed to come on the trip and will have to wait for another turn. If Jasmine decides to take a juice can into grandmother's trunk, she is allowed to come. The game continues to travel around the circle with each player continuing to add to the trunk until the group catches on to the condition necessary to go on the trip.

CATEGORIES

This is a good game that promotes group cooperation. The rhythm in the game, as well as its non-competitive nature, allows the group to have fun with cooperation.

Ask the players to sit or stand in a circle and appoint someone to go first; this person will be the leader. The leader thinks up a category such as animals, countries, colours, etc. Once the category has been chosen, that person is ready to start the beat. The beat is marked out by first slapping both hands on knees, then clapping hands together, then snapping the fingers on one hand, and then the other hand. The rhythm goes slap, clap, snap, snap, slap, clap, snap, snap, and so on.

To begin the leader chants, "Let's play (slap) categories (clap) such as (snap) animals (snap). Keeping in time, the next player must chime in at the appropriate time with the name of an animal, for example (slap), (clap), (snap), tiger, (snap), (slap), (clap), (snap), elephant, (snap), and so on around the circle. It is best to start this game at a slow speed. If the slap, clap, snap, snap rhythm is too difficult, children can merely clap in time.

CATERPILLAR RACE

This is a lively game that relies on teamwork and the cooperation of team members. This game may take two or three attempts to master.

Divide the group into small teams. Instruct the teams to squat down, one behind the other, and to put their arms around each other's waist. Each team is then to practice moving up and down in unison. Once they have mastered this skill, have them learn to hop forward together. Suggest that counting "one, two, three, hop" may help the team to time the jump. After the teams have developed skills in moving forward, line the teams up and have a series of races, such as, first team over the finish line wins, the front of one caterpillar must tag the rear of another caterpillar, or teams must only hop to the finish line.

PEOPLE PACKAGES

This is another game that is enjoyable and non-threatening. Group decisions are important, and the dynamics of how particular groups make decisions can be enlightening for all.

This activity requires several newspapers, wrapping paper, string, scotch or masking tape, and any other types of packaging materials.

Divide the group into two teams of four or five members. Provide each team with the packaging materials. Instruct the teams to decide on one member to be the package. On a signal from the facilitator, the teams are to begin to wrap their package using the materials provided. When the packages are completed, or when the time limit is up, encourage members to look around at the other packages and to comment on their handiwork.

CREATIVE BLOCK BUILDING

Sometimes language and how it is interpreted can hamper relationships. This interesting activity stresses the importance of clear and detailed instructions.

This activity requires sets of wooden blocks; each set should have the same number and types of blocks. This activity can also be completed with pairs, each pair having a set of blocks.

> "Friends you and me... you brought another friend...and then there were three... we started our group...our circle of friends ... and like that circle .. there is no beginning or end."
> – ELEANOR ROOSEVELT

Instruct the group to form a circle. Ask for two volunteers and ask them to sit back to back in the middle of the circle. Give each volunteer a set of blocks. Appoint one volunteer to be A and one to be B. A is to build a structure with the blocks and to give B the necessary instructions in order to build an identical structure. Neither A or B is allowed to turn around, and only A may speak (for young children and those experiencing difficulties, allow dialogue between A and B).

Discuss with the children how instructions can sometimes be misunderstood. Discuss how clear communication can add to better understanding.

COOPERATION

This is an excellent activity to study and teach group dynamics. Cooperation is essential for the group to succeed in this activity, and strategies for cooperation can be discussed once the activity is completed.

The facilitator will need to prepare a number of envelopes depending on the number of participants—one envelope for each group. Each envelope is equipped with a set of 4 or 5 (same number as group participants) cardboard squares, each square cut randomly into 3 pieces. This activity works best with a table or place on the floor where each small group can work on their puzzles.

Divide the group up into small groups of four to five members. Group members are to organize themselves around the table or on the floor so each member has a spot to complete his/her puzzle. The object of the game is for each member to have a completed puzzle in front of him/her by the end of the allotted time.

The rules are:
• No one is allowed to move from his/her spot
• No one is allowed to speak
• Gestures and other forms of nonverbal communication are allowed
• Participants may give up pieces to other members but they
  may not take pieces from others
• Participants may not put their pieces in the centre for others to pick up
• Pieces may only be given from one individual member to the other

Pass out the envelopes and determine a time limit. Once time is up, ask the group to come together and discuss their experiences.

Group Development: Stage Three

SURVIVAL

This activity can provide the facilitator with a wealth of knowledge about the particular dynamics of the group. A good time to present such an activity would be when the facilitator feels that the level of comfort in the group is sufficient to warrant their handling of this sometimes very frustrating exercise. A role-play or re-enactment of an actual situation makes this activity more exciting (see "The Voyage" below).

This activity requires paper, pencils, and a list of the supplies either posted or on individual sheets of paper. I have found, with younger children, that it helps to have pictures or objects to represent the items available to take on the raft.

Divide the children into groups of five – eight members and ask the children to imagine that they are on a boat that is sinking in the middle of the ocean. Each group has a life raft that is big enough to hold all of them and enough room for six other items. Their task is to choose which six items they will take from the following list. Instruct the individual members to go through the exercise alone first and to prioritize the items they would choose in order of importance:

• Purification tablets for drinking water (8 tablets)

• Food (enough for three days)

• Puppy

• Motor for raft

• Gas for motor (12-gallon tank)

• Paddles (2)

• Fishing rod and hooks

• Life jackets (8)

• One woolen blanket

• Waterproof matches

• Compass

• Water jug

• Swiss Army Knife (pocket knife with several attachments)

After each child has numbered the items in order of importance, instruct them to join their small groups. The task of the group is to collectively agree on six items to take with them in the time allotted. When appropriate, the facilitator should signal when five minutes of the time allotted remains, and when one minute is left.

The children should be given the opportunity to express their feelings concerning the exercise.

This exercise can be lengthy, and it would be best for the facilitator to place time limits on the group. Consensus in decision-making is necessary, and this should be explained to the group members before they start the group exercise.

THE VOYAGE

This is a more challenging activity than "Survival" as it requires members to be more creative and more cooperative. It is a role-play activity and provides the facilitator with some insight into group development and leadership within the group. There is very little structure, which allows the children to control, to co-operate, to withdraw, or to do whatever they wish. It might take props and some enthusiasm to motivate the group and to help more inhibited children to feel comfortable.

Instruct the group to lie down and relax in order to help them to fantasize the voyage. Conduct a guided fantasy (see Chapter 13, "Relaxation, Imagery, and Guided Fantasy"), and ask the group to fantasize a trip to a lost continent, to outer space, or to travel back in time. Give them enough information in the fantasy that will allow them to complete their mission, which is to locate food and water, materials for a shelter, and possible locations to place a signal to contact their allies. When the fantasy is completed, ask them to get up and interact with each other as if they had just arrived, and say that their mission is to survive long enough for their allies to join them in two weeks.

Allow 20 minutes to one hour, depending on group involvement, for the drama to be played out.

GROUP MASSAGE

This works well for ending a group, especially after more physically strenuous activities.

Ask the group to form a circle and sit down. Instruct group members to make a quarter turn to the left so that they are sitting facing the back of the person that was beside them. Now instruct the members to reach out and begin to give the person in front a back massage. Encourage members to instruct their "masseur/masseuse" to make sure they get a good massage. Once the group appears to be finished, ask them to make a half turn to the right and massage the person to their right.

POT LUCK PARTY

This activity requires a large sheet of paper, pencils, markers, masking tape, balloons (enough for each member), several sheets of paper, and a box of toothpicks.

Instruct group members to sit in a circle. Pass out pens, paper, and balloons to each person. Set up a scenario, something like this:

"You have all been invited to a pot-luck party, but instead of bringing food to share, you will be bringing yourself and one strength you believe you contribute to this group. For example, you may be a creative thinker, or well organized, or able to keep others motivated. On a slip of paper, write down one strength or talent that you will bring to the party. Once you have written it down, carefully place it into your balloon, blow the balloon up, tie it off, and put it in the circle."

Allow 5-10 minutes for the group to complete this activity. When everyone is done, designate one person to select a balloon from the pile, pop it, and read the slip inside.

After a slip has been read, ask the author to step forward, share a little more, and then write his name and strength on the large sheet of paper. This person becomes the next player to pop a balloon from the pile. The activity proceeds until all players have contributed. Post the paper somewhere in the play space.

This activity can also require players to choose more than one strength and also may require players to comment on one or more of their weaknesses.

LETTING GO

This exercise requires a certain level of trust among group members; therefore, take some time beforehand to decide on dyads that will work well together.

When the dyads have been assigned, one partner lies down and slowly relaxes (you may wish to conduct a short relaxation exercise; see Chapter 13, "Relaxation, Imagery, and Guided Fantasy"). When relaxed, that person will allow the partner to lift up his/her arm and to move it without needing to control the movement of the arm; it is totally limp. Repeat this procedure for the other arm and the two legs. If the partners are really trusting, they can allow each other to gently cradle their head in their two hands, gently rocking it back and forth.

TRUSTING

This exercise also requires a healthy degree of trust among group members. Discuss with the group the seriousness of the risk involved.

Divide the group up into triads, and have them decide who will be A, B, and C. A positions him/herself between B and C so that B is facing the front of A and C is facing the back of A. There should be about 60-100 centimetres between A and B and A and C.

When A is ready, A is to fall forward into B's outstretched hands; B, in turn, supports A and gently propels A backward into C's outstretched hands. B and C push A forward and backward gently. B and C can start out standing close together and then slowly move back to a safe distance as A's trust in them increases. All three decide when they move and how far back they move.

The activity continues until all have had a turn.

TRUST WALK

Once again trust and maturity is a must for this exercise.

Divide the group into pairs, and give each pair a blindfold. The pair decides who will be blindfolded first. The guide will stand close to the person blindfolded and will hold on to this person or keep in touch physically with the blindfolded person at all times.

The guide then leads the blindfolded person on a discovery journey. The guide points out various aspects of the environment and encourages the blindfolded person to experience it without eyes.

Group Development: Stage Four

ROCK THE BABY

Here is an excellent activity to complete a program. This is a very powerful exercise; a healthy attitude and gentle nature is necessary.

Divide the group into two lines and have the lines face one another. One group member at a time volunteers to lie down between the lines of players and close his/her eyes. The two lines of players squat down and gently place their hands underneath the body of the person lying. On the count of three, the group slowly lifts the group member until all members are standing. The group gently rocks the person to and fro; if it is a large group, they gently pass the person down the line to the last person standing.

WARM FUZZY BALL

This is a good activity to use at termination or after the group has spent some time together. A ball is required for this activity.

Instruct the group to form a circle and sit down. Explain to the group that if they would like to say something positive to a member of the group, they can roll the ball to them and make their comment or observation, for example, "I had a lot of fun playing cards with you last night," or "You have beautiful skin," or "I really like your singing voice." When the ball is rolled to a player, then it is their turn to roll it to someone else in the group and make a positive statement about them.

BEGINNINGS AND ENDINGS

This is an excellent exercise for termination. There will need to be paper and pencils provided to each member.

Ask the members to write down two lists. One list is of those things they are going to stop doing, and the other list is what they are going to begin to do or continue to do; for example, a

> It is within groups that competencies, attitudes and values are formed.
>
> — **DAVID & FRANK JOHNSON**

"beginning" might be, "I am going to begin to take better care of myself," and an "ending" might be, "I am going to stop putting myself down." Group members are encouraged to make at least three beginnings and three endings.

Once completed, the group will form a circle, and members will list off one at a time each of their beginnings and endings.

Variation: This variation will need paper and pencils for each member and either a wastebasket or a campfire.

Players are instructed to compose two lists on separate pieces of paper, one a list of things they want to take with them after the group leaves, and the other a list of the things they wish to leave behind. For example, a "taking" might be, "I am going to take the memory of our last campfire with me when I leave," and a "leaving" might be, "I am gong to leave behind the memory of cleaning the latrines."

Once completed, the players form a circle around the campfire or a wastebasket. Designate or ask for a volunteer to lead. The leader begins by reading the list of things he/she wishes to take home. Once the leader completes the list, he/she keeps the list. Next the leader reads off the things he/she wishes to leave behind, and when completed, this list is thrown with much fanfare into the fire or the wastebasket. The process continues until all have had a turn.

Chapter 9, "Leader and Leaderless Games" provides the facilitator and programmer with a compilation of exercises that involve shared leadership and cooperative activities. These activities work very well in stage two and stage three of group development and are designed to build cooperation and teamwork in any group.

Leader and Leaderless Games

This chapter focusses on leadership in the group. Its aim is to develop the individual group member's ability to lead and, for the group as a collective, to feel comfortable with each member taking on a leadership role. The leaderless games are designed to allow the group to function as a unit without the need to have one person as a director.

The games and activities are designed to allow for various degrees of competition within the group. The first series of activities are leaderless and have little or no competitive elements in them. The next level of games offer competitive experiences, but they do not fall into the win-lose category where the loser is eliminated. The final level involves team games where one team is in competition with the other.

Programmers and facilitators are cautioned to introduce competitive games into their curriculum when they feel that this will not disrupt cohesiveness within the group as a whole. It is far better to leave the team-competitive activities to the later stages of the group's development. Various techniques can be utilized to make the team activities less competitive in order to make them more enjoyable for the whole group.

> I suppose leadership at one time meant muscles; but today it means getting along with people.
>
> – GANDHI

Activities

Leaderless Games

FACE FLASHING

The group sits in a circle; players decide on the weirdest looking face they can make. Player number one starts the game by turning to the player on his/her left and makes a weird face. This player, player number two, turns to the player on his/her left and mimics player number one's face. Player number three reacts to the face and turns to the left and mimics player number one's face. This continues around the circle until player number one's weird face has come full-circle. Now it is player number two's turn to make a face and have it mimicked by all the players as before. The group plays until each person has had a turn.

Variation: This activity begins in the same manner, but player number two reacts to player number one's face by imitating it and then turns to the player on his/her left and makes his/her own weird face. Player number three imitates the face of player number two and turns to his/her left and creates his/her own weird face. The game continues until everyone has had a turn.

TEN SECOND LOOK

Ask the group to form a circle. Hand out sheets of paper and pencils to each group member. One player begins by secretly drawing a simple sketch of a house, a tree, a person, etc., so that no one can see what they have drawn. The artist then allows the group member on the left to sneak a peek at the drawing for the count of 10. This player then in turn draws what he/she saw, secretly so that no one can see. This artist in turn allows the player on the left to see the drawing for 10 seconds. This player repeats the procedure until the drawing has gone completely around the group. The originator of the drawing compares his/her drawing with the drawings of the other artists. The more complex the original drawing, the more distorted the final drawing.

ELECTRICITY

The group holds hands and one person is designated to begin to set the charge off. The player does this by squeezing the hand of the person on his/her right. This player in turn squeezes the hand of the person on their right. The electrical current runs around the group and finishes back at the leader who may send the current back through the circle again, only this time sending it in the opposite direction.

SCULPTING STATUES

Ask the group to form triads and identify each other as A, B, or C. A is to be the sculptor, B is to be the model, and C is to be the clay. B and C are asked to stand close to each other, allowing enough room for A to move in between them. A, with closed eyes, is to be positioned facing B and C. B is to take on a pose, the more bizarre the better. Just by using the sense of touch, A is to manipulate C into a similar pose.

GROUP PULL-UPS

Divide the group into pairs, and ask each member to sit back to back on the ground. Instruct each pair to reach back and lock arms. When they are ready, each pair is to stand up as one unit while remaining back to back. When they have completed this task, they are to assist whoever needs help until the whole group is standing. Now divide the group into threes and then fours until the whole group is sitting back to back. The final stand is the group pull-up.

BALANCE AND SUPPORT

Divide the group into pairs according to height. Instruct the pairs to face each other and to stand with their arms extended and their palms facing up. The partners touch their palms together and slowly walk backward with their weight supported by their outstretched hands. The pair continues to move backward as far as possible. Next the pairs are asked to join another twosome to form a four-person balancing structure. The group continues to build from fours to eights until all group members are standing in a tight circle supported by each other's palms.

GROUP DRAWING

The group is asked to form a circle. One player is given a pencil and a piece of paper. This player draws a simple drawing, like a man, a house, or a tree. This player then passes it to the player on his left, and this player adds to the drawing. The drawing continues around the circle until everyone has had a chance to add to the drawing.

Variation: This same game is more exciting when each player has a piece of paper and a pencil. The players pass the papers around as before, and the group drawings are finished when all the papers have gone completely around the circle.

CIRCLE LAP SIT

Ask the group to form a tight circle, standing shoulder-to-shoulder, and then instruct them to make a one-quarter turn to the right. Instruct group members to bend slightly at the knee until they are sitting on the person's lap directly behind them. This game usually needs a few trial runs.

Once the group has mastered the move, put on some lively music. Ask them to now move as a group to the beat of music around in a circle until the music stops. When the music stops, they are to sit back on the other's lap.

BODY ROLLING

It may take a couple of practice runs before the group is able to master this activity.

Instruct the group members to lie down on the ground beside one another shoulder-to-shoulder with about 10-20 centimetres between them, in one continuous line. Choose one person to go first, and instruct him/her to lie down across the line of bodies beginning at the front of the line. The group is then instructed to start to roll, all in the same direction so that the back of the line is rolling towards the front. This rolling propels the person on top right down to the end of the line. The person gets off and lies down with the group, and the player at the beginning of the line stands up and lies across the bodies for a ride.

CONVEYER BELT

This activity requires coordination and teamwork, and it may take the group a few practice runs before they master it. The activity may also need players on either side of the conveyer belt in case it breaks down.

Instruct group members to form a single line standing shoulder-to-shoulder with every other person facing the alternate direction. Now the group is asked to lie down on their backs in the same formation (facing alternate directions). Players are instructed to reach their arms upward with their palms facing upwards. These outstretched hands are the conveyor belt.

A player is asked to be the leader and take the first ride on the conveyor belt. This player lies on the conveyer belt (players outstretched hands), face up, and once positioned (he/she may need assistance getting on the conveyer belt), the conveyer belt starts up and propels him/her on down the line. That person takes his/her place at the end of the line, and the next player, at the front of the line, goes next.

Shared Leadership

BACK TO BACK

Ask the group to choose a partner and to stand facing one another. Assign one member to be the leader—if there is an even number, the leader's partner can connect with another pair to form a triad. The person who does not have a partner is then designated as the leader. The leader calls out commands (e.g., touch hands to hands, touch feet to feet, touch back to back). When the leader calls out "Switch," everyone is to find a new partner, including the leader. The person who is left now becomes the new leader. The game continues like this until the allotted time has elapsed.

THE CLOWN GOT SICK

Ask to the group to form a circle, and assign one of the participants as the leader. The leader is directed to stand in the centre of the circle and call out, "The Clown Got Sick!" The group is instructed to reply, "How did he get sick?" The leader responds,

"He got sick by doing this," and then makes a silly movement (e.g., hopping up and down, winking an eye, etc.). The player on the right now becomes the leader and shouts out, "The Clown Got Sick." The group responds, "How did he get sick?" The leader calls back "He got sick by doing this" and mimics the first player's silly action and says, "and by doing this," and adds one of his/her own silly actions. The game continues on to the last player who must mimic all the other silly actions and add one of his/her own.

HAVE YOU EVER?

Ask the group to form a circle, seated. Select a player to be the leader, and ask the leader to sit in the centre of the circle. Inform the players that if the leader asks them a question, they must answer honestly. The object of the game is to see who can stay the leader longest.

The leader is instructed to ask a question that can be answered by yes or no. The leader asks the question, for example, "Have you ever been to Alaska?" If any of the group members answer yes, the leader must leave the centre, and the players who answered yes must try to be the first to sit down in the middle of the circle. The player who is first is now the leader. If no one, for example, has been to Alaska, then the leader can continue and ask another question.

BUZZ

The group is asked to form a circle and assign someone to be the leader. The leader is asked to choose a number (e.g., 5) and whenever that number (5) and any other number containing it (15, 25, 35,) is spoken, it must be replaced with the word BUZZ. The leader begins the count with 1, the player to his/her right counts 2, and so on until the count reaches the chosen number (5); this player must respond with BUZZ. The count continues until the group reaches another number containing the chosen number (15), which also must be counted out as BUZZ. If a player fails to respond appropriately, then the count continues but switches directions (left to right).

SPUD

The object of this game is for each player to spell out the word Spud. Ask the group to make a tight circle and select someone to lead. The leader is given a ball and is asked to stand in the centre of the circle. The leader then throws the ball high into the air, calling out the name of one of the members of the group. The rest of the group members try to run as far away from the ball as possible. Whoever is named runs for the ball, and when that person has it, he/she is to yell out "SPUD." When the player yells "SPUD," all other players must freeze in their tracks. The player with the ball is allowed to take four steps in any direction. Then he/she is to throw the ball at one of the players. If the ball misses, the thrower becomes the leader and scores an "S." If the player is hit, then that player becomes the leader and scores the "S." The game continues until each member gets S-P-U-D. The group gathers after each shot, and no one is eliminated. Whoever gets the letter is the new caller and can call out any name.

LUCKY HANDSHAKE

You will need a coin for this game. Ask the group to close their eyes and secretly select one member to be the leader. The leader is given the coin and is secretly given a number (whispered in his/her ear by the facilitator). The number determines how many handshakes he/she must receive before passing on the coin. Ask the group to open their eyes and instruct them to mingle and shake hands with one another. Once the leader has passed on the coin, he/she whispers another number to the new leader, and this number determines the number of handshakes required before the coin is passed on.

HEADS AND HIPS

Have the players sit in a circle, and appoint a leader to stand in the middle of the circle. Instruct the leader to spin around and to point, with one hand, to someone in the group, and to put the other hand on his/her own head or hip. If the leader puts a hand on his/her head, the person pointed to must say his/her own first name. If the leader puts his/her hand on his/her hip, the person pointed to must say his/her own last name. The leader is allowed to have as many turns as there are players and then must choose someone else to take on the role as leader.

> A leader is best when people barely know he exists, when his work is done, his aim fulfilled, they will say: we did it ourselves.
> – LAO TZU

LEADER

Ask the group to form a circle. This game can be played sitting or standing. One member is asked to go first, to stand in the middle of the circle, and to close his/her eyes. Now select a group leader by pointing to one of the players in the circle. The group members are instructed to imitate any action made by the leader. The leader is then asked to begin a series of actions (e.g., clap hands, scratch forehead, slap knees, etc.). Once the group is all imitating the leader, the player who has his/her eyes closed is asked to open them and try to determine who is leading the actions. The leader at any time may change the series of actions. Four guesses are allowed, and if that person guesses correctly, then the "leader" becomes the next person who guesses in the new game. If he/she guesses incorrectly, then that person must choose someone to stand in the centre of the circle who will then attempt to guess the new leader. The new leader will be appointed in the same way as in the beginning of the game.

FRENCH BLIND MAN'S BLUFF

Ask the group to form a circle, and assign someone to lead. The leader is blindfolded, given a stick or cane, and designated the blind man. Place the blind man in the centre. Instruct the group to join hands and to move around the blind man. Tell the blind man to tap his/her stick on the floor, and when the tapping stops, the group is to stop moving. Once the group has stopped, the blind man points his/her stick towards a member of the group. The member who is pointed to must say, "Blind man, blind man, guess who I am." If the blind man guesses correctly, that person continues as the blind man. If the blind man guesses incorrectly, then he/she must appoint someone else to be the blind man.

AIR, EARTH, AND WATER

Ask the group to form a circle, and appoint someone to be leader. Instruct this player to turn to the person on his/her left and say one of these words, earth, air, or water. The person on his/her left must then name an animal if the leader calls out earth, a bird if air, and a fish if water. If the player answers correctly, he/she is now the leader and must turn to the person on his/her left and say, earth, air, or water. If the player is incorrect then the person on his/her left is now the new leader.

TOUCH AND TELL

Ask the group to form a circle, and choose someone to lead. The leader is blindfolded and placed in the centre of the circle. The rest of the players are then told to slowly walk around the circle to the right, and then they are signalled to stop. The blindfolded player is then told to walk forward with arms outstretched until he/she touches somebody. The player continues to touch the person until he/she can guess who it is, and if the guess is correct, that person may go again. If the guess is incorrect, the person that was touched becomes the one who is blindfolded.

DOG IN A MANGER

Draw a circle on the floor with chalk, approximately 1-2 metres in diameter; this is to be the manger. Ask for a volunteer to be the dog. Instruct the rest of the group to form a larger circle around the manger.

Inside the small circle, place a small item (e.g., pine cone, stick, pebble, coin, etc.). The object of the game is for one of the group members to snatch the item from the manger without the dog touching him/her. More than one person may sneak up on the dog; however, only one person at a time can snatch an item out of the manger. If the dog touches that person before he/she is out of the circle, that person must go back to his/her place. The person who successfully snatches the item out of the manger without being touched becomes the dog, and a new turn begins.

RHYMING RIDDLE GAME

Ask the group to form a circle. Appoint one member to be the leader. The leader begins by asking the group member on the right to solve a rhyming riddle, for example, "I'm thinking of a (pet) that rhymes with (log)." Answer: dog. "I'm thinking of something that's found in the (kitchen), and it rhymes with (pink)." Answer: sink. The player must solve the riddle on his/her first guess. If the player answers correctly, he/she is now the leader and must turn to the person on his/her right and ask them to solve a riddle.

DROP THE HANDKERCHIEF

Ask the group to form a circle. Someone is chosen as the leader. Players are either standing or sitting. The leader walks around the outside of the circle. At some point, the leader drops the handkerchief behind one of the players. Once the player realizes the handkerchief was dropped, he/she must chase the leader and tag him/her before the leader reaches the chaser's spot in the circle. If the chaser is successful in catching the leader before he/she reaches his/her place, then the leader must try again to give away the handkerchief. If the chaser is unsuccessful, then he/she becomes the leader.

Variation: This game can be played with young children while singing a song and using an envelope rather than a handkerchief. While the leader walks around the circle the group sings:

I wrote a letter to my love,
And on the way I dropped it.
A little doggie picked it up
And put it in his pocket.
He won't bite you and won't bite me,
But he'll bite the one who's got it.
So hurry up and drop it.

STORMY WEATHER

Instruct the group to sit in the form of a circle. Assign someone to be the leader. The leader begins by rubbing his/her hands together to make a swishing sound. The person to the left of the leader imitates the leader, and now both of them are rubbing their hands together to make swishing sounds. The next player to the left starts to rub his/her hands together and so on around the circle.

Once the whole group has completed this action, they are to practice until they can make the swishing sound start with the leader and travel around the circle back to the leader again. The group can experiment by making the sound travel to the left and to the right. The leader then suggests that the swishing sound will represent the sound of the rain. The leader then repeats the above exercise only replacing the action of rubbing hands to clapping the hands. The leader suggests that the hand clapping sound can represent the thunder.

The exercise is repeated again using finger snapping to represent lightning and again using thigh slapping to represent heavy rainfall.

Once the group has become proficient at making all the sounds travel around the circle, instruct the leader to speed up the process beginning with raindrops that get progressively faster and louder as they go around the circle. Each player must watch the other players closely and imitate exactly what he/she sees the person on the right is doing. The leader experiments with the sounds to create the illusion of a thunderstorm by inserting thunder and lightening along with the rain. When the level of skill with this exercise increases, members can take a turn at creating their own storms.

FAVOURITE GAMES

This activity gives the players a chance to lead one of their own favourite activities. Each child is to think of a favourite game, activity, stunt, skit, etc. It must be one that takes less than 10 minutes to play and one that can be easily taught to the group. Children are also allowed to make up their own version of a popular game.

Ask for a volunteer, or randomly assign a player to go first, and ask them to teach his/her game to the group. This continues on until time runs out, or the group has played all the games. This activity may need to go on for more than one session so all players get a chance to teach their activity.

Team Competition

PIG PIN

This is a game played in many countries in many different forms. It is good fun for groups of all ages. You will need some wooden croquet balls, baseballs, or any other suitable substitutes (one for each participant) and a plastic bowling pin, milk carton, or a stick in the ground placed several feet from the starting line.

Divide the group into two teams and assign a leader. Instruct the leader to ask his/her group to form a line, one behind the other, on the starting line. The object of the game is to roll the ball as close to the pin as possible. The leaders begin followed by the players behind. Players may knock each other's ball away from the pin.

The game can be elaborated on by adding more balls or drawing a circle around the pin and giving points to balls remaining in the circle at the end of each turn.

PAPER SNOWBALL FIGHT

Divide the group into two teams and assign two leaders. Establish a line down the centre of the play area. Instruct the leaders to hand out two pieces of scrap paper to each player. The leaders are asked to instruct his/her teammates to crumple each sheet of paper into a paper snowball. Explain to the group that their goal is to get as many paper snowballs as possible past the centre line and into the other team's territory in five minutes.

RED ROVER, RED ROVER

Make sure all watches and rings, etc. are taken off before playing this game. Choose two captains and ask them to pick teams. The teams face each other at a distance of about 20 feet. Instruct each team to form a chain by locking hands, wrists, or arms. Play begins with one player from one of the teams calling out to the opposing team: "Red Rover, Red Rover, please send (name of someone on the opposing team) over." The person whose name was called then runs toward the opposite chain in an attempt to break the chain. If the runner manages to break the chain, that person returns to his/her team, bringing one of the players of his/her choice from the opposite team. If the runner is unsuccessful at breaking the chain, he/she is "captured" and becomes a member of that team. Eventually, one team is down to one member and the game ends.

RATTLESNAKE TAG

Appoint two leaders and ask them to choose two teams. Each team forms a line or snake behind its leader. Players attach themselves to the teammate in front of them by putting their hands on the shoulders or waist of that player. Both teams must begin side-by-side and facing in the same direction with the leaders at the front of the line. On the word "Go," the leader of each team must try to touch the last person in line or the tail of the opposite team. The first leader to tag the trailing member of the opposite team wins. If the either chain breaks, the leader may tag the last player linked up with the leader of the opposing team.

Chapter 10, "Convalescent and Special Needs Children" is a collection of activities that can be played with children who have impaired abilities or who are in a state of recovery or convalescence. All of these activities can be played and adapted to complement almost any situation or environment that children find themselves in.

> A genuine leader is not a searcher for consensus but a molder of consensus.
> – MARTIN LUTHER KING, JR.

Convalescent and Special Needs Children

The type of therapeutic activity programs intended for this group of children allow all participants to engage meaningfully, actively, and in a way that challenges them individually. Modifications should be applied to the activity to insure that all participants have an equal opportunity to benefit and compete. The vast majority of games and activities presented in this book can be adapted by creative facilitators to suit the needs of any group of children that they are working with.

The games in this section are designed for groups of children whose mobility is limited by their environment or by other restrictions. These children are often not included in activities or given subordinate roles. This may also be true of incarcerated youth or children confined in some way. When children are restricted, excluded, bedridden, or confined, they are easily bored, and they often resort to television or other passive forms of leisure entertainment. These passive exercises can reinforce feelings of helplessness and add to the individual's feelings of depression or feelings of low self-worth. When the children's minds are challenged during these periods of inactivity by activities suitable or adapted to them, it can increase feelings of competence and self-worth. Some children resort to aggression or misbehaviour to deal with their being limited. When the environment can be structured to allow for some movement or exchange among the group members and when the activities can be presented in such a way as not to disadvantage any of the participants, these individuals have an opportunity to combat the frustrations of their confinement and to be empowered.

> What lies
> behind us
> and what lies
> before us are
> tiny matters
> compared to
> what lies
> within us.
>
> – RALPH WALDO EMERSON

Tips for Facilitators

Hurdle Help (Redl, 1952), discussed in Chapter 7, "Bridges and Anchor Points" is an excellent concept when working with groups of children with varying abilities. A race between a child in a wheelchair and an excellent runner of the same age can be adapted so that each has an equal chance of winning. For instance, the child in the wheelchair may have a head start, or the runner must run carrying another child on his/her back. A child with limited motor skills, for example, can compete with a child who is an excellent basketball player by requiring the more skilled player to use only his/her non-dominant hand. The foul line can be adjusted along with many other potential adaptations, which can make the activity much more exciting and interesting.

During demonstrations, free play, or trial runs, the observant student will note which children need accommodations. It is also possible to bend the rules without drawing too much attention to the change. The practitioner who is acting as referee or judge may give some children more latitude than others. For example, in a game that involves quickly catching and throwing a ball, you might allow a player more time to hold on to the ball before he/she passes it on to the next player.

Some of your participants may need extra assistance for cognitive activities such as word games, memory games, or games that require more complex cognitive skills. You can help kids with memory challenges or limited vocabularies and also those who are shy about speaking in front of others by picking a word or phrase or question out of a hat or coaching by whispering. Or, the child could whisper the word or phrase he/she chooses to the leader, so the leader can play as a partner. Having or helping the child draw the word or brainstorming a list of questions, words, or phrases before the game begins, are other possibilities. The best adaptations are often those that do not single out any one participant but help the entire group.

The child's support network, including fellow leaders, teachers, parents, special support staff, and most importantly, the child him/herself, should be informed and be part of a discussion on how to adapt activities to suit them.

Finally, Hurdle Help should be coordinated with the entire group so that all players know that some adaptations will be made to the activities as a way to make them more fun and challenging. Also try to include a variety of activities so that all players at some point will have an accommodation made to assist them specifically.

Activities

BEDSIDE BEANBAG BASKETBALL

Attach a string to a beanbag or to a small ball, and attach the other end to the bed or chair. Place a pail or wastebasket close enough to the bed or chair so that the player can easily score a basket. The basket can be moved and the string lengthened as his/her skill level increases.

This game is a lot of fun between beds where the player has to be the first to make a basket to gain the point.

GUESS THE WORD

One child leaves the room or plugs his/her ears, and the group decides on a "magic" word. The person comes back into the group and can ask anyone a question about any subject. The answer given must contain the magic word. After several questions, the person can guess what the magic word is. The player is allowed three guesses before another person leaves the room.

Variation: Instead of using a certain word, there is a common gesture that everyone will use in the answer (e.g., always scratch an itch during the answer, always cross or uncross the legs, look to the left before answering).

JUST LIKE ME
Chorus:
Everybody do this, do this, do this.
Everybody do this, just like me.

Repeat a few times until the group has the chant memorized. Assign a leader to go first, and they will make an action such as wave hands, stomp feet, clap hands, flap arms, cluck tongue, or run fast; the trick here is that it has to be an action of some kind that the group can imitate. Once the leader has decided on an action, the group begins by chanting the chorus. Then the leader adds his action (wave arms) as the group chants.

Everybody (wave arms, wave arms, wave arms).
Everybody (wave hands), just like me.

The group chants the chorus again, and the player on the leader's left takes the lead and adds his/her action.

Everybody (stomp feet, stomp feet, stomp feet).
Everybody (stomp feet), just like me.

Every fourth round the group can combine the preceding four players' actions into a chant like this.

Everybody (wave arms, stomp feet, clap hands).
Everybody (flap arms), just like me.

GUM ART
Give each participant a piece of bubble gum to chew, several toothpicks, and a small piece of paper or index card. Allow the group 10 minutes to chew the gum and make a design out of the gum on the index card using only toothpicks.

MAN AND OBJECT
Assign someone in the group to begin as leader. In this activity the leader thinks of a famous person, someone well known to the participants, or a distinct group of people, and something identified with this person or group, for example, Stephen Hawking—the big bang, or music teacher—piano, or Inuit—igloo.

The leader begins by giving one of the words as a clue, and the group must guess the corresponding word. The number of guesses allowed depends on the developmental level of the group. When someone guesses correctly, the leadership rotates to the person to the left of the last leader.

LAUGHING FACE
This is a pencil-and-paper game using the name of a person, place, or thing. Each player thinks of a famous person, place,

or thing that everyone in the group knows about (e.g., television show, local landmark, or teacher's name).

The person who goes first indicates the number of letters and words in the name by drawing a short line to indicate a single letter and a space between the short lines to mark off one word from the other. For example, MARTIN LUTHER KING would be:

_ _ _ _ _ _   _ _ _ _ _ _ _ _ _ _

The group is asked to decide who this famous person is by guessing letters of the famous person's name. If a member guesses a letter and it is not in the word, then a part gets added on to the laughing face.

The parts of the laughing face in order are: head, left eye, right eye, nose, left ear, right ear, and mouth. When the laughing face is completed, the group gets one last guess. If they still don't guess correctly, the player may go again or pass the pencil on to the next person. If a member of the group is able to guess the name before the laughing face is completed, then that person may take a turn.

HORSE, PIG, DONKEY, PENNY/BALL TOSS

This game is simple and can be played in the style of "Bedside Beanbag Basketball." Each player may use a penny, ball, or object, or the group may wish to share an object. A target is established (e.g., a wastebasket, a mark on the wall, a hoop, etc.). Players are given letters for each successful hit on the target. The group decides which word they are to spell out. The first player to spell out the word is the winner.

THE MINISTER'S CAT

This is an alphabet game. "The Minister's Cat is a ___ cat." The blank has to be filled with an adjective that starts with the next letter of the alphabet (e.g., an annoying cat; a big cat; a crazy cat).

Next, the group can add two adjectives (e.g., an annoying, anxious cat or a big, beautiful cat). With each round, a new letter of the alphabet can be added (e.g., an annoying, big, crazy cat).

LEFT-HANDED

Write down the names of common objects on pieces of paper such as man, woman, tree, store, car, house, etc., and place them in a bowl. The group will need paper and pencils for this activity..

Left-Handed begins with the person chosen to lead drawing a paper from the bowl. The leader must draw the object with his/her non-dominant hand. The group is allowed one guess each to try to guess the object drawn. When a group member guesses correctly, the leadership rotates to the player to the left of the last leader.

Variations: The leader must draw the object blindfolded or with his/her foot.

DICTIONARY

This game requires pencil and paper for the participants and a dictionary. This game works well in groups of 4-6. One player is chosen to lead. The leader selects an uncommon or obscure word from the dictionary and says the word out loud to the rest of the group. The leader copies the definition of this word from the dictionary onto a piece of paper. The remaining players make up a definition, and write their definitions down. The leader collects all the meanings and he/she reads them out to the group. The players must then decide which one is the correct meaning. The leadership rotates to the left for the next turn.

CONCENTRATION

This game is played with a deck of cards and is best in pairs or triads. The leader is appointed and lays out the first 20 cards in this manner: four rows of cards, with six cards in each row, not overlapping one another, with the cards face down. Players take turns, one at a time, turning over two cards on each turn to try to make a match. The card must be turned face up so that all can see. If players make a match on their turn, they can go again until they are unsuccessful at making a pair. The leader will replace each pair with two new cards face down on the table. The game continues until all cards are matched.

WHERE AM I NOW? WHERE DO I WANT TO BE? WHAT IS STOPPING ME?

This activity will need pencils, paper, and art materials. The three questions in the title are those that children may be asking themselves, especially when they have a lot of extra time or feel disempowered. It is like the game or question, "What do I want to do when I grow up?" or, "What I want to do when I get out of here?" Adding an element of planning or forethought, "What is stopping me?" is useful for those who want or need to have a plan of action to achieve their goals. Finally an evaluation of possible roadblocks that could hamper the child from achieving his/her goals is accomplished with the question "What is stopping me?"

Ask the group the following questions. It may be useful to write them down or give the group materials to write them down.

i) Where am I now?
   What is happening in my present life?
   What are my likes and dislikes?

ii) Where do I want to go?
   What are my aspirations for the future?

iii) What is preventing me?
   What are the challenges that await me?
   What do I have to do to attain my goals?

While the group members are pondering these questions, pass out three sheets of paper or one large sheet and art materials.

When the group has finished contemplating the last question, ask them to draw on their sheets of paper, or on the large paper divided into three, pictures, symbols, or colours that would illustrate their thoughts on the three main questions: Where am I? Where do I want to be? What is stopping me?

JENKIN'S UP

Divide the group into two teams and seat them opposite one another at a table.

One team is given a quarter, and they must pass it from person to person with their hands under the table. At any time someone from the opposing team can call "Jenkin's Up," and the team must raise their hands, fists closed. The opposing team then calls "Jenkin's Down," and the players must put their hands, palm down, on the table.

The opposing team has to guess who has the quarter and in which hand it is. The team gets one guess. If they are correct, they score a point. If they are incorrect, the other team scores a point. The quarter is then passed over to the other team for their turn.

ZIT AND DOUBLE ZIT

Ask the players to form a circle or stand in a line, and appoint one player to be leader. Ask the leader to choose two categories, (e.g., food and colours). The first category is called ZIT, and the second category is called ZIT ZIT (a food is ZIT and a colour is a ZIT ZIT). Instruct the leader to begin by pointing his/her finger at one of the group members and at the same time naming one of the categories (a food or a colour). The player who was pointed out must respond appropriately (ZIT for the food or ZIT ZIT for the colour). The leader may try to trick the player by naming something that is not a food or a colour (a train); the correct response to a word that is not one of the categories is silence. If the player responds correctly, the game continues. If the player responds incorrectly, they are asked to be leader.

CHARACTERS

Assign different roles to all of the players (doctor, athlete, teacher, etc.) in secret (e.g., whisper the roles in the children's ears or write the roles on cards to be picked out of a hat). Instruct the players to mingle and greet one another in character. After a few minutes, ask the players to guess the roles that were acted out by the different players.

DANCING HANDS

Ask the group to form a circle and sit down. Demonstrate that there are many ways to dance your hands (wave hands, clap hands, spin hands in circles, slap thighs, etc). Each player, one at a time, will demonstrate one way to dance his/her hands, and then the group will all imitate the dance.

SNORT

Instruct players to sit down in the form of a circle. A leader is chosen to go first and begins the game by snorting at the person on his/her left—a snort is a harsh sound made by rapidly blowing air out through the nostrils. This player must then turn to his/her left and snort at that person; the snorting proceeds until it has made one revolution. The game continues with another round of snorting, but this time a double snort changes the direction around the group, and a triple snort means the group must snort all at once.

Variations: Players can pair up and have a "snort-down"—one player tries to out-snort the other. Small groups of children can have snorting conversations with one another.

GUESS WHO?

This activity provides an opportunity for group members to share a bit more information about themselves. This activity is a good guessing game, and it encourages the improvement of memory skills.

Pass out paper and pencils, and instruct group members to write down three things about themselves that the other group members may not know, for example, middle names, hobbies, places visited, secret ambitions, etc. Instruct the group members to keep their answers confidential, to write them down on the paper provided, to fold the paper, and to place it on the table. When all papers are handed in, mix up the papers and read them to the group one at a time. Each member of the group is given a turn to guess who the author is, until someone guesses correctly. If they are unable to guess, the paper goes back into the pile. The activity is completed when all the players have been guessed.

> A true friend knows your weaknesses but shows you your strengths; feels your fears but fortifies your faith; sees your anxieties but frees your spirit; recognizes your disabilities but emphasizes your possibilities.
>
> – WILLIAM ARTHUR WARD

KIM'S GAME

Collect a wide variety of small objects, the number depending on the group's developmental level. Place the objects on a table or the floor a distance from the group, and cover them with a piece of material so the group members cannot see them. Hand out paper and pencils, and ask the group members to come forward one by one or in small groups. Lift the material off the objects for 1-2 minutes, and then cover them again. Players are then asked to go back and write down as many objects as they can remember from the collection. Teams may confer with one another.

COMMUNICATION

Instruct the group to form pairs and find a comfortable place in the room where they can have a conversation. Once the group is ready, inform them that they cannot speak to one another but must communicate nonverbally. Suggest that they tell their partner what they did over the weekend. They will have one minute to communicate to their partner.

Once this is completed, ask the group to find a new partner. Hand out a piece of paper and pencil, and suggest to the group to continue to discuss the original topic what I did on the weekend, but they can now communicate to their partner with drawings. This time they are given 30 seconds to communicate.

Once completed, ask the group to form new partnerships. Instruct the group that they can now choose 4 words to communicate to their new partner what they did on the weekend. Inform the group that they have one minute and you will keep time.

A new pair can use 8 words and have 30 seconds.

THIS IS THE HOUSE THAT JACK BUILT

Group members sit in a circle. One player begins with the sentence "This is the house that Jack built." The next player adds on to the line, for example, "This is the Ferrari that is parked on the street in front of the house that Jack built." The next player adds on a bit more information to the developing scene such as, "This is the driver that sits in the Ferrari in front of the house that Jack built." The game continues until all of the players have had a turn.

BACK-WORDS

Divide the group into teams of 3-5 players. Ask the teams to form a line one player behind the other. Communicate to the player at the end of the line a common name, either by whispering in the players' ears or handing out a written word. The player at the back is asked to trace the word on the back of the player in front. That player is then asked to print the word on the back of the person in front of them. The person at the front of the line is asked to speak the word aloud.

Variation: The list of words can be replaced with names of common objects such as, an apple, a smiling face, or a garden rake, and players are asked to begin with the last person in the line tracing the object on the back of the player in front of them.

EXCUSE ME; WHAT ARE YOU DOING?

Ask the group to form a circle and appoint a player to lead. The leader turns to the player on his/her left and mimes an action (e.g., washing his/her face, hitting a baseball, etc.). The player to the left of the leader asks, "Excuse me; what are you doing?" The leader must respond with anything other than what he/she is really doing. For example, if the leader were miming washing his/her hair he/she might respond by saying, "Putting on my make-up." The person to the left of the leader must then turn to the player on his/her left and mime putting on make-up. That player in turns asks. "Excuse me; what are you doing?" The player is to respond with something other than what he/she is doing. The game proceeds around the circle until everyone has had a turn.

ME SWITCH

Instruct the players on how to give three signals: one, wrists crossed with arms out straight; two, right hand under left elbow, left hand raised; and three, left hand under right elbow, right hand raised. Ask the players to pair up and stand or sit in front of their partners. Each player takes a turn and calls out, "Me switch!" On the word "switch," each player must signal with one of the three positions. The object is for the caller to match his/her partner's signal.

Players can keep score or just enjoy outsmarting their opponent.

WOULD YOU RATHER

This game asks players to decide between the lesser of two evils or the better of two conditions. Some examples are: "Would you rather lose your eyesight or your hearing? Would you rather have a great body or a great mind? Would you rather be 8 feet tall or 3 feet tall?"

Ask the group to form a circle, seated. Introduce the theme of the game, and ask for a volunteer to lead. The leader begins by asking the person directly across from him/her a "would you rather" question. This player can answer, pass, or counter with his/her own "would you rather" question. If the player answers the question, then he/she can ask anyone in the group a "would you rather" question. If the player passes, the person on his/her left has a chance to answer. If the player responds with his/her own "would you rather" question, both players must answer, and the turns rotate to the left of the leader.

GROCERY STORE

Form the group into two lines of equal number of players and have the lines face each other. Players are to number off.

The facilitator will call out a number and a letter. The number determines which two players can answer. The first player to call out the name of something in a grocery store that begins with the letter called out scores a point, if it is correct (e.g., peanut butter, oranges, soap, etc. for P, O, and S).

FAVOURITES

This is another good "getting to know you" exercise. It allows participants to share more personal information. There are a number of ways to present this activity: in dyads, triads or small groups. Please feel free to add or subtract from this list.

My favourite food is...

My favourite drink is...

My favourite shape is...

My favourite colour is...

My favourite animal is...

My favourite bird is...

My favourite automobile is..

My favourite toy/possession is...

My favourite story/fairy tale is..

My favourite dinosaur is...

My favourite musical instrument is...

My favourite movie/television show is...

My favourite cartoon is ....

My favourite game/sport is..

My favourite song is..

My favourite hero/star/famous person is..

My favourite musical group is...

My favourite subject in school is...

My favourite friend is...

My favourite relative is..

My favourite character trait in others is...

My favourite character trait in myself is...

My favourite physical characteristic is...

Variations: Any one or all of these favourites can be drawn or sketched to make the discussion and the experience more meaningful.

I AM VERY TALL, VERY SMALL

Ask the group to form pairs. One of the pair must shut his/her eyes. The other player either holds his/her arm straight up in the air or lets it drop to his/her side. If the player with his/her arm up straight says "I am very tall," and the player with his/her eyes closed agrees, then that player wins and takes a turn. If the player with eyes closed disagrees, then the player who is standing tall can take another turn. Conversely, if the player with their arm held straight up says, "I am very small," then the opposing player must disagree in order to win the round.

HAWKS AND DOVES

Randomly divide the group up into two groups or four groups, depending upon group size, and assign a leader for each group. This is an informal debate, and facilitators will want to pick issues that are relevant to the group composition (e.g., attending school year round, lengthening the time for recess, or extending bedtime or curfew). One group is called the hawks, which are loud, boisterous, and aggressive, by nature. The second group is called the doves, which are nonviolent, quiet, and passive by nature. Divide the room in half so that the hawks are on one side and the doves on the other. The hawks can only give forceful and aggressive solutions to the problem, and the hawks are allowed to lose their tempers. The doves must try to remain as calm as possible and give nonviolent peaceful solutions to the problem. Group leaders will allow each group member to give an opinion. Play begins with one side giving their solutions to the problem. Once the first group has offered their solutions, the next group is allowed to give their opinions.

When each group member has had a turn, then ask the sides to switch roles. The hawks become the doves, and the doves become the hawks. Repeat the process giving each group equal time. Once each group member has had a chance to speak on both topics, conduct a brief discussion with all group members. Some possible questions are:

What emotions and internal images were present when role-playing a hawk and a dove?

How is the outside world like this game?

How is our country like this game?

How is the neighbourhood, classroom, or family like this game?

SELF-LOVE, SELF-HATE DRAWING

Children who have experienced self-hatred, self-doubt, and self-blame often get stuck in this state of mind and are unable to feel positively about themselves. This exercise offers the child a vehicle (art) in which to express their negative feelings and then, in turn, express self-appreciation. Have art materials ready.

Relax the group with a relaxation exercise (see Chapter 13, "Relaxation, Imagery, and Guided Fantasy").

"Now that you're feeling relaxed, I want you to concentrate on the times you get angry at yourself. You might get angry because of what you said or did or because you wished you had said or done something differently. Remember as many situations as you can."

"Become aware of how this feeling of self-hatred makes you feel."

"Where do you feel it in your body?"

"What do you see? [pause, pause] Hear? [pause, pause] Feel?"

"Think of what a picture of all this anger and hatred would look like."

"What shapes are in your picture?"

"What colours? [pause, pause] Sounds? [pause, pause] Words?"

"Now slowly erase that picture, remembering exactly how it looked, and when you are ready, draw that picture on the paper provided."

Relax the group a second time using a similar relaxation technique.

Ask them to get an image or feeling of their positive self. Instruct them to remember the situations when they felt good about themselves, and proceed in much the same way as in the first exercise. When they have completed the fantasy, the group is to draw this picture on the other side of the paper provided.

Discuss with the group first their drawing of self-hatred, and then their drawing of self-love. Ask them how these parts integrate to become the person that they are.

Chapter 11, "Teen and Young Adult Play" is especially for those older teens and young adults who either do not want to play the more juvenile games or who have played them all and want something more adult oriented or more challenging. Teens and young adults are usually very social and enjoy the type of activities presented in the upcoming chapter.

> ...inclusion is about a community where everyone is recognized for their differences and everyone is recognized as belonging...
>
> **– JOSEPH PETNER**

CHAPTER 11

Teen and Young Adult Play

Teenagers and young adults can benefit greatly from a structured recreational program that integrates socialization with self-expression. Their stage of development is often focussed on what society labels "mature" behaviour. Yet the small child that dwells within them still longs to be able to play. Once structure and opportunity are provided, this age group has a wonderful time playing old childhood games and learning and inventing new ones. Many of the games already presented in this section can be used or adapted to suit this age group. This age bracket can usually handle competition, and therefore challenging activities often provide useful opportunities for the group to get in touch with their playful Self. Competition can be tempered, and humour can be added to the activities so the group can focus on enjoyment rather than winning. Large groups can be periodically broken into small groups or dyads to allow the members a variety of social experiences. "Who am I?" and "How do I fit into the larger group?" are developmental questions that this group is most concerned with. World affairs and local issues are also areas of interest that this age group enjoys discussing, and these issues can be adapted into many of the games and exercises in this book.

> You may strive to be like them, but seek not to make them like you. For Life goes not backward nor tarries with yesterday.
>
> **– KAHLIL GABRAN**

Activities

MACHINES

Instruct the group to form a circle and designate someone to lead by standing in the centre of the circle. The leader is instructed to begin by making a motion and repeating it at regular intervals (e.g., moving arms up and down or from side to side repeatedly). The next person joins the leader and must attach to this person in some way (e.g., placing one hand on the person's shoulder). Once attached, the player is asked to begin a motion of his/her own (e.g., moving the other arm in a circular motion).

The rest of the group in turn joins the moving group members to form a machine. Once the machine is running smoothly (the group may need a rest depending on how long the machine has been running), suggest that each part of the machine should make a sound. Beginning with the leader, the parts begin to make their own special sounds.

Finally, instruct the machine to dismantle; however, they must do this by the leader exiting first. Each player disconnects from the machine one at a time until the machine and its sound fades to the last player.

BODY OBSTACLES

Instruct the group to create an obstacle course using only their bodies as the obstacles. Encourage the creative use of bodies, and help organize the set up. Make sure of safety, especially for anyone with back problems or physical limitations. Once the course is created, select one player to begin, and ask them to run through the course. Once the group has had a turn, suggest that dyads attempt the course, with one of the pair blindfolded.

WHERE'S WALDO

This is an activity with lots of physical contact and is a way for the group to physically connect with one another.

Instruct the group to spread out over the play area. Explain that you will ask them to close their eyes and that you will touch one of them on the top of the head and that player will be "Waldo."

The group is then asked to wander around the room with their eyes closed and their arms extended. If they bump into someone, they are to ask that person, "Are you Waldo?" If the player is not Waldo, he/she is to respond, "No, I'm not Waldo." If the player is Waldo, he/she will not respond. In this case the first player who has discovered Waldo will go behind Waldo and attach his/her hands to Waldo's hips. This player is now Waldo as well. As each player finds Waldo, he/she must connect to the last player's hips, which will require players to find their way to the end of the chain to attach to Waldo. Once everyone is attached, the game is complete.

FRIENDLY PHRASES

This is a good activity to allow group members to share their previous and current interpersonal relationships. It allows them to discuss what they see as important in friendships. This activity can give all group members useful information about each other.

Pass out the pencils and copies of the list below to the group members, and ask them to complete the sentences on their own.

Having a friend helps me to...

My best friend always...

One thing I like about my friend is...

It is important to cooperate because...

I like being with people when...

Helping others is ...

One way to make a friend is ...

My best friend can be counted on to...

Other people are important because...

A person I learn things from is...

My family is ...

I can help most people by...

The world would be better if...

One thing I can teach someone else is...

Groups of people are...

Allow the group plenty of time to finish. Suggest to those who are finished early that they draw a picture of a friend on the back of their sheet. Discuss the answers with the group as well as what each member looks for in a friend.

TOUCH IT

Divide the group into groups of four. One player is chosen as the chaser, and the other three players join hands to form a triangle. Now, one of the three members of the triangle is chosen as the leader. The object of the game is for the chaser to touch the leader and for the players in the triangle to prevent this from happening. The chaser may not reach through the triangle, nor may he/she tag the leader's arms or hands. The chaser must touch the leader by running behind the triangle and tagging him/her on the back.

TWO TRUTHS, ONE LIE

This is a good game to get to know more about fellow group members.

The group is asked to form a circle and think about two facts about themselves that they want the group to know. Once they have decided which two they wish to share with the group, they are to make up something about themselves that is not true. Explain that the subtler the difference between the truth and the lie the more difficult it is to detect. Each person takes his/her turn telling two truths and one lie, and the group is asked to try to determine which two statements are true and which one is the lie.

HUMAN MASS

Divide the group up into two teams of equal numbers of members. Designate one team A and the other team B. Team A sits in a tight circle locking arms and legs until they are one human mass. Ask team A to close their eyes and imagine that they are one and cannot be taken apart. Team B is now instructed to do just that; they begin by each getting behind one member and trying to pull them apart from the human mass. Rings, belts, jewelry, and any potentially dangerous clothing should be removed, and players are instructed not to jerk or twist arms or legs.

BLOW YOUR SOCKS OFF

Hand out a collection of work socks one pair for each group member. This is a giant free-for-all where members try to take each other's socks off. The group is divided into pairs, and they begin by putting on a pair of work socks. Then, kneeling on all fours, they must attempt to get their opponent's socks off. If a person has both socks removed, he/she may now help others to remove the socks of remaining players.

FUNNY INTRODUCTIONS

This activity is usually initiated after other group name-games but can be used on its own.

Instruct the group to think of a fruit that best describes them as a person or what their favourite fruit is and why. Now ask group members to pair up and introduce themselves. Players begin by stating, "My name is Maurice and my favourite fruit is _____ because _____ ."

Now ask the group to change partners, but instead of a fruit, they are to select a television show or movie and introduce themselves to their new partner.

Ask the group to pair up again and this time to select a brand name or popular toy to include in their introduction to their new partner.

NEWSPAPER STORM

Before the activity, draw a line or designate a mid-point boundary somewhere in the middle of the play space that separates the area into two equal halves. Cover the entire play space with newspaper.

Divide the group into two teams and instruct the teams that their goal is to try to get all the newspaper from their side of the room to the other team's side. Play continues until one team is successful or time is called.

WHERE ARE MY SHOES?

Ask the group to form a circle, sit down, and remove their shoes. The players then throw their shoes into the middle of the circle. Instruct the group to close their eyes and to proceed on all fours to the middle of the circle and find any two shoes and place them on their feet. Once they have the two shoes on, they can open their eyes, stand up, and wait for the rest to finish.

Once finished, the group members are asked to find the mate to the shoe they are wearing on their left foot and to stand beside the person so that both shoes are together.

Once everyone has paired up using the left shoe, the group members are instructed to find the mate to the shoe they are wearing on their right foot and to stand beside the person so that both shoes are together.

Finally the group as a whole is asked to find both mates to the shoes they are wearing and discover a way to stand beside both pairs.

CONTACT ACTIVITIES

Divide the group up into pairs and, after each exercise, have them change partners.

1. Off Balance: Stand face-to-face. Place your palms against your partner's palms and push against each other as hard as you can. The object is for one member to try to put his/her partner off balance.

2. Slap Hands: Stand face-to-face, feet slightly astride. One partner (A) extends arms with palms raised—the other (B) extends arms and places palms down over partner's palms leaving a space of 5-10 centimetres between palms. The object is for B to slap A's hands before they are withdrawn. A is to try to prevent B from slapping his/her hands.

3. Thumb-Wrestling: Partners hold hands in a handshake position, and raise thumbs vertically. Touch thumbs together three times. On the count of three, each partner tries to force the other's thumb under theirs and hold it there.

4. Arm-Wrestling: Players are asked to sit at a table across from one another or to lie down facing their partners. Each player is instructed to raise up his/her right arm and place his/her elbow on the floor or table in front of his/her partner. Players are then instructed to clasp hands and attempt to force the back of their opponent's hand on to the floor or table top without moving any other parts of their bodies.

Once completed, players are asked to repeat the exercise using their left arm instead of their right.

5. Indian Leg-Wrestling: Partners lie down on their backs facing opposite directions. They should be close enough together so that their hips are touching. The partners raise their legs to meet each others, and on the count of one, two, and three, they are to lock ankles and try to overturn their opponent.

Once completed, players are asked to repeat the exercise but using the other leg.

6. Knee-Boxing: Partners are instructed to face each other and bend forward at the waist, arms swinging free. The object of this activity is for players to slap their partners' knee before their own knee is slapped.

7. Duck-Bunt: Partners are instructed to face each other and squat into a full knee bend. Players are now asked to cross their arms in front of them at shoulder height. The object of this activity is for players to knock their opponent off-balance.

8. Toe Tag: Instruct the dyads to stand facing one another, clasp hands, but to not interlock the fingers. Choose one foot to be A and the other foot to be B. The object of this game is for players to tag the A foot of their opponent with their B foot before being tagged by their opponent's B foot.

THE MURDERER'S WINK

Instruct the group to form a circle and designate one person to begin as leader. The leader is then asked to leave the room or turn away from the group so the group is no longer visible to him/her. Inform the group that one of them will be singled out as the murderer for this round. If the murderer winks at a group member, they are to act as if they have been murdered and fall down dead.

Ask the group to close their eyes, and inform them that the person who is touched on the top of their head will be the murderer. Once that person is designated, ask the group to open their eyes and for the leader to come into the centre of the circle. The object is for the leader to determine who the murderer is before everyone is dead. The leader has three choices to guess the murderer.

CROSSING THE SWAMP

To play this game, you will need two planks approximately three metres long (planks 20 cm. wide are easier to walk on) or two benches approximately three metres in length for each team.

Divide the group into teams of 8 to 10 members. The imaginary swamp is nine metres wide. The team is told to cross the swamp making use of the materials provided. They are not allowed to step off of the planks or benches, and they must travel the full nine metres as a group. The first team to cross the swamp without stepping into the water wins.

FLASHLIGHT TAG

You will need a flashlight to play this game; it takes the same form as a game of tag, except that it is played in the dark. The person who is designated as the leader is equipped with a flashlight. A home base is established. The leader hides his/her eyes and counts to 100 by 10s. The rest of the group hides while the leader is counting. When the leader flashes the light on one or more of the players and identifies them by name, they are caught. Those who get to home base before being caught are home free.

This game can be also be played by two teams. One team has flashlights, and the other team hides. Home base has a fluorescent flag which, when captured by a team member before being caught, ends the game. The teams then switch.

SCAVENGER HUNT

Divide the group into teams of three to five players. Each team gets a list of items to be collected on the hike. The first team to return home with the required number of items is the winner.

The teams can be asked to return at a specific time; those closest to the time and who have the most items collected are winners.

Each team can be given a letter of the alphabet and asked to list as many items that start with the letter that they observe on the hike.

COMPASS HIKE

You will need a set of directions or topographical map and a compass for each player/team.

Construct the hike prior to the activity using the compass points as directions, for example, (walk due north 20 paces, then travel east 45 paces, and turn southwest for 10 paces, etc.). Each team player is given the set of directions and is required to follow the directions to a home base.

The same can be accomplished with a topographical map, a compass, and a series of checkpoints.

SECRET CONFESSIONS

Each player needs a paper and pencil for this game. The group is instructed to sit in a circle and to print their names at the top of the page. Instruct the group members to fold the paper once in order to cover their name. When completed, players are asked to pass their papers to the person on their left and continue to pass the papers around until told to stop. Once the passing has stopped, players are instructed to write a true confession (e.g., something they did which was dangerous) at the top of the sheet closest to the fold. When they are finished, they are to fold the paper again so as to cover up the confession. Players are instructed to again pass the papers around and to stop when signalled to do so. Play continues until the sheets are full. The group is then instructed to pass the papers around for one last turn and signalled to stop. Each player unfolds the paper and in turn reads the name at the top and the list of confessions.

I think being a teenager is such a compelling time period in your life--it gives you some of your worst scars and some of your most exhilarating moments.
— STEPHENIE MEYER

FAMILY HISTORY

This activity is done over a period of time. The group members will need time to gather the necessary information. This family history goes back two generations but could go back further depending on the availability of the information. Begin by instructing group members to speak with their parents and grandparents in order to get the following information: names and birth dates of all family and extended-family members; marriages, separations and divorces; deaths, dates and causes of death; occupations of all members, their education, religion, and language(s) spoken; moves and reasons for moving; achievements of specific members; and adventures taken.

When this information is gathered, it can be placed on a family tree or gene-o-gram. The information is shared and presented in small groups or in the large group.

TEAM CHARADES

Divide the group into two teams; you will need two separate rooms or areas for this activity. Instruct teams A and B to go to their different rooms and to decide what action they will mime (e.g., fixing a flat tire, building a house, erecting a tent, building a campfire, etc.). Team A then decides which team member will act out the mime. Team A calls in one member from Team B who watches the mime. When it is finished, the member from Team B calls in one of his/her teammates and acts out the mime for that person, who, in turn, calls in another member from the team and acts out the mime for him/her. This continues until the last member of Team B comes into the room, and and tries to guess the mime. Usually, by the time this member tries to guess the mime, it is quite different from the original. If this person is unable to guess Team A's mime, any player from Team B can try to successfully guess it.

Once completed, teams switch roles, and a player from team B acts out the team's mime for the first player on team A.

PARTS DRAWING

Divide the group up into small groups of four or five. Distribute art materials, and instruct the group that they are being asked to draw a composite drawing of a person. Each member agrees to draw one of the following body parts: the head, the torso, the right arm, left arm, right leg or left leg. The team members are asked to scatter and instructed not to collaborate in any other way and not to share their drawings until the facilitator asks them to do so.

When their individual drawings are completed, they are to reassemble as a group and tape the body parts to the wall to form their person. Once formed, the group is to agree on a name and a profession for their character.

GREETINGS

Divide the group into smaller groups of six to eight members. Instruct each group to design and develop one of six forms of greetings. Designate a greeting for each group.

Group #1: Your job is to create a unique handshake or way of greeting that will convey good wishes for the upcoming day.

Group #2: Your job is to create a greeting that is unique and special for good friends—something that will express or communicate a sense of closeness and a familiarity with one another.

Group #3: Your job is to invent a special handshake that will be energizing and bolstering for participants whenever the group needs a boost.

Group #4: Your job is to create a nonverbal greeting that says, "I'm not doing so well today (hung-over, ill, frustrated)."

Group #5: This group is to create an unusual nonverbal message that is used to communicate good luck.

Group #6: This group is to create an unusual nonverbal message that is used to bid people farewell at the end of the meeting.

IMAGINARY ANIMAL

Divide the group into small groups of four to five members, and ask the group to share among the members the name of their favourite animal and what it is about that animal that they like.

Once they have discussed their animals, ask them to come up with a composite animal that includes some or all of the animals named. They are to form this animal using themselves as parts of the animal. For example, they may make a deer-dog-fish or a horse-budgie-lion-cow or a unicorn-crow-badger-trout.

Once completed, each small group will share their animal with the entire group.

EMPTYING MY SOCK

This is a fun activity that can bring out the competitive spirit. In preparation, fill a number of work socks with identical items. You might want to use objects such as coins, pebbles, shells, nuts, beans, etc. Make a list of these items for reference. There should be only one item of each kind in each group's sock.

Divide the group into teams of equal numbers of members, and ask them to line up one behind the other. Instruct the first players of each team to take one sock and stand three metres away facing their teammates.

The facilitator will call out the first object on the list. Players must run over to their teammate holding the sock, reach into it to feel the item called for, and pull it out of the sock. Players who guess correctly place the item back into the sock, and now they are to hold the sock while their teammate runs to the back of the line.

This can be played in heats (one item at a time) or can be a free-for-all (facilitator calls out the next item once the first player guesses correctly).

NIGHT WATCHMAN

Select one player to be the "Night Watchman." The rest of the players are asked to spread themselves around the playing area, strike a pose, and hold it. The group is informed that this is a haunted museum and they are statues. The Night Watchman's task is to catch any statue that moves, and if caught, they become Night Watchman too. When the Night Watchman's back is turned, the statues can sneak around and move into different positions, but they must be frozen before the Night Watchman turns around.

THE BIG DEBATE

This is an entertaining activity, especially once the group has become familiar with one another.

Select current issues or dilemmas—political, social, religious, or from the world of entertainment, or you may want to ask the group for ideas and write them individually on a piece of paper

Divide your group in half, Group A and Group B. Group A is against the topic of discussion, and Group B is for or pro the topic. One group member is assigned to be the Judge (to assist the group in maintaining the rules of debate), and this role will be rotated amongst the group members.

Rules of Debate: Only one player can speak at a time and only one team can speak at a time. The Judge is required to enforce the rules and act as a timer. Each group member must present their BEST argument, even though they may not feel it is the correct one. Both sides must remain silent when the other side is giving their reasons for supporting their argument. Both groups will have two minutes of uninterrupted time to put forth their argument and one minute each to rebut the other group's argument.

I AM NOT A ROPE

Arrange the group in a circle, and explain that this activity requires that they use their imaginations to come up with as many ways to transform the rope as possible.

The game requires a rope or some other suitable object. Explain that the rope will be passed around the circle and that each participant is to imagine what the rope might be transformed into, for example, a snake. Each player is to begin by saying, "This is not a rope, it is a _____ ." The participant not only states what the rope has been transformed into, for example, "I am not a rope, I am a snake," but must also move the rope as if it were a snake.

VAMPIRES

Instruct the group to close their eyes and wander around the play space. Inform the group that you will touch one of the players on the top of their head to indicate that they are the "Vampire." The Vampire must also keep his/her eyes closed, but when he/she bumps into someone else, the Vampire grabs on to the victim and let loose a bloodcurdling scream or howl. The vampire's victims become vampires too and join the prowl. However, if two vampires bump into each other, they become mortals again.

EVOLUTIONARY CHAIN

This game begins with everyone starting at the bottom of the food chain, for example, a plant. The plant evolves into an animal and the animal evolves into a human. Instruct players to form groups of three. The way players move up and down the food chain is by winning at rock, paper, scissors, (see Chapter 7, for a description of how to play Rock, Paper, Scissors). The player who wins at rock, paper, scissors moves up the food chain; players who lose stay where they are. Once a player reaches the top of the chain, he/she must win each time or move down the chain once for each loss. Play continues for a designated period of time.

I AM SIMPLY AMAZING

This is a fun activity to end on and gives everyone a chance to say something special about themselves.

Ask the group to form a circle, seated. Ask someone to lead, and explain to the group that they will be asked to complete this sentence, "I am simply amazing because ...." When the player completes the sentence, everyone is to reply in unison, "Amazing!" Everyone gets a turn to tell the group one thing that makes him or her amazing.

The upcoming chapter, Chapter 12, "Dealing with Feelings" moves the therapeutic programmer and facilitator into a higher level of concentration on the therapeutic elements of play and the advantages of the using therapeutic programming to develop awareness and express feelings.

"The main characteristic of play—whether of child or adult—is not its content but its mode. Play is an approach to action, not a form of activity.

– JEROME BRUNER

PRACTICE

CHAPTER 12

Dealing with Feelings

My uncle had a favourite mule, which he named Sentient Sam. This animal was clearly his own boss. Sam did whatever he wanted, whenever he wanted. Uncle Mel and Sam were much alike in this way. Sentient Sam was a beautiful and proud beast who stuck out in the herd as an animal unique in many ways. He could be very gentle and affectionate, and he could also be ruthless and mean.

It was very difficult knowing how to be with Sam, and I found myself being very fearful of his ways; yet, Sam intrigued me. I dreamt of him and thought of him for most of four years of my life. All the kids were a little afraid of "Ol' Sam," and we didn't venture too far into his territory. However, there was something about Sam that was very alluring for us as kids.

When we were old enough, Uncle Mel took us to Sam. He showed us how to approach Sam and how to wait him out if he looked too scary. We felt comfortable when Uncle Mel was with us because he knew Sam. He and Sam acted like old friends; they were little kids at play and fierce rivals, all in one day. Eventually we were able to stay in the corral by ourselves with Sam, and in time, he let us rub his nose.

Uncle Mel told stories of how Sam had saved the herd and how he kept Uncle Mel from freezing one night. "Sam teaches me how to live life," he would often say. They were comfortable with one another, Uncle Mel and Sam. They grew up together and truly loved each other.

> **Feelings reflect a need, a loss, or satiation, and are a form of energy which can be used to help us act effectively to take care of ourselves.**
>
> – HENDRICKS & ROBERTS

We experience our lives in our bodies (sensations) and in the interpretation of our sensory experiences (emotions). Children need to be able to get to know their feelings, to express and to experience them, and to befriend them, as Uncle Mel did with Sentient Sam and us. Teaching and reinforcing emotional and sensory regulation is the heart of child and youth work—emotional and sensory experiences are the heart of us all. In many ways, feelings are the experience of the life force within us.

This chapter on feelings underscores the importance of feelings when working with children. It provides discussion on the appreciation of sensory experience as separate from, but connected with, emotion. The importance of emotional regulation will be stressed and techniques provided to assist the learner to facilitate ways in which children can learn to use their feelings to support and understand their thoughts and behaviours. This chapter discusses the use of feelings in group play experiences and provides strategies to initiate emotional expression and discussion in children's groups. Children have a much better appreciation of their feelings and have much more potential for using feelings as a means to attain homeostasis—balance. This chapter also provides the student and novice programmer and facilitator with 20 therapeutic interventions focussing specifically on assisting children to express and learn from their feelings. Chapter 16, "Special Programs" offers a six-week therapeutic play program focussed on the connection that exists among feelings, thoughts, and behaviours.

The Importance of Feelings

Sensory experiences are particularly important for children because they are the initial building blocks to learning. The child experiences the world through the five senses and interprets the sensations in a meaningful way. Therefore, encouraging sensory experiences in children, especially children who have deadened or numbed their senses, has considerable merit.

Feelings inform and guide children as to how to experience life (Artz, 1993; Rolls, 2005). Physical sensations let the child know whether the experience was pleasant or unpleasant. Emotions tell children what it is that they want or need, which gives them clues on how they should behave, think, and live in the world. Feelings can inform children as to what they need to change and what not to change. They tell them how to react to certain individuals and in certain situations. They tell children what they like and do not like, what experiences to avoid and what ones to embrace, what makes them feel safe and what makes them feel unsafe. They are a form of energy that can motivate and create, that can immobilize and destroy. When feelings are accepted, expected, and cherished, the individual feels acknowledged and validated. As in all areas of child and youth care, the facilitators must be in touch with their own feelings and be able to readily express them.

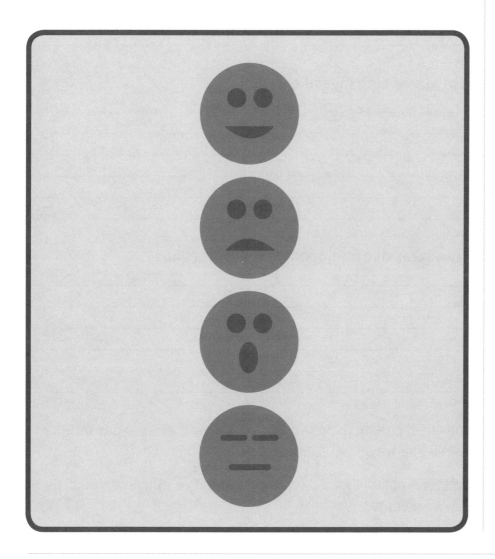

Personal Reflection – Managing Emotions

Take a few minutes to relax and review your past week, highlighting the emotional experiences. Write down all the emotions that you experienced (see the list of emotions in "Distinguishing Between Emotions and Sensory Experiences" in this chapter).

Emotions experienced:

_____

_____

_____

_____

_____

_____

_____

_____

_____

_____

Do I have healthy ways of expressing myself emotionally?

_____

_____

_____

_____

_____

_____

What can I do to be more expressive and open about my feelings?

_____

_____

_____

_____

_____

_____

Put a star or asterisk (*) beside those emotions you listed above that were powerful or that strongly affected you in some way.

From the starred list, select an emotion that did not have a positive outcome, recall the episode, and answer these questions:

Did I express all my emotions concerning this episode? If not, what emotions did I repress?

_____
_____
_____
_____
_____
_____
_____

How can I express these emotions right now?

_____
_____
_____
_____
_____
_____
_____

How would I have liked to express my emotions at the time that I experienced them?

_____
_____
_____
_____
_____
_____
_____

Talk to a friend and debrief this episode. Can you develop a non-judgmental, non-blaming way of handling this emotional episode?

_____
_____
_____
_____
_____
_____

Feelings and Thoughts

When children are exposed to violence, trauma, abuse, and neglect, the memory of that experience is retained primarily in the body. Any treatment of these types of problems in children needs to include the individual's feelings (Levine, 1997, 2010; Rothschild, 2000; Steele, 2003; van der Kolk, 1994). The right hemisphere of the brain, responsible for emotional expression and creativity, is more fully developed and develops quicker than the left hemisphere of the brain that governs logical and linear thinking (Chiron, Jambaque, Nabbout, Lounes, Syrota & Dulac, 1997). This makes the use of feelings (and creative expression, see Chapter 15, "Art, Drama, Movement, and Music Therapy") a more meaningful and productive intervention than thinking the problem through logically. So feelings need to be released through the body and expressed emotionally.

Children experience pressure to control their emotions, their whims, and their physical sensations in most of their environments: at home, "... a child should be seen not heard," at school, "… sit quietly in your desk," and in the community "... bullies, bullies everywhere." This capping of the life force requires a great deal of energy and can cause serious stress when children are not provided with outlets and vehicles with which to experience and express their emotional and sensory selves. Stifled, suppressed, and unexpressed emotion can surface in the child in a myriad of ways. Anxiety, depression, and social withdrawal all have their roots in sensory and emotional "dis-ease." The aggression and violence that are plaguing our playgrounds at school and on the internet at home are but one outcome of our culture's inability to accept, embrace, and value children's emotional worlds.

Thoughts in the culture are given more credibility than feelings—"I think therefore I am." Feelings are given labels like negative, inappropriate, bad, undesirable, and useless. Children learn to deny, to conceal, and to suppress their feelings in order to survive. Yet medical research shows conclusively that the ability to express emotion has a great deal to do with the recovery from, and prevention of, serious medical conditions (Boyle

& Joss-Reid, 2004; Chapman, 1976; Dowling, Hockenberry, & Gregory, 2003). As well, recent research into the brain and the effects of trauma clearly underscore the essential role that physical sensations and emotions play in the cause and recovery from traumatic events (Levine, 1991, 2010; Porges 2007, 2011; Steele, 2003; van der Kolk, 1994). "Children who are encouraged to attend to their instinctual responses are rewarded with a life-long legacy of health and vigor!" (Levine & Kline, 2007). Unlike thoughts or cognition, feelings are a direct experience of reality whereas cognition is an interpretation or an analysis of life experiences. Yet we continue to support a cognitive behavioural approach in most of our dealings with children.

Distinguishing Between Sensations and Emotions

It is important to make a distinction between the general term, feelings, and the more specific terms, sensations and emotions. Sensations refer to our sensory experiences that are validated and recorded in the limbic system of our brains. They are the visual, auditory, kinesthetic, gustatory, and olfactory experiences (see Chapter 6, "Therapeutic Relationships" on sensory modalities). "Sensations simply describe the physical way the body feels (its ins and outs), free of interpretations or judgments," (Levine & Kline, 2007). Our sensations might be hazy and blurry or solid and clear; they might be loud and abrasive or soft and soothing; they might be prickly and jumpy or tingly and smooth; they may be bitter and gagging or sweet and flavourful; or they may be pungent and stinky or sweet and fragrant. Sensory experiences are often very personal. What is a pleasant smell to some could be quite unpleasant to others. What feels good to one child may be irritating to another.

It is helpful for children to learn to express how they are feeling physically and to be able to communicate these experiences and instinctual responses. Here is a short list of sensations to assist the facilitator in teaching effective sensory communication.

VISUAL: colourful, colourless, round, square, wavy, glossy, lacy, shadowy, tiny, massive, lean, blurry, dazzling, gaudy, smudged, radiant, hazy, solid, clear, shimmering, sparkling, indistinct, misty, cloudy, flashy, faded, feathery

AUDITORY: crash, chime, thud, hiss, roar, whimper, scream, giggle, cry, whisper, whistle, crackle, hiss, gurgle, mutter, rant, squeal, howl, shout, sizzle, yelp, rustle, bang

KINESTHETIC: twitchy, smooth, sandy, gooey, soft, cold, hot, oily, thick, waxy, thin, sharp, dull, itchy, numb, fuzzy, cuddly, feverish, hairy, greasy, fluffy, icy, moist, prickly, jumpy, clammy, sweaty, spongy, silky, velvety

GUSTATORY: bland, tasteless, sugary, bitter, spicy, tangy, succulent, fishy, sour, burnt, vinegary, gingery, piquant, refreshing, ripe, salty, stale, tangy, rotten, zesty, nauseating, creamy, savoury, flavourless, luscious

OLFACTORY: sickly, moldy, fresh, spoiled, briny, medicinal, dank, putrid, fragrant, musty, rank, sweet, perfumed, spicy, reeking, rancid, pungent, fetid, aromatic, musty, foul, fishy, flowery, rotten, piney, lemony, fresh

Emotions are states of consciousness that combine sensory experiences with cognitive interpretations. They are often an intellectual interpretation of our sensory experiences. We sense something, for example, a slap on the face. We feel the sting on our skin and, along with other information, interpret that sensation as an act of hostility and experience the emotion of anger, embarrassment, fear, etc. Emotions inform children as to how they are experiencing their worlds. Emotions are neither good nor bad; they can be however pleasant and unpleasant. The emotion felt depends on our cognitive interpretation of the situation. Take the example above of a slap on the face. The same sensory experience, stinging skin from a slap, in the context of a flirtatious situation might lead to emotions of excitement, anticipation, and affection. It is the context and our interpretation of it that determines the emotion felt.

Children can be taught to value, express, and benefit from their emotional experiences, which will increase the purpose and pleasure in their lives. Here is a short list of emotions that will assist the facilitator in discussing and labelling them with children.

PLEASANT EMOTIONS: adored, affectionate, amazed, attractive, blissful, boastful, bubbly, calm, cheerful, compassionate, courageous, delighted, determined, eager, ecstatic, empathetic, enchanted, excited, fascinated, humoured, innocent, joyful, pleased, proud, relieved, satisfied, surprised, sweet, thrilled, zesty

UNPLEASANT EMOTIONS: agitated, aggressive, betrayed, bored, cowardly, cruel, dejected, disappointed, discouraged, dismal, depressed, embarrassed, empty, envious, foolish, frustrated, gloomy, guilty, hostile, infuriated, intimidated, insecure, jealous, lonely, miserable, overwhelmed, panicky, petrified, terrified, worthless

"

The greatest single source of difficulties in interpersonal relationships is dealing with our own and others' feelings.

– JOHN L. WALLEN

Personal Reflection – Emotions' Sensory Qualities

Find a relaxed area and get as comfortable as possible. Begin with a favourite relaxation exercise. Once relaxed, start with the sense of sight, and ask yourself the following questions.

"What do emotions look like?" List the primary emotions (i.e., sadness, anger, fear, happiness) one by one and comment on what they look like to you. You may wish to make a small sketch of what they look like. If you want, include the more subtle categories of emotions such as embarrassment, surprise, loss, frustration, exhaustion, exhilaration and so on.

_____

_____

_____

_____

_____

_____

_____

"What do emotions sound like?" As with sight, recall the primary feelings first and then the more subtle feelings.

_____

_____

_____

_____

_____

"What do emotions feel like?" This is feeling in the tactile sense.

_____

_____

_____

_____

"What do emotions taste like—smell like?"

_____

_____

_____

_____

Feeling Myths

There is a popular misconception that some feelings are bad or inappropriate and others are good or appropriate. Adults convey this message to children, and eventually, some grow up believing that it is bad to get angry, to cry, to feel afraid, and in some instances, to feel pleasure. This same understanding is sometimes carried to the extreme with thoughts and behaviours, where some children see themselves as a type of split personality, the good-me and the bad-me. When this misconception is applied to gender stereotypes, we find males expressing anger and females expressing sadness more than any other emotion. These predominant emotions are often secondary to the original emotion. This happens in the male child who is prompted to express anger even when he feels afraid, sad, or alone. The female child also experiences this when she is prompted to express sadness and fear through her tears, when actually she may be feeling angry, frustrated or misunderstood.

Another misconception is that it is acceptable to feel anger, but not to be too angry, or to feel sorrow, but not feel too much sorrow, or to feel grief, but not to grieve too much. This misconception also interferes with the essential information and messages that emotions convey.

Children need an environment that allows them to become familiar with all of their emotions and to learn to decode the messages they send and receive. This will allow them opportunities to develop effective, socially acceptable, behavioural strategies and thought processes in response to their experiences in life. Programmers and facilitators need to promote an environment that makes the expression of emotions a natural and spontaneous act.

> The deeper that sorrow carves into your being, the more joy you can contain.
>
> – KAHIL GIBRAN

The Importance of Self-Regulation

Children with social, emotional, behavioural, or cognitive problems often have difficulty regulating their feelings, thoughts, and behaviours. This inability to self-regulate causes them to overreact or under react. Hypersensitivity or hyposensitivity at a feeling level interferes with their daily functioning. When children can self-regulate, especially at a feeling level, they are much better equipped to manage their feelings as well as their thoughts and behaviours. Remember the main goal for all children is to find balance or homeostasis—self-regulation is a most important skill to master.

Children who have numbed themselves to feelings need to be able to appreciate that physical sensations and emotional experiences are transient. These sensations do not remain constant but fluctuate depending on the type and amount of stimulation. Children who deaden their feelings have lost the confidence that this is so and worry that if they allow themselves to feel certain sensations or emotions that these feelings will remain with them. They fear being overwhelmed by these powerful experiences. They fear being hyper-aroused and so learn to deaden their feelings (Levine, 1997).

Children's sensory and emotional experiences can be modulated in such a way as to assist them to slowly allow themselves to feel more and more. Levine (1997) describes a process of "pendulation" between unpleasant feelings and pleasant ones. This can begin with vocabulary, giving children labels for their feelings. This gives the child a concrete word to attach to their physical, but sometimes ambiguous, experience. Then sensory experimentation can take place. There are a number of sensory activities at the end of this chapter which allow children to begin to feel physical sensations enough to know that they are transient, that they do pendulate (ebb and flow), and that there are ways to relieve the stimulation if it is painful. Children can learn that they can have more and more intense physical experiences and still be able to control them.

The same is true of emotions. Children can be taught to experience emotions in their fullest range and to always be able to return to balance and homeostasis. Emotions not only affect the psychological Self and the sociological Self, they also have effects on the physiological Self. "One of the ways we stop ourselves from experiencing our feelings is through body tension and blocks" (Hendricks & Roberts, 1977, p. 136). The physical Self, in order to control rage, may create muscle tension in the back of the neck, in the shoulders, or in any other part of the anatomy. This tension becomes the physiological reaction to that particular emotion. For example, the body's way to control fear or anxiety might show up in the breathing patterns of an individual. A block in a breathing pattern manifests itself with limited or restricted breathing, shallow breathing, or gasping. Breath is life giving, and when breathing patterns are blocked or arrested, this directly affects the physiological Self. The act of controlling emotions by tensing the body or by restricting breathing only adds more stress to the individual and is a maladaptive strategy. Chapter 13, "Relaxation, Imagery, and Guided Fantasy" offer a series of breathing exercises to assist programmers and facilitators.

There is an interrelationship between emotion and motion. When motion is restricted, so too is emotion. Muscular tensions and erratic breathing patterns restrict motion. A more productive strategy for structuring emotions is by using movement as a form of expressing the emotional Self (see Chapter 15, "Art, Drama, Movement, and Music Therapy"). The expression of emotion through movement and the arts, through imagery, fantasy and relaxation, and by means of intellectual discussion and experiential learning are all effective ways to channel and structure emotional experiences.

There are activities at the end of this chapter that will assist the child and youth care professional in teaching children to self-regulate. Relaxation and the ability to self-sooth are critical components to self-regulation. When children can be taught to relax and slow down feelings, thoughts, and behaviours, they can be taught to use their internal voice to speak to themselves in an affirming and supportive manner. Relaxation and self-soothing will be discussed further in Chapter 13, "Relaxation, Imagery, and Guided Fantasy." The setting is also critical to the child's ability to self-regulate—the task to self-regulate depends on "… the fit between the child, her or his environment, and the interaction between the child and the environment" (Mash & Wolfe, 2013, p. 47). For more on this, see Chapter 2, "Therapeutic Play Environments" and Burns (2006).

Personal Reflection – Stress in the Body

Find a comfortable place, take a relaxed position, and relax your body. Close your eyes and imagine that you are able to scan your body like a CAT Scan. Start with your feet, and very slowly and very thoroughly scan your feet for signs of tension or the effects of stress. Travel the length of your body, scanning portions at a time. Take particular care when you scan your organs to notice the areas of your body where you hold tension. When you have completed this, make a diagram of your body and mark on it the parts or areas where you noticed the tension.

Where are your big stress areas on the diagram? Comment on these areas remembering times when they were particularly painful or bothersome.

_____

_____

_____

_____

_____

_____

_____

_____

_____

_____

Examine your diagram, and think how you could exercise/stimulate the areas of stress. Make a list of four ways you could relieve the tension in each area identified.

_____

_____

_____

_____

_____

_____

_____

_____

_____

_____

Make a resolution to try to reduce stress and to express physically what you experience emotionally.

Discussing Feelings in Groups

Group experiences that focus on emotions in a logical and sequential way can be awkward for both child and adult at first. The intellectualizing of emotions can also be traumatizing in some way. The child's act of sharing his internal world, fact or fancy, should be treated with reverence and respect. The group climate and milieu are essential areas of consideration for the success of Feeling Groups. The group must have achieved a basic level of trust in the facilitator, and reasonable levels of trust with each other, in order to be able to freely express emotions with group members. The milieu needs to reflect an atmosphere of calm, warmth, and safety. The size of the group should be small, and the intellectual level of the group participants should be homogeneous.

When discussing feelings, it is useful to have group members seated in a circle. This allows for better eye contact with one another, and members are positioned on the same physical plane. If the group is seated on the floor, cushions or mats can be provided for their comfort. The concept of the circle provides a feeling of unity and equality. Even if the group is on the 12th floor of a high rise, sitting on the floor will bring the child closer to the earth. This closeness to the earth has calming, comforting, and non-threatening qualities that are useful in this type of group activity.

If the group is just starting to discuss feelings in a structured way, many will need guidance in how to behave. Here are some useful guidelines and points of discussion to present the group:

• Feelings are real, and it's okay to have them.

• There are no right/wrong, bad/good feelings.

• Group members have the right to choose not to talk about their feelings.

• Feelings discussed in the group are private for the group members only and are not talked about outside of the group.

• When one group member is speaking, the other members need to be silent and to listen.

• Group members should agree to refrain from judging each other's feelings, thoughts, and behaviours.

> "Genius is the ability to renew one's emotions in daily experience.
>
> – PAUL CEZANNE

Discussions concerning emotions do not always have to take on the structure presented here. In fact, impromptu discussions can often be less threatening and more productive. Finally, when structured activities are presented to the group, it is best to monitor their effects on group members. Some children, particularly those who have been traumatized, can be reminded of their experiences in these discussions. The group facilitator may need to provide some added support for such children. It may mean spending some time alone with them, or it may mean alerting their caregiver. Feelings are very personal and wonderful experiences. Their expression and symbolization in group process can be meaningful and can help the child to mature.

As in all good activity programming, pacing the group and the activities allows the group to begin at its level of understanding and maturity and to progress at its own pace. When planning for these types of more sedentary exercises, the programmer may want to reverse the order suggested in Chapter 3, "Designing Therapeutic Programs." The warm-up to the activity could be a centring or relaxation activity, and the cool-down might include an active game.

Expressing Emotions in Groups

The expression of emotion initially by children may not result in them expressing themselves in a socially acceptable manner. Children may use swear words to express their emotions, they may need to smash and break objects, they may say regrettable things to one another or the facilitator. They may need encouragement and permission from the facilitator in order to allow their emotions to flow. Extreme latitude needs to be given in the initial stages of emotional expression. Over time, children can be taught to regulate their emotions and express them at appropriate times in acceptable ways. Initially however, they may need to be allowed to express them in whatever way seems best to them at the time. Naturally, physical and emotional safety is paramount, and all measures need to be in place before encouraging children to freely express their emotions. Depending on the intensity of the group experience, some members may need time to debrief and discuss their feelings and reactions to the session.

Sometimes there is a backlog of emotions, and children may need to spend more time on a particular emotion to fully express themselves. Maintaining emotional equilibrium and developing emotional regulation is the goal for all children who have experienced emotional trauma, emotionally intense experiences, or have not been allowed to express their emotions. The exercises at the end of this chapter provide the facilitator with resources for beginning this emotional expressive work with children.

Emotions can be represented through all modalities. A picture, a colour, a movement, or a shape, can all be stimuli for emotions. A song, a sound, a voice, a smell, a taste, a way of being touched, all can cause feelings. Therefore, when discussing emotions in a group, all modalities represented in the presentation of the topic and in the discussion make for a richer and fuller experience of the feelings.

Use happy pictures, songs, sounds, smells, tastes, etc. when discussing happiness. Pictures of people weeping, dark colours, sad songs, slow and serious voice tones, all enhance a discussion on sorrow. Discussions on sorrow, as well as fear, end nicely with a group hug for comfort and support. Yelling out loud, drawing angry pictures, and stamping your feet make discussions on anger more real. Scary music, dark and bright colours, pictures of hospitals, accidents, or fires creates an atmosphere more amenable to expressing fears. When using these techniques, certain cautions must be adhered to. Emotional levels of the group must be respected at all times. Techniques such as pictures, sounds, and sensations should be introduced one at a time. It is important not to overload any one emotion for the child. Slow and easy steps when introducing the different modalities are very important to the emotional well-being of the child.

Exercise 12:1

Select an age group of participants (early childhood, middle childhood, late childhood, early adolescent, late adolescent, or young adult). Design a four-session program (see Chapter 3, "Designing Therapeutic Programs") introducing the theme "Feelings: Sensory and Emotional Experiences". Assume the group is in the early stages of phase three of group development (see Chapter 4, "The Therapeutic Group). Sessions are to be one hour in length. Provide a brief outline of each group session below, listing topics of discussion and activities.

Session One

_____

_____

_____

_____

_____

Session Two

_____

_____

_____

_____

_____

Session Three

_____

_____

_____

_____

_____

Session Four

_____

_____

_____

_____

_____

Review

• Feelings are classified into two categories, sensory experiences and emotional experiences.

• The body and the mind have memory of feeling experiences.

• Children are given mixed messages regarding feelings.

• Children sometimes repress their sensory experiences.

• Unexpressed emotions can lead to psychological and physical discomfort and may cause repression of feelings.

• Children should be given opportunities to learn about and to express feelings.

• Emotional regulation is a key factor in recovery for emotionally troubled and traumatized children.

• Expressing emotions in a group setting may be difficult initially for some children.

The therapeutic techniques and interventions discussed in this chapter can, in many cases, be greatly enhanced when relaxation, imagery, and guided fantasy are added to the program. Chapter 13, "Relaxation, Imagery, and Guided Fantasy" broadens the facilitator's and therapeutic activity programmer's skillset to include these very powerful interventions. These techniques have the potential to increase the effectiveness of most interventions as well as that of the entire therapeutic program.

The following are a series of therapeutic interventions intended to act as resources for the student or novice practitioner who wishes to practice his/her skills in dealing with feelings.

> " The importance of being put in touch with the pain and pleasure in life, with your feelings and experience as they really are, is that it frees you to make the most realistic and positive adjustment to the world. "
>
> — DAVID VISCOTT

Therapeutic Interventions

Sensory Experiences

DESCRIBE IT

This activity requires either a photograph or a list of persons, places, and things. Pictures are easier to describe than just a name, so start with the pictures, and as the group members develop their skills, switch over to just the names printed on a sheet of paper or whispered into the leader's ear.

Ask the group to form a circle and choose someone to be the leader. The leader is given a picture of a person, place, or thing. The leader must describe the person, place, or thing to the group without actually naming it. Group members guess until successful, and then it is another participant's turn.

BUBBLE-WRAP HOPSCOTCH

This activity requires a roll of bubble-wrap, a black magic marker and a small stone, beanbag, or coin for each group. Use the magic marker to draw out the hopscotch court on the bubble-wrap.

There are several ways to play hopscotch, and this is one way to play. They can wear socks for this or use bare feet.

Divide the group into smaller groups, or have them play as one group. The first player begins by tossing the coin onto the first square or space on the hopscotch court. The coin must land in the appropriate space and may not be touching any of the boundary lines. The player then hops through the course but does not step on the section where the coin landed. Once through the course, the player must then turn around and hop back through the course until he or she reaches the square where their coin landed. The player must then pick up the coin and continue through the course until back at the starting point.

The player must not step on any of the boundary lines of the course. If a player does step on any of the boundary lines, they must stop there and allow the next player to begin. When it comes back to their turn, they must continue where they left off. The game is completed when a player has completed the entire court.

STORY SOUNDS

This activity requires some preparation. Record a series of sounds from the internet such as screams, sirens, laughter, cheering, dogs barking, cats purring, etc.

Play each sound individually, and the group or one of the group members makes up a story incorporating or explaining the sound.

WHAT'S THAT SOUND?

This activity requires a variety of objects, such as metal plates, coins, chopsticks, plastic toys, dried beans or rice in a container, sandpaper, etc. These objects should be kept out of sight from the participants.

The group is asked to turn their backs and face away from the facilitator. The facilitator will make a sound with the materials provided, such as dropping the metal plate on the floor, shaking the container of rice, etc. The participants will guess at what made that sound.

WHAT'S IN THE BAG?

This activity requires a cloth bag filled with several common items, for example, small human figures, cars, coins, etc. There should be at least as many items as there are players for this activity. Specific items can be used to create a theme or reflect a particular incident. The bag needs to be sewn shut so the objects cannot be removed.

Pass the bag around the room, and ask each player to identify one item in the bag. The facilitator answers whether the player's guess is correct. The bag continues around the circle until all items are identified.

FEEL-IT AND SAY-IT

This is an easy tactile activity that takes little effort and requires little clean up. You will need several pails, large opaque jars, or containers that do not reveal their contents. Place a variety of dry, clean media such as, sand, birdseed, beans, pasta, rice, etc. into the pails. Place the pails in a line on a table.

Instruct the members to stand around the table and come up to the various pails one at a time, close their eyes, and put their hand into the pail. They are then asked to describe the contents to the group without saying what it is. Each player has one guess, and if the contents have not been identified correctly, the next player comes up and repeats the process.

Variation: Players can tell a story that would assist the group in identifying the contents.

EWWWW OR AHHHHH

This activity requires some preparation. Gather 4-5 pans or containers and some tactilely stimulating substances such as jelly, wet spaghetti noodles, mud, peeled grapes, liquid soap, etc. Place the substances individually into a pan and set the pans out so participants have access to them. Supply a blindfold for participants, and also include a roll of paper towel.

Blindfold participants and, one at a time, allow them to put their hands into one of the pans. They are required to respond with either "Ewwww!" or "Ahhhhh!" or some other appropriate exclamation.

ROUGH AND SMOOTH

This is a wonderful activity to assist those children who have deadened their feelings or have numbed them. It requires various objects that will feel either rough or smooth on the skin, objects such as a hairbrush, sand paper, piece of concrete, tree bark, hemp rope, emery board, etc. for rough objects, and feathers, pieces of silk, glass bottle, polished metal, plastic object, ball, etc. for the smooth ones

This activity can be accomplished individually, or if you have enough supplies, the whole group can do it all at once. One caution is that some children may use the rough surfaces to purposely hurt themselves.

Begin by asking the children to form a circle. Distribute the rough objects first, and ask the group to gently rub their forearms with the rough object and then describe the feeling. Once the child has described the physical sensation, ask them how their forearm feels now (without the rough object stimulation).

Next, have them experiment with the smooth objects and describe their feelings during the stimulation and shortly after.

SCENTS

Before conducting this exercise, it is always a good idea to check into any children who may have asthma or allergies to various scents. This activity requires some preparation. You will need a collection of zip-lock bags and a variety of materials with distinct scents, for example vanilla, peppermint, tobacco, cough medicine, chocolate, vinegar, etc.

Ask the group to form a circle and to sit down. Instruct the participants to close their eyes, and, when a plastic bag is handed to them, they are to open it up and cautiously smell the contents. Once they have smelled the contents, the players are asked to zip the bag back up and pass it on to the next player. Once the bag has made it around the circle, the participants are asked to identify the smell. They can also comment on the first thing they thought of when they experienced the smell.

FOOD FINGER PAINT

Make sure you check the group for any food allergies. This activity requires some preparation. Place out on a cookie sheet, plate, or a sheet of finger-paint paper, a scoop of several different tasting substances such as whipped cream, apple sauce, oatmeal, spaghetti sauce, Jell-O, pudding, etc. Include small spoons for each participant and have them one-by-one or in a group taste each sample and comment on their experience.

Variation: Distribute finger-paint paper and assist participants to collect a sample of each of the tasting materials. Encourage group members to make a finger-paint taste-composition or work of art from the materials.

Emotional Expression

EMOTIONAL IMAGES

This is a good opener for new groups of children. You will need a few photographs or sketches depicting people experiencing emotions in a variety of situations. This allows the children to talk about the emotions of others and distances them initially from talking about their own emotions. Here they can guess how the various characters may be feeling.

Present the images to the group one at a time, and ask the group to volunteer comments on the emotions of the various characters. You may want to ask the group to comment on what the characters may be saying or thinking.

EMOTIONAL LANGUAGE

This activity is a good beginning for teaching children about their emotions. It is often easier to talk about emotions initially before actually experiencing or re-experiencing them—it usually makes it safer.

Begin with the basic happy, sad, angry, proud, frightened, and relaxed/calm emotions. Ask group members to share their experiences with each of these emotions. Whenever possible, point out the more subtle names for emotions, for example, anger can be annoyance, agitation, rage, etc. Also assist children to define, expand, or re-label their emotions when appropriate; for example, a child who experienced embarrassment might label the emotion as anger and may not be aware that he/she was initially embarrassed and then became angry.

THE CONTINUUM OF EMOTIONS

This exercise gives children a chance to evaluate their feelings at the moment, or how they might feel in specific situations. When this exercise is repeated over a period of time, children become more aware of the continuum that their feelings run along. As well, in more advanced discussions, they can become more aware of how intensely they feel and more aware of those feelings that they avoid.

Ask the group to rate themselves individually in the following areas. This rating can refer to their overall assessment of themselves or to how they feel at the moment. The rating is from 1 to 10, e.g., happy/sad, 1 would be most happy and 10 would be most sad:

happy/sad

angry/calm

fearful/fearless

aggressive/passive

talkative/quiet

friendly/unfriendly

worried/carefree

confident/unsure

EMOTIONAL PLACES AND SITUATIONS

Sometimes emotions are anchored to situations or places in that, whenever someone enters into the situation or the place, it brings up certain emotions. For example, "Whenever I walk past a funeral home, I feel sad and miss my father," or, "Every time that woman comes in my yard, I could scream!" or, "As soon as I walk into my bedroom, I feel safe."

Begin by reviewing the basic emotions, and ask members to comment one at a time on places or situations that conjure up a specific emotion. Depending on the cognitive level of the group, the discussion can include a brainstorming session on specific ways to deal with or avoid the unpleasant situations and continue or increase the incidence of the positive situations.

BODY AND EMOTIONS

This activity requires coloured pencils or crayons and a body map. This can be a piece of paper (216 mm x 279 mm) for them to draw an outline of a human figure, or you may want the group members to trace their bodies on large pieces of paper, or you may want to give them a printed picture of an outline of an androgynous body.

Begin by explaining to the group that they are going to be asked to experience specific emotions, and if for any reason they do not want to feel any of the emotions listed, they can open their eyes, sit up, or signal that they will pass on this specific emotion.

Ask the group members to look around and find a safe spot in the play space where they can lie or sit and feel comfortable. Once they have found their spot, ask the group to close their eyes and recall a time they felt happy. Ask them to visualize where they are, who they are with, what sounds or voices they hear, and finally to imagine where in their bodies they feel their happiness. Then ask them to imagine that this emotion has a colour and to identify what colour their happiness is.

The group members can then, using that colour, colour on their body map where they feel their happiness. This exercise can be repeated to include a variety of emotions.

EMOTIONAL MOTION
This activity works best with music but can be used effectively without it. Make a list of emotions, taking into account the level of emotional sophistication of the group members.

Ask the group to form a circle, and inform them that a variety of emotional words will be called out (or songs depicting emotion will be played). When the group members hear the word, they must move around the room as if they are experiencing that emotion.

When completed discuss the group's experience with this exercise.

EMOTIONAL ABSTRACTS
This activity requires sufficient paper and paint, pastels, markers, or crayons for the participants. Music can work well with this activity.

Ask the group to take a few minutes to relax and think back to a time when they felt a strong emotion (fear, anger, jealousy, joy, pride, etc). Suggest that they recall a total of three experiences with the same emotion.

Now distribute the materials and ask participants to depict that strong emotion. Suggest that they try to use colour, texture, and symbol to depict an abstract picture of their emotion (fear, anger, jealousy, joy, pride, etc).

EXPRESSING EMOTIONS IN PRIVATE

This activity requires a variety of equipment specific to the emotion that the group will be expressing. For example, if the emotion were anger, punching bags, newspaper (for ripping), pillows of various sizes, music that would evoke anger, recorded angry sounds, stuffed animals, soft foam balls, etc. would be required. If the emotion is sorrow, then lots of tissue, recorded sad and mournful sounds, pictures that evoke sorrow, stuffed animals, soft blankets, etc. would be needed. This activity usually works best by beginning with a relaxation exercise (see Chapter 13, "Relaxation, Imagery, and Guided Fantasy").

Ask the group members to find a comfortable safe place in the room, and there they may sit, lie down, or stand, whatever is most comfortable. Relax the group and ask them to picture a time when they felt (insert emotion, e.g. anger). Ask them to see where they are, who they are with, any sounds that are in the environment, and finally, to feel that emotion in their bodies. Once the feeling is very strong, they are to get up and use any one of the materials available to express that anger from the past.

EXPRESSING EMOTIONS IN PUBLIC

This is primarily a cognitive, problem-solving exercise but can be presented as a role-play. Participants can also be asked to practice any one of the strategies and report back to the group.

Ask the group to think about a specific emotion, such as embarrassment. Have them discuss ways of expressing this emotion in public that would allow them to recognize and express the emotion but in a manner that would not have negative consequences. The term "in public" should also include at home when guests are present, in the classroom, in the playground, as well as being out in public places such as when shopping, riding the bus, hanging out at the mall, etc.

> One is certain of nothing but the truth of one's own emotions.
>
> – E. M. FOSTER

OWNING EMOTIONS

One way to empower children regarding their emotions is to help them to take ownership of their emotions. This activity is usually conducted with a more advanced or emotionally savvy group. It is important for children not to take ownership or blame for causing the emotion. For example, we do not want John to feel responsible for his dad's anger or his dad's expression of this anger, only that he can choose not to feel certain emotions when his father gets angry.

The group participants will need a pencil and 2 sheets of paper or papers prepared for them with the appropriate phrases.

Ask the group to list the number of people (specific individuals), places, and situations (such as world hunger) that make them angry, sad, happy, etc. Instruct members to number their list.

When the group is ready, ask members one at a time to read out all or some of their list. They are to say, for example, "(Mom) makes me (angry) when (she makes me do my homework)." or "(People) make me (sad) when (they don't help one another)."

Now ask group members to read their lists one at a time, exchanging "(Mom) makes me (angry) …" for "I choose to get angry when (mom insists I do my homework.)"

Depending on the cognitive level of the group, the discussion can address the following questions.

Do we choose to feel anger, or do people really have the power to make us angry?

If people do have the power to make us angry, how can I take ownership of the emotion and act on it? Can anyone really make us do anything?

CHAPTER 13

Relaxation, Imagery, and Guided Fantasy

My grandfather was a very patient and passionate man and prided himself on being a good problem-solver. Often I would come to him as an adolescent with one problem or another, and he was always there to listen and loved giving me advice. I can still hear his voice, "When matters get confusing, my grandson, and you're not sure which way to go, remember these words: SLOW DOWN, FEEL, and THINK!" Grandpa was known for his dramatics, and he usually got quite animated during this part of his monologue.

"Slow down; slow down your movements and your breathing. Relax those good muscles of yours, and sit or lie yourself down. Get comfortable, and when everything is quiet on your outside, start to slow down your insides. Feel your breath enter and escape from your lungs as your whole being begins to experience total relaxation.

"Now it's time to experience your emotions. Allow your feelings to enter as you address the problem. Do not block them; just allow them to surface on their own. Laugh, cry, shriek, pound, tremble, whatever it takes to give them expression, and then imagine your emotions flowing out of your being until there is only quiet peace.

"All is ready now for creative thinking. Focus your awareness on what appears to be the problem. Open your mind to any and all solutions, allowing your thoughts to flow freely. Decide on a course of action and the problem is halfway solved now."

"Act on your new awareness, and remember—slow down, feel, and think."

> **Relaxing images actually produce physiological changes in the body.**
>
> – MIKE & NANCY SAMUELS

Relaxation is that state of rest or slowing down of the physiological Self. Imagery is the ability to construct visual, auditory, and kinesthetic representations in the brain. Combining relaxation and imagery form the conditions necessary for guided fantasy. Guided fantasy was Grandfather's favourite technique. He would relax me with his manner and language in order to lead me on an internal voyage of discovery.

This chapter introduces the reader to the concepts and practical uses of relaxation, imagery, and guided fantasy. It provides the learner with the theory behind, and the uses of, these three concepts. The text provides the learner with opportunities for experiences that will assist in a better appreciation of the relaxation, imagery, and guided fantasy processes. Techniques in each of these areas are provided to aid the facilitator in offering effective interventions. The chapter concludes with scripts for breathing exercises, relaxation, imagery, and guided fantasy exercises ready-made to use with groups of children.

The use of relaxation, imagery, and guided fantasy as a method of improving and enriching lives is as old as human kind. Socrates emphasized to his young students that their first duty was to relax and to reassure their patients. Women from the Lakota Indian tribe of North America whispered cheerful thoughts to their young children as they slept; these were words to comfort, to relax, and to strengthen the child. Buddhist monks use relaxation and imagery to become more spiritually aware. The medical sciences utilize the power of relaxation, imagery, and guided fantasy to promote and sustain health.

Children can learn to relax themselves as a method of self-soothing when they are frightened or overwhelmed, as a preparatory process to problem-solving, and as an overall stress-reducing agent. They can be trained to use imagery to augment their performance in academic, athletic, and artistic endeavours. Imagery can also assist children in dealing with highly stressful events whether from the past, in the present, or in the future. Guided fantasy can assist children to regulate their emotions and reactions to novel situations. It also helps them to benefit from the stress-releasing and problem-solving qualities of relaxation techniques, story, and fantasy. Children can benefit in many areas of their lives by experiencing and using the techniques outlined in this chapter.

Relaxation

In the late 1960s, Dr. Herbert Benson of Harvard Medical School categorized a series of physiological changes that he called the relaxation response. He noticed that when relaxed, his subjects decreased their oxygen consumption, decreased their carbon dioxide production, lowered their blood pressure, decreased their heart rates, lowered the levels of lactate in their blood systems, and intensified their alpha brain waves (Benson, 2000). "One of the implications of Benson's work is the understanding that a person is able to control, in a general way, their body physiology" (Samuels & Samuels, 1975, p. 222). This ability provides opportunities for children to lower their levels of stress and lessen the effects that stress is having on their bodies. Elkind, in his book The Hurried Child, points out the dramatic increase in stress levels for children based on the ever-increasing demands placed on them to become more adult-like (Elkind, 2006).

The pressure to grow up, to achieve academically, to be future oriented, asks children to become adults before their emotional and intellectual Selves have had time to develop. Parents, teachers, media, and society in general are expecting more and more of children than they are developmentally capable of, resulting in the excessive stress created by trying to achieve the impossible.

Children in certain dysfunctional families are under such extensive stress and duress that they become hypervigilant. They are so tuned to the emotional climate of the family that they are sensitive to the slightest discomfort in their parents and siblings.

Quiet and calming activities presented in peaceful and trusting environments provide children opportunities to slow down, to forget about the future, and to experience the present. And most children can master relaxation; however, obvious differences in developmental levels dictate the length and type of relaxation methods used. The ability to relax oneself easily, quickly, and deeply can have a considerable effect on the child's overall stress levels.

The ability to relax physically has life-long implications for the child. The ability to lower stress on the central nervous system is crucial to lessening or avoiding many forms of heart and respiratory problems. It can drastically lower the possibility of strokes and various types of stress-related diseases.

On a cognitive level, relaxation can assist children in many areas of their academic life by increasing memory, by intensifying creative thinking, and by promoting assimilation of learning. Children will find less difficulty in subjects such as mathematics and physics if they are able to slow down and concentrate.

Another approach to relaxation, used for centuries by many eastern religions, involves the "simple" act of breathing. Breathing is an important factor in assisting children to relax. Children can be taught to slowly reduce their rate of breathing and to alter their breathing as a means of relaxing.

Personal Reflection – Relaxation

Find yourself a comfortable spot and take all the time you need to squirm around until you feel settled and relaxed. When it feels right, soften your gaze and focus your vision on one spot, one object before you. As you softly gaze at the object, quiet your thoughts, and in your own time, quietly close your eyes. With your eyes closed, begin to focus your attention on your breathing. As you inhale, be aware of the air entering your lungs, filling your blood system with oxygen. And as you exhale, concentrate on the air that is expelled from your lungs, releasing the carbon dioxide to nurture plant life. Try to fill the lung cavities so that there is air in the top and bottom portions, and exhale so that the lungs are completely empty. Control your breathing so that you are able to fill the bottom portions of the lungs first, then the middle, and finally, the upper portions. As you exhale, empty the lungs from the top portions down to the bottom portions of the lungs.

Continue this technique for 10 breaths. De-focus your concentration on your breathing, and allow your breath to regulate itself. Now, as you inhale, imagine that your breath is travelling through your body, in through your nostrils to the crown of your head and down through your throat to the tips of your toes, and as you exhale, feel the air escape from every pore of your being. Use this technique for 10 breaths.

When you are ready, slowly awaken yourself, taking all the time you need to reintegrate with your surroundings before you open your eyes and become slowly accustomed to your external reality.

Practical Uses of Relaxation

Relaxation techniques with children greatly increase their ability to sleep soundly. Soothing words, physical touch, and relaxing stories and language allow the over-stimulated child opportunities to prepare for restful sleep. Meal times too can be more relaxing, increasing digestion and health to the body. One might prepare children for meal time by listening to the day's events before the meal is served, by playing quiet, relaxing music before and during the meal, and by slowing down their activity levels through hugging and giving backrubs before the meals. Finally, a prayer to give thanks to the provider of life and recognition to the cooks and attendants sets up more possibilities for healthier meals.

In addition to the earlier comments made about stress, children can be assisted by relaxation before writing tests or examinations, before public speaking or talking with parents, and when coping with the stress of doctor and dentist appointments. Relaxation also helps with coping in a dysfunctional family, when dealing with the effects of trauma, poverty, separation and divorce, or while dealing with situations of adjustment and change to the environment. Relaxation can be used to enhance creativity by slowing the child down before the creative experience.

There are a number of relaxation techniques and exercises in this book and in the activity section at the end of this chapter that can be incorporated into daily routines, school curriculums, and leisure activities that can make life more meaningful, less stressful, and more pleasurable.

Personal Reflection – Relaxing Routines

Make a list of your daily activities and routines from the time you wake up until the time you sleep at night.

_____

_____

_____

_____

_____

_____

_____

_____

_____

_____

Place a check mark or star beside the routines or activities that you find relaxing.

Approximate the length of time for each relaxing activity and routine. Calculate how much you relax in your waking hours.

_____

_____

_____

_____

_____

Ask yourself this question; "Do I wake up in the mornings feeling rested?" Go back to your list and place an arrow or an X beside daily activities that need to become less stressful. Brainstorm and strategize how you could incorporate simple relaxation exercises or techniques to release the stress.

_____

_____

_____

_____

_____

_____

Incorporate your new ideas into your daily life and periodically evaluate by repeating this exercise.

> Imagery is not past but present.
>
> — GEORGE MEAD

Imagery

The ability to relax enhances the next state of mind discussed in this chapter, imagery. Imagery is an internal process that requires the individual to see with the mind's eye, hear with the inner ear, and feel the inner Self. It involves manipulation of the senses by conjuring images, sounds, emotions, and sensations. The child creates an internal reality. Imagery can be as simple as remembering and picturing in the mind a familiar face, or hearing a familiar voice, or feeling a familiar feeling, and it can be as complex as seeing, hearing, and feeling an entire episode or series of episodes in the child's life. Children can be taught to image themselves being successful, confident, and clear-thinking. Imagery can assist in creating a state of internal relaxation and concentration. Although imagery can be used when the body is active, to begin, children should learn to relax their bodies and minds when they are sitting, lying, or standing passively. Imagery is a part of all guided fantasy exercises and can be used individually to help the child focus on one particular task. This focussing of attention can help the child to learn more about the task or situation.

A relaxation exercise can assist children to make more compelling images and usually precedes formal sessions on imagery. There are exercises and techniques throughout this book that require imagery, and there are more specific exercises for children in the activity section found at the end of this chapter. Imagery, like relaxation, can be used in conjunction with other activities in order to make them more meaningful, effective, and less stressful.

Personal Reflection – Problem Focus

Recall a difficult situation from the past that is likely to occur again for you in the future, for example, confronting a co-worker, having a job interview, or dealing with a difficult adolescent. Briefly describe the situation.

_____

_____

_____

_____

Find a comfortable spot and relax yourself fully. Recall the incident from the past and become aware of all that was visible at that time.

Now remember what was said, any background noise, or anything you were saying to yourself.

Now recapture your emotional and tactile awareness at the time.

Once you have a real and rich representation of that time, imagine yourself as an independent observer and recall the situation from start to finish. Write down or articulate to a friend what you observed that was interesting or new.

_____

_____

_____

_____

Relax yourself again, and imagine that you have all the internal abilities to be successful in a similar situation in the future. Create such a situation in your mind's eye using imagery, and see yourself being successful. Arrange the situation so that your objectives are met fully to your satisfaction. Draw a quick sketch of you being successful.

Repeat this process several times until you have a successful vision of the future.

Guided Fantasy

Guided Fantasy is a structured form of imagery where children are told a story or given a series of directions that allows them to fantasize or recreate internally what is being said.

In a guided fantasy, the child is asked to experience and benefit from the story or directions in a way that best suits that individual. This type of approach leaves the child open to all the possible variables of benefitting from the experience. Guided fantasy is usually preceded by a relaxation exercise. Here is an example of an introduction to a guided fantasy.

"Now that you are here and relaxed in a positive way, I want to tell you a story. You can become characters in the story if you wish; or, you can pretend to be objects in the story; or, you can listen and learn; or, you can drift off to your own story world, enjoying and learning all the time what is important for you as a happy, healthy, and lovable child. You may choose to make pictures and sounds, and smells and tastes, and feelings out of the words you hear to make the story real. Or, you may choose not to choose. Breathe deeply and feel comfortable while listening to my voice."

In the example above, the dialogue gives the child a series of suggestions as choices of ways of responding. All of these choices are presented as ways in which the child can benefit from the story. The element of choice is very important in guided fantasy, because it allows the child to easily respond to what is being asked. The statement, "You may choose not to choose" covers the child who is experiencing difficulty relating to any of the choices given. The introduction to the guided fantasy should further relax the child and prepare him/her to gain the most from the experience. The idea of benefitting from the story or fantasy is suggested so that the child might attend to any morals, examples, ideals, or directions presented in the story.

Guided fantasies can also be stories that the facilitator or programmer has written especially for a specific child or group of children. The facilitator must always be aware of the power of guided fantasy and take precautions when dealing with material that might re-awaken traumatic or otherwise negative experiences from the child's past. One way to guard against the possibility of children reacting negatively to an otherwise harmless story line or element is to prepare them for possible adverse reactions to the fantasy and to provide the option that they may open their eyes and sit quietly if necessary. This element of choice should be made clear in the introduction to the guided fantasy. The subject of using story and metaphor as a teaching or healing technique is discussed further in Chapter 14, "Therapeutic Storytelling."

CENTRING: Centring, a form of guided fantasy, is a technique that helps the child to feel balanced, confident, and in charge. It focusses the child's energy on a given task or subject so that he/she may deal with it in the best way that they know how. A centring exercise is preceded by a relaxation exercise and by an introduction. The introduction to a centring exercise is similar to that used in a guided fantasy in that a series of choices are presented to the child. The choices relate to finding and/or creating a state of inner balance, strength, and calm.

The state of being centred is one of strength, calmness, concentration, and relaxation. "There is a feeling of balance, a feeling of inner strength that we feel when we are centered" (Hendricks & Wills, 1975, p. xi). In The Centering Book (1975) and The Second Centering Book (1977), Gay Hendricks et al. presents centring as a way for children to achieve "a solid integration of mind and body" (Hendricks & Wills, 1975, p. xi). This state of being is more than feeling calm and relaxed; it is more one of a concentration of energy and a combining of inner resources. This type of focus of energy can be used to help the child achieve a desired goal.

A child can experience various states of this centred feeling. A physical centre, where the child feels grounded or anchored to his/her environment, is sometimes referred to as grounding. Many grounding techniques use imagery and visualization in order to assist the child to reach this state of physiological well being. The child in this state is asked to experience a somewhat heightened state of physical awareness while imagining absorption of strength and energy from the environment. This technique strengthens the child's sense of physical awareness. Through its repeated use, a child can begin to feel more comfortable and confident with his/her physical Self.

Cognitive or intellectual centring focusses a relaxed mind and body on specific subject material or concepts. It can be a form of brainstorming, asking children to free-flow think in respect to a specific theme. It can be used as a way of desensitizing them to feelings or emotional blocks that hamper learning. It has obvious benefits in the classroom, which makes it popular with educators. Its potential outside the classroom is far-reaching when it is applied to socialization, the arts, mental health, self-concept, and countless other areas.

Emotional centring allows children to experience a balance in their emotional life. Its techniques of integrating mind and body allow children to make better choices in their emotional responses. When used extensively, it presents the child with a wide range of emotional experiences and the ability to deal effectively with emotion. Some children become so skilled in this technique that they can centre themselves at will.

Centring can also take on a spiritual or meditative aspect. The child can be asked to centre him/herself on God, the Universe, Nature, Beauty, the Meaning of Life, Death, Light, and so on. The nature of this type of activity allows children to experience their own individual awareness of certain ideals, and in time, they are able to express these awarenesses in order to apply them to their own thoughts and behaviours. See the imagery exercises at the end of this chapter for examples of the various types of centring techniques.

Conducting Relaxation, Imagery, and Guided Fantasy Exercises

When beginning a relaxation, imagery, or guided fantasy exercise, try to use your voice to match the child's state of awareness. If they are loud and excited, begin with a loud and excited voice. If they are quiet and slow moving, adjust your voice and timing to suit them. Once you have matched their state sufficiently, you can lead them to the state that you feel is most beneficial for the particular exercise.

When using relaxation, imagery, and guided fantasy, try to make your instructions fit the child's immediate experience. If the children are lying down, have the character or characters at some point in the story lying down or integrate it into the directions. If they are fidgeting or moving their feet, have the character do the same. If it is warm or the sun is shining down on them, have this fit into the storyline as well. This technique is more useful at the beginning to assist those children who are having difficulty with relaxing or participating.

Another useful technique is to include statements that further replicate the child's reality, for example, "As she takes in each breath her arms slowly unfold." or "The sun was shining, and she crossed and uncrossed her legs," or "Lying on the ground, he felt the sun shine on his face." You can also make statements that verify the child's external and internal realities; examples of this are: "As she crossed and uncrossed her legs, she wondered what would come next"; "The sun is shining and her brain was active"; or "Lying down, she began to slowly, very slowly, think peaceful thoughts." This technique allows children to make easy, small steps towards relaxing, imagining, and fantasizing in a way that fits in with their present state of awareness. Eventually, the facilitator includes less of the external experience and more of the internal experience until the group or individual is fully relaxed or in sync with the fantasy.

Voice tone can be varied to suit the child's present state and then slowly altered to a slow, rhythmic pace with increasingly longer pauses. The breaking up of sentences with pauses also allows the child to slow down or to catch up. A good technique is to match the tempo with the child's breathing rate and to slowly change tempo in order to match a relaxed breathing rate. Key words and phrases can be marked out by changing the voice tone, by pausing before or after the word or phrase, by clearing the throat, by tapping lightly on the desk, or by any other action that is somewhat out of context with the present state of awareness. For more information on the effective use of voice tone, body posture, and timing see Chapter 14, "Therapeutic Storytelling."

Through careful observation, limited expectations, and a slow pace, the therapeutic activity facilitator can assist the most impulsive, overactive child to learn to slow down, think and relax.

Relaxation, Imagery, and Guided Fantasy with the Atypical Child

THE OVERLY ACTIVE CHILD: Children experiencing attention problems must initially have limited goals but with the long-term expectation that they will be able to slow themselves down as effectively as their peers. Since these individuals tend to be very active, the facilitator should meet them at this state. Providing exercises that incorporate music and movement allow the child to move but give the facilitator some control over this movement. Chapter 15, "Art, Drama, Movement, and Music Therapy" will be of assistance in generating ideas for using music to help the child relax.

The tempo of the music and the texture of the music can be slowed down or softened, slowing down the overactive child. Eventually, the child can be asked to sit and to move only his/her hands to the music and then to lie down moving either hands or legs to music. Movement is slowly decreased to the point where the child is lying or sitting and merely imagining that he/she is moving to the music. Slow steps with as many aids as possible allow children to gain more self-control over their movements.

Children with attention and activity-level difficulties may require physical aids and cues to assist them to relax. A back rub slowly reduced to a hand on their shoulder, reduced to periodic touching, can greatly assist these children. Often the child can identify what other aids may be needed in order to slow down and to concentrate. A stuffed animal, a blanket, a picture, a mandala, or a favourite object can often assist in helping them to relax. Breathing and active relaxation exercises included at the end of this chapter, as well as the centring and grounding activities, are particularly useful for children with these types of problems. Note that these children often have a weak sense of self-worth, therefore patience and limited expectations will allow them to make progress. Also, any activity that increases their sense of Self will assist in this and other areas of their lives.

THE IMPULSIVE CHILD: Children with poor impulse control can be assisted in much the same way as the overactive child; however, these children can often relax and use imagery much more effectively. Imagery and guided fantasy exercises that emphasize thinking before acting, talking to oneself about possible solutions or reactions, checking with your feelings before acting, slowing down and holding on to emotions, can be most useful. The "Imaginary Doctor" exercise, included in the interventions at the end of this chapter, can be used to encourage the child to contact their inner wisdom to give them clues to controlling impulsive behaviour. "Heroes," included in this chapter, can be used to help the child gain control by internalizing the strengths of others. "Magic Buttons," also included in this chapter, can assist this type of child in gaining more impulse control. Grounding, centring, and relaxation exercises also add to this child's ability to be less impulsive.

THE LETHARGIC AND POORLY MOTIVATED CHILD: Imagery, affirmations, and external centring help these children to access their creativity in order to better motivate and activate themselves. Children with these types of difficulties often experience negative self-talk, that negative internal voice that tells them that they are bad, lazy, or stupid. This experience often causes them to get stuck in unpleasant emotions or in a mild depression, and thus they become lethargic or poorly motivat-

> A mind never thinks without a mental picture.
>
> – ARISTOTLE

ed. The negative self-talk causes the child to feel upset, which promotes more negative self-talk. These two strategies feed on one another causing chronic problems. Visual and auditory activities can take these children out of this self-destructive thought process.

Mobilization too helps to promote motivation; such things as creative movement, art, and large-muscle activities help to get children motivated. These children are often skilled at visual imagery; however, many times these images are non-supportive, so it becomes a task of changing those negative images to positive ones. "Magic Buttons," "Grounding," and "Heroes" included in the activity section are useful exercises for working with children who are passive. Art and musically oriented activities can assist in energizing and motivating them. Many of these children can learn to meditate and increase their energy levels through centring exercises.

THE FEARFUL CHILD: The most important factor in working with children who are fearful is to understand clearly what fears are normal for their age or developmental stage. Children from toddlers to middle childhood often experience fearful stages as part of normal development. Fear is not to be seen as an aspect to eliminate from the child's life. It is often very wise to be fearful. A supportive and flexible environment helps considerably to allow children to express and to explore their fears.

Art and drama are excellent mediums to use in the expression and exploration of fears. Relaxation and centring allow the child to gain some control over intense fear responses. Grounding exercises help the fearful child to feel more connected to, and supported by, his/her environment. The "Heroes" exercise in this chapter can help the child to gain strength internally, which assists in stabilization. "The Dream Arm" exercise, included in Chapter 7 ("Bridges and Anchor Points"), can be an excellent technique for the facilitator to add affirming messages to the child's internal processes. The "Imaginary Doctor" exercise, found at the end of this chapter, can stimulate the child to search for alternate strategies for expressing their fears. Positive imagery and the exercise, "Magic Buttons," give the child added support in adjusting to fearful situations. Also, consult Chapter 12, "Dealing with Feelings," for useful strategies for expressing fear. There are a wide variety of ways to allow children to understand, to appreciate, and to live more comfortably with their fears.

THE AGGRESSIVE CHILD: Aggressive children, much like overactive children, will need to start with a higher level of activity in their relaxation exercises in order to provide them with the several small steps that prepare them for grounding, centring, and guided fantasy exercises. Grounding and centring give the aggressive child a sense of self-control. Art, drama, and creative movement allow for creative outlets of emotion. The aggressive or angry child is often reacting to fear, sorrow, or abandonment, which is expressed through anger. The "Magic Buttons" exercise, included in the activity section, provides children with alternatives that counter emotions rather than masking them with anger and violence. The "Imaginary Doctor" as well as the "Heroes" exercise from this chapter can provide an added sense of personal strength and healthy role models to help them deal with their emotions. Also, consult Chapter 12, "Dealing with Feelings," for productive ways of expressing anger. Aggression and violence are very complex issues and a multi-dimensional approach to the problem is often most effective.

Exercise 13:1

Select one of the above categories of atypical children (you may select the age) and, using the exercises in the intervention section, plan and develop a series of four sessions for a group of 8 participants—each session 60 minutes in length (see Chapter 3, "Designing Therapeutic Programs," for assistance in program development). Provide a brief outline of each group session below listing topics of discussion and activities.

Session One

_____
_____
_____
_____
_____
_____

Session Two

_____
_____
_____
_____
_____
_____

Session Three

_____
_____
_____
_____
_____
_____

Session Four

_____
_____
_____
_____
_____
_____

Review

- Relaxation, imagery, and guided fantasy can assist a child to regulate feelings, thoughts, and behaviours.

- Relaxation slows down physical, emotional, and intellectual activity.

- Children may have difficulty initially relaxing and may require some assistance.

- Imagery and guided fantasy can assist children in dealing with past, present, and future stressors.

- Relaxation, imagery, and guided fantasy exercises can be enhanced by the use of the voice and the environment.

The upcoming Chapter 14, "Therapeutic Storytelling," incorporates the skills developed in this chapter and utilizes their therapeutic advantages in the use of storytelling as a therapeutic intervention.

The following are a series of therapeutic interventions intended to act as resources for the student or novice practitioner who wishes to practice his/her skills in the use of relaxation, imagery, and guided fantasy.

> "At the center of your being you have the answer; you know who you are and you know what you want.
>
> – LAO TZU

Therapeutic Interventions

Breathing Exercises

Please note, each "[pause]" is approximately three seconds.

ZEN BREATH COUNTING

This is an easy breathing exercise to use with children, and one you can return to time and time again.

"Find yourself a safe and comfortable position. This exercise is usually done from a sitting position, but you may lie down if you wish [pause, pause, pause]. Slowly close your eyes and take a few deep breaths [pause, pause, pause]. Now allow your breathing to return to normal [pause, pause]."

"Now I want you to breathe deeply and count your breaths, both inhalation and exhalation. When you breathe in, you count silently to yourself, "1," and when you breathe out, you say silently to yourself "2." Practice this technique up to the count of 5 [pause, pause, pause]."

TAI CHI BREATH

"This exercise requires you to fill your lungs by making 3 separate inhalations through the nose without exhaling. On the first inhale, lift your arms from your sides, straight out in front at shoulder height. On the second, open your arms out straight to the sides, keeping them at shoulder height. And on the third, lift your arms straight over your head."

"Now exhale through your mouth while slowly lowering your arms down to your sides again. Repeat this process for 5 breaths initially, and slowly increase to a maximum of 10 breaths."

RAPID BREATH

"Inhale and exhale rapidly through your nose, keeping your mouth closed but relaxed. Your breaths in and out should be equal in duration, but as short as possible. This is a noisy breathing exercise. Try for three in-and-out breath cycles per second. This produces a quick movement of the diaphragm, suggesting a bellows. Breathe normally after each cycle."

"Do not do this for more than 15 seconds on your first try. Each time you practice the Rapid Breath, you can increase your time by 5 seconds or so, until you reach a full minute."

WHOOSH

"Exhale all the air from your lungs through your mouth, making a whoosh sound. Close your mouth and inhale quietly through your nose to a mental count of 4.

Hold your breath for a count of 7.

"Exhale completely through your mouth, making a whoosh sound again, and exhale to the count of 8."

Repeat this exercise 3 – 4 times.

DEEP BREATHING

"I want you to pay attention to your breathing [pause]. Your lungs are shaped like a pear [pause], wide at the bottom and narrow at the top [pause]. Imagine breathing in through the nose and sending the air right down to the bottom of your lungs [pause], right down to the biggest part of them [pause]. And then, exhale through your mouth [pause]. You can fill your lungs up the same way you would pour water into a glass. Breathe in through your nose, filling your lungs from the bottom right up to the top [pause]. Now release your breath through your mouth, and allow the air at the top of your lungs to escape first [pause], and empty your lungs of air right from the top to the bottom."

Repeat this several times until the group is able to easily accomplish this exercise in breathing.

Variation: Using the same script as above add this dialogue: "As you breathe in, count to 4 out loud while inhaling, 1, 2, 3, 4; now let the air out to the count of 5 - 1, 2, 3, 4, 5. Now breathe in to the count of 5, and exhale to the count of 6 [pause, pause]. Now breathe in to the count of 6, and exhale to the count of 7 [pause, pause]. Breathe in to the count of 7, and exhale to the count of 8."

Relaxation Exercises

Please note each "[pause]" is approximately three seconds.

MOVING RELAXED

This is a good beginning for developing relaxation skills, especially if the participants are coming from a very active situation or have trouble relaxing.

"Walk around the room as quickly as possible, and be careful not to run into one another [pause, pause, pause]. Now run [pause], or speed walk [pause, pause, pause]. Now slow your pace down a bit [pause, pause, pause], now slower [pause], and slower [pause], slower still [pause]. Now walk in slow motion [pause, pause, pause]. Slow right down to a stop [pause]. Take a deep breath, and let your breath go right down to your toes, and let your body relax."

Repeat or reverse, walking in slow motion to running.

FAST-SLOW TECHNIQUE

This is an excellent exercise to help those more resistant participants or those that have difficulty slowing themselves down. These can be used as bridges to the other relaxation exercises.

"I want you to wave your arms back and forth really fast [pause], faster [pause], faster [pause]. Now slow them down [pause], slower [pause], and slower [pause, pause]. Now move them as slowly as you possibly can [pause], like they are in slow motion [pause]. Take a deep breath, and send it right down to the bottom of your lungs [pause]. Let your body completely relax [pause, pause, pause]."

Repeat or reverse, waving arms from slow motion to really fast.

RELAXATION CLOUD

These are two brief relaxing exercises, Relaxation Cloud to use with children, and Tropical Island with teens. These exercises are intended to act as bridges to the longer and more detailed relaxation exercises that follow. They are also very useful for those participants that are accomplished at relaxation and only need a short time to fully relax.

"I want you to imagine that you are sitting on a cloud [pause, pause], a soft, fluffy cloud, and you are safe and sound [pause, pause]. The cloud is slowly drifting across the sky, and as it moves, you become more and more relaxed [pause, pause, pause]"

Variation: Tropical Island

"Imagine yourself on a warm, comforting beach [pause, pause]. You can hear the waves softly rolling in and out [pause, pause, pause]. All your needs have been taken care of [pause, pause, pause]. Absolutely no worries [pause, pause, pause, pause]."

RELAXATION ONE

This is a good exercise to begin formal relaxation techniques. It can also be incorporated into guided fantasy, yoga, grounding, and centring exercises. It is also useful as a cool-down for gym programs.

Ask the group members to find a safe and comfortable place in the play area and sit or lie down. Explain to the group the importance of quiet in this exercise. Proceed using the following dialogue:

"Close your eyes and get ready for a journey through your body [pause]. We will begin at your feet. Tighten all the muscles in your feet [pause]. Now, relax them [pause]. Tighten all the muscles in your legs [pause]. Now, relax them [pause]. Tighten all the muscles in your mid-section, beginning with your buttocks and moving right up your back [pause]; now relax them [pause]. Moving your concentration up your body to your stomach, tighten it [pause], and now relax, your chest [pause], and now relax [pause]. Take a deep breath and let it out [pause, pause].

"Now, tighten all the muscles in your arms, your shoulders, and your neck [pause]. Relax [pause]. Now your face; tighten all the muscles in your face [pause], and relax [pause, pause]. Now let your mind drift back to one good thing that has happened in the past hour (or whatever the length of group time) [pause, pause]. Now slowly begin to wake up your bodies [pause]. Take all the time you need; there is no rush [pause]. When you feel ready, open your eyes and focus your attention on me."

RELAXATION TWO

This relaxation exercise is more detailed than the others and is useful for groups or individuals who are accomplished at relaxation.

"Find yourself a comfortable position either sitting or lying down [pause], whichever you feel will allow you to relax most easily. While you are relaxing, allow your eyes to slowly close [pause], as the muscles in your body begin to relax. I want you to send a message [pause] from your brain [pause] to the muscles in your feet [pause], asking them to slowly relax. The tendons, veins, arteries, and muscles [pause], will them to relax [pause, pause].

"Now, as the muscles in your feet begin to relax [pause], I want you to slowly move your attention to the muscles in your legs. Your calf muscles, shin muscles, and the biggest muscle in your body [pause], your thigh muscle [pause]; send them all relaxing messages [pause]. If you are finding it difficult to relax your leg muscles [pause], you can tighten them up first really tight, and then let them go [pause].

"As you are relaxing [pause] all the muscles in your feet and legs [pause], I want you to pay attention to your breathing [pause]. Your lungs are shaped like a pear [pause], wide at the bottom and narrow at the top [pause]. Imagine breathing right down to the bottom of your lungs [pause], right down to the biggest part of them [pause]. You can fill your lungs up the same way you would pour water into a glass [pause], filling your lungs from the bottom [pause], right up to the top [pause]. Continue to breathe using this method, and at the same time, focus your attention on relaxing the rest of your body [pause].

"Now focus your attention on your torso [pause], the middle section of your body [pause]. Relax the muscles in your buttocks, groin, and lower back area; [pause] send a soothing message to this part of your body [pause], willing it to relax [pause]. As you are breathing slowly and evenly [pause], and your muscles are relaxing [pause], I want you to imagine your internal organs [pause], your heart, lungs, liver, stomach, and all the organs in your body [pause, pause]. Ask them [pause] to relax [pause, pause]. The muscles in your lower back, your abdomen, your chest and your shoulders [pause]—send them a message to let go [pause] of the tension [pause, pause].

"Your breathing is relaxed [pause], your body is relaxed [pause], and your mind is beginning to relax [pause, pause]. Focus [pause] your attention [pause] on the muscles in your shoulders, arms, and hands [pause], your biceps, triceps, and the muscles in your forearms [pause]. Let all the tension out of your body [pause], and clear your mind [pause]. Now focus your attention on the muscles in your neck [pause], your jaw [pause], and your face [pause, pause]. Allow your jaw to drop [pause], and your neck muscles to relax [pause]. Your brain can relax too [pause, pause]. From the tips of your toes to the top of your scalp [pause, pause], will your body to relax [pause five seconds].

"As your body is relaxing [pause], allow your mind to drift [pause, pause]. Let your thoughts travel; [pause] try not to hold on to them; [pause] just let them drift [pause, pause]. In a minute I am going to ask you [pause] to focus your attention [pause], but for now [pause], just let your mind [pause] drift [pause for 30 – 60 seconds]."

Imagery Exercises

Please note, each "[pause]" is approximately three seconds.

EXTERNAL CENTRING

This exercise is sometimes useful for the distractible child who is having difficulties with the relaxation or centring process. It can also work well with the child who has a short attention span.

"Walk around the play area and explore the room using all of your five senses [pause, pause, pause]. Use your eyes to notice the entire area and also the small details [pause, pause, pause]. Remember this is a quiet exercise. There is to be no talking [pause, pause, pause]. Notice the people, the colours, and the movement happening around you [pause, pause, pause].

"Now focus on your hearing; use your ears to record all the sounds within the area [pause, pause, pause]. Listen to even the smallest and to the weakest sound [pause, pause, pause]. Listen to any changes in the sounds [pause, pause, pause].

"Now feel your feet as they touch the ground [pause, pause], feel the temperature of your skin [pause, pause], feel the textures and the shapes of the objects in the room [pause, pause, pause]. Feel the muscles in your body as you move about [pause, pause, pause].

"Breathe in and smell all of the different smells around you [pause, pause, pause], the faint ones and the stronger ones [pause, pause, pause]. Note the different tastes in your mouth [pause, pause]. Your mouth can be dry and still there can be a taste [pause, pause, pause].

"Spend a few more minutes exploring the world around you and when I signal to you, come back and form a circle."

SENSORY CENTRING

This exercise allows the child to centre or focus on different sensory experiences. It is useful to help distractible and impulsive children centre in on things in a light and non-threatening manner. Begin with a relaxation exercise that suits your group's level of attention.

"Now that you are feeling relaxed, I would like you to imagine that you can see with your mind's eye, some of the people and things that make you feel happy [pause, pause]. Focus your mind as clearly as you can, and you may see pictures in colour, or black and white, and for others, the pictures will be a little unclear [pause, pause, pause].

"Now think of a funny face, one you have never seen before [pause, pause, pause]. Listen to the laughter inside of you [pause, pause]. Do not be surprised if you hear bells or singers [pause, pause, pause].

"Can you make up a special sound that only you can hear inside of your head [pause, pause, pause]? Breathe in deeply and imagine that you can feel any emotion that you want to [pause, pause, pause].

"Remember a time when someone touched you in a special way and it felt good [pause, pause, pause].

"Imagine what a moon rock feels like [pause, pause, pause].

"Think about the last time you tasted a delicious treat [pause, pause, pause]. Allow yourself to remember and almost taste that treat again [pause, pause, pause].

"Breathe in through your nostrils, and be aware of any smells that you can imagine [pause, pause, pause]. Remember pleasant smells that bring back pleasant memories [pause, pause, pause].

"Take a deep breath and listen for more pictures, sounds, smells, tastes, or sensations [pause, pause, pause]. Take a few more moments to remember anything else you would like [pause, pause, pause], and then slowly come back to this place [pause, pause, pause].

"Raise your hands when you can see my face."

GROUNDING EXERCISE

This is also an excellent exercise for distractible, impulsive children. It allows them to feel, however fleeting, their first experiences of being grounded and firmly rooted. This exercise needs to be repeated several times in order for some children to get the full benefit of it. The paragraphs are written so that the facilitator can use any one, or a combination, of them to create shorter exercises.

"I want you to find a safe comfortable spot in the room and stand still in that place [pause, pause, pause]. In order to feel more solid and connected with the universe, your concentration is needed. For a short time, I would like you to imagine yourself as a tree, a flower, a shrub, or any living plant that gives you a good feeling [pause]. Decide which type of plant you wish to be [pause, pause, pause].

"I want you to experience for a moment the feeling of what it's like to enjoy life as a living plant [pause, pause]. Concentration can be done with either the eyes opened or closed [pause, pause]. As you stand there feeling your body responding, imagine the different parts of the plant [pause, pause, pause]. Your feet, now planted firmly on the ground, may start to send roots deep down into the earth [pause, pause]. Imagine that you can feel these roots attaching your body solidly to the floor [pause, pause, pause]. A plant has an entire network of roots and rootlets that nourish the plant. Imagine how firmly the deep roots create a sound grip on the earth [pause], such a firm hold that even the strongest wind or the hardest rain cannot shake them loose [pause, pause, pause].

"Imagine the plant can feel the energy flow from the earth and travel up the root ends into the plant [pause, pause, pause]. Listen for any messages being sent up from the earth, and notice how firmly planted this plant is [pause, pause]. If it feels comfortable, reach your arms up as the branches [pause], leaves [pause], stems, and buds of a plant. Feel the energy from the sun and the air [pause, pause, pause]. Your arms in the air can receive energy from the atmosphere and send it flowing down the plant to the ends of the roots, allowing the plant to feel as if it were one unit [pause], one solid flexible unit [pause, pause, pause].

"You can remember, whenever you choose, to feel grounded and one with the earth. Stand as you are standing now, and remember this feeling all over again [pause, pause, pause].

"When it feels right, I want you to slowly return your attention to this place where I am [pause, pause, pause]."

PHYSICAL CENTRE

This is a good exercise for children to explore their physical Self. It can be most useful, when repeated daily or at regular intervals, to allow the children to centre themselves. Begin with one of the relaxation exercises.

"Now that you are relaxed, I want you to attend to your breathing [pause]. Breathe deeply into your lungs, and allow your body to be energized [pause, pause]. By breathing slowly, you can fill your lungs up with air, and then let all of the air out [pause].

"There is a spot just below your navel that is the centre of your body. Imagine now as you breathe deeply that you are sending energy to this spot [pause, pause, pause]. Breathe into your centre and feel the energy rise [pause, pause, pause]. Once you have located the centre and are able to send the energy from areas of the body to the centre, you may relax and enjoy that feeling [pause, pause, pause].

"Draw your attention to the inside or interior regions of your body [pause], and feel the different organs and parts of the body [pause, pause, pause]. You can choose to feel relaxed and centred whenever you desire [pause]; all you need to do is to remember the feelings and visions and voices from today and find yourself feeling much the same as you are now [pause, pause, pause].

"Taking enough time to understand what is necessary for you to be fully relaxed and energized [pause, pause, pause], I want the group to slowly bring your attention [pause] back to the room [pause], and when you are back, open your eyes."

CLEANSING

This imagery exercise can be used for any of the internal organs or as a guided fantasy for the whole body. It relaxes and eases stress in specific areas and sets up a series of physiological reactions. Begin with one of the relaxation exercises, and conduct it with the group seated.

"Sitting there, feeling comfortable and relaxed, I want you to prepare yourself to travel inside your body [pause, pause], inside to the area we call your [insert the name of the organ or area of the body you wish the group to explore for example, lungs, mind, heart, muscles, etc.].

"Travel to that place right now [pause, pause]. Imagine that part of you being cleaned by imaginary cleaners [pause, pause, pause]. Allow yourself to feel soothed and comforted [pause, pause], relaxed [pause, pause, pause]. Send a message to your imaginary workers to clean and repair that part of you so it's working perfectly [pause, pause, pause]. See that part of you, and thank it for being such a good part [pause], such a useful part [pause], such an important part [pause, pause]. Imagine it being slowly and lovingly cleaned and repaired [pause, pause], soothed, and relaxed [pause, pause, pause].

"When the time feels right, slowly return your attention back to this room."

Variations: The children can be asked to imagine themselves as tiny enough to travel inside their bodies as characters such as tiny men, women, or imaginary characters that can be called on to do the cleaning. For more in-depth imagery, the facilitator can seek medical assistance and advice as to how to best word this fantasy to fit each particular child, especially those with medical problems.

Guided Fantasies

Please note, each "[pause]" is approximately three seconds.

MY SPECIAL PLACE

Ask the group to find a safe and comfortable place and lie or sit in a comfortable position. Conduct a relaxation exercise and follow the script below.

"As you find yourself slowing down [pause], slowing down your thoughts, you can begin to prepare yourself to travel in your mind to a special place [pause, pause]. It can be an imaginary place or a real place, but it is a place that makes you feel good, safe, and confident [pause, pause]. Look around, with your mind's eye, and explore your surroundings [pause]. Are there colours, or is it black and white [pause, pause]? Notice what is moving and what is staying still [pause, pause]. Explore your special place by looking all around you [pause, pause, pause].

"Listen. What sounds do you hear in your special place [pause, pause]? Are there voices, or is it quiet [pause]? What, if anything, are you saying to yourself [pause, pause, pause]? Take a moment and listen to the sounds in your special place [pause, pause, pause].

"If you have not already done so, step into the picture you have imagined, and become you in your special place [pause, pause]. What does it feel like to be in your special place [pause, pause]? Enjoy all the positive feelings associated with your special place [pause, pause, pause].

"Take a last look around and know that you can return to this place whenever you wish [pause, pause]. All you need to do to visit your special place is to sit down or lie down and remember this exercise [pause, pause, pause].

"Now, slowly, taking all the time you need, return your thoughts to this place in the here and now."

ANIMAL FANTASY

This is a good exercise for exploring self-esteem. There are several ways to approach this exercise. Here is one example.

Ask the group to form a circle, conduct a relaxation exercise, and use the following dialogue.

"Now that you have been able to relax your body, I want you to slow down your thoughts and imagine an animal, any kind of animal you want [pause, pause, pause]. Slowly begin to imagine your animal [pause, pause]. What is it doing [pause, pause]? What does it look like [pause, pause]? Is your animal making any sounds [pause, pause]? Is it saying anything to itself [pause, pause, pause]? Is it speaking to you [pause]? Are there any sounds or noises in the environment [pause, pause, pause]?

"Now I want you to become that animal [pause, pause, pause]. Just imagine yourself stepping into the picture and becoming that animal [pause, pause]. How are you feeling as the animal [pause, pause, pause]?

"Use your imagination to move around and explore your world [pause, pause, pause]. Can you smell anything [pause]? Taste anything [pause]? Enjoy being that animal [pause, pause, pause].

"Is your home nearby [pause]? What is it like [pause]? Move into your home if you have one [pause, pause]."

"In a few seconds, I am going to ask you to come back to this time and place, but for now, explore your world as your favourite animal [pause, pause, pause]. Take a final look around, and then step out of your animal body [pause, pause, pause]. Say good-bye to your favourite animal [pause, pause].

"Now I want you to come slowly back to this place again. Slowly [pause, pause, pause], take all the time you need [pause, pause]; there is no rush [pause]. When you are back, you can open your eyes."

IMAGINARY DOCTOR

This activity is an excellent way of centring children and giving them a vehicle for contacting their inner wisdom. Relax the group with a favourite relaxation exercise.

"Now that you are feeling quiet and relaxed, I want you to go off in your mind, to a spot where you feel safe and comfortable [pause]. Go there now [pause, pause, pause]. Notice any sounds or voices [pause, pause]. Take in all the colours of this place [pause, pause, pause]. Be aware of how you are feeling and how it feels to be here [pause, pause, pause]. Get as clear a picture as you can, and make this comfortable place look, sound, and feel any way you want [pause, pause, pause].

"In a short time, you are going to meet a very special person in your place [pause]. This person will be very wise and will be there especially for you [pause, pause, pause]. We will call this person your imaginary doctor [pause, pause, pause]. Take all the time you need to experience this person [pause, pause, pause]. If the imaginary doctor does not materialize in your mind, just make believe—it's OK to pretend [pause, pause].

"Once you have become aware of this person, ask him/her if there is anything special or important that you must do [pause, pause, pause]. Ask the doctor any questions you want [pause, pause, pause]. Spend as much time as you need to finish with your imaginary doctor [pause, pause, pause]. Take one last look [pause], speak one last word [pause], get one last feeling for what it is like to be in the doctor's presence [pause, pause, pause].

"In a minute I am going to ask you to come back to the room [pause, pause, pause]. Come back slowly, remembering your experience [pause, pause, pause]."

HEROES

This exercise invites the child to model and take on the positive attributes they see in their role models. Children can be encouraged to emulate aspects of these characters and to incorporate their positive characteristics into their own individual personalities and characters. Begin by relaxing the group and repeat the following:

"Now that you are feeling relaxed and comfortable [pause, pause], soothed and quiet [pause], I want you to take some time to think about a hero of yours, a character that you would most want to be like [pause, pause]; it can be any character you wish, imaginary or real [pause, pause]. Take some time, all the time you need, to think of this character [pause, pause, pause, pause].

"If you have not already done so, imagine that you can see that person in your imagination [pause, pause]. How does your hero look [pause, pause]? Make the picture as clear and as colourful as you wish [pause, pause]. Are there any sounds in this picture [pause, pause]? Are you saying anything to your hero [pause, pause]? How do you imagine your hero is feeling [pause, pause]? What is it you most like about this character [pause, pause, pause]?

"Imagine that your hero can give those talents, abilities, or traits to you [pause, pause]. Now imagine that you are your hero [pause, pause]. Step into the imaginary picture you created, and become that person [pause, pause]. Imagine you are taking on the strengths and positive abilities of your hero [pause, pause, pause]. Feel yourself becoming like that person [pause, pause].

"Now go back to being yourself, except take with you those parts or abilities you wish to keep [pause, pause]. Take some time to feel yourself taking on these qualities [pause, pause], changing slowly [pause], not all at once [pause], but little by little [pause], day by day, develop your abilities to match your character [pause, pause].

"Now picture your hero again [pause, pause]. Thank that person for helping you [pause, pause]. Ask if you can visit with him or her again in your imagination [pause]. Take the last few moments to be with your hero [pause, pause]. Now slowly return your thoughts to this room."

MAGIC BUTTONS

This is a more advanced exercise and is more beneficial after children have mastered relaxation. This is a deep relaxation exercise and should be preceded by Relaxation One or Relaxation Two. This exercise focusses on only one attribute, confidence; however, any feeling, talent, or attribute can be inserted to replace the word CONFIDENCE/CONFIDENT.

"Now that your body is feeling nice and relaxed, let your mind drift off to a very peaceful and contented time for you [pause, pause]. Notice your surroundings, and arrange them in any way that you wish until you begin to feel the small muscles in your face and your jaw let go and relax [pause, pause, pause, pause].

"Now that your muscles are relaxing, I would like you to think of someone who you feel has a lot of CONFIDENCE [pause, pause]. Picture how this person looks and sounds [pause, pause]. Make that picture with those sounds, and add the feelings as clear as it needs to be for you to appreciate this person [pause, pause]. Imagine you are that person and can feel his or her CONFIDENCE [pause, pause, pause, pause].

"When you can feel the CONFIDENCE begin to grow inside of you, press your finger firmly on one of your knuckles [pause, pause]. As this feeling of CONFIDENCE grows in you, press your knuckle harder [pause], and harder, as the CONFIDENCE builds [pause, pause]. This knuckle will now be your CONFIDENCE button. Each time throughout this exercise when you feel CONFIDENT, press your CONFIDENCE button in order to make it stronger.

"Take another look at this person, and notice any detail that you may have missed [pause, pause]. Listen closely to the sound of your person's voice, and be aware of its CONFIDENCE [pause, pause]. Be aware of how it might feel to possess this degree of CONFIDENCE [pause, pause]. Let that feeling build [pause, pause].

"Remember that in the future when you want to feel CONFIDENT, just remember that person and press on your knuckle really hard."

> "Tension is who you think you should be. Relaxation is who you are.
>
> – CHINESE PROVERB

CHAPTER 14

Therapeutic Storytelling

Brownie, my father's working buddy, would always send us home a treat in Dad's lunch box. An apple, a pear, a sandwich, a banana, and even the occasional Molly'O bar were handed out to us as "treats from Brownie." Dad usually had a story for us about Brownie, his life, his family, the happy times, and the unhappy times in his life. Dad's Brownie stories would make us laugh, about the funny situations Brownie found himself in, or when Brownie told a good joke that day. We felt sad too when Brownie's brother had to have an operation and when Brownie did not have enough money to fix his car. We cried when Brownie's dog Max died. We all loved Brownie very much and looked forward to Dad's stories each night.

We never did meet Brownie in person, only heard about his life through Dad's stories. I guess we all assumed that when we got older we would meet him. The stories lessened over the years as we grew up to be teenagers and perhaps were not home when dad arrived home from work or were too busy to hear the latest from Brownie.

It was not until shortly after my father's death that I realized that Brownie was actually my father and that his stories were his way to communicate some of his own life experiences, his lessons, his morals, and his ideas to us. We did hear many stories from Dad about his life growing up and his adventures as a child and teenager, but he communicated some of his messages, probably the ones he did not want us to be concerned about, through Brownie. His stories allowed us to deal with events later in our lives that were similar to the trials, tribulations, and celebrations of our old friend Brownie.

> "The purpose of a storyteller is not to tell you how to think, but to give you questions to think upon."
>
> — BRANDON SANDERSON

The birth of the story runs concurrent with the beginning of humankind's ability to communicate with signs and movements. Since that early beginning in human history to the present date, stories have been an integral part of human existence. The faded markings on cave walls are testimony to our need to recreate the past and to tell stories of possible future exploits. Over the centuries, these chronicles have taken on many forms of expression. In the beginning, most of our stories were told to transmit cultural values and beliefs, to give meaning to life's mysteries, or to justify our actions. Other stories were meant purely for entertainment, sometimes giving us a chance to laugh at our follies. And some were meant to instruct and to point the way to a useful and meaningful life, as in the Brownie stories.

This chapter on storytelling presents the therapeutic advantages of the use of stories with children. It discusses ways to select stories that will suit the specific group of children or individual child. The use of voice and body to enhance the impact of the stories' messages is presented as well as a technique to link the audiences' reality with that of the story. Finally it provides ideas, techniques, and templates to facilitators who wish to write their own stories, tailored to the individual group's needs. The chapter concludes with a section on interventions that provides storytelling activities to conduct with the group as well as 10 therapeutic stories to give facilitators material to begin right away to communicate through story.

Knowledge of the variety of types and styles of stories provides storytellers with countless opportunities to communicate, to teach, and to heal the children in their care. Stories can be told to entertain, to build rapport, to create closeness, to change the mood, and to build self-esteem. They can be used to desensitize children to fear and other feelings, and to express, feel and understand their emotions. Stories can also be used to teach, to communicate, to motivate, to redefine problems in a creative way, to provide alternative solutions, and also to stimulate the imagination of children in order for them to make sense and purpose out of their worlds.

Personal Reflection – Stories from the Past

Place yourself in a relaxed posture, and slowly count backwards from 10 to 1; with each number you will find your muscles and skin relaxing deeper and deeper. Begin ...10...9...8...7...; with each breath your body and mind slow down and relax ...6...5...4...3...; eyelids are getting heavy ...2... and 1.... Drift back to a happy time in your childhood and recall the storytellers and the stories that were told to you as you grew to adulthood.

Listen to one or two of those stories now, but hear them with the ears of an adult. What wisdom or lessons do you hear in the story line?

_____

_____

_____

_____

_____

_____

_____

Were there any stories that you wanted to hear over and over again? What was it about those stories that appealed to you?

_____

_____

_____

_____

_____

_____

_____

Who was the best storyteller, and how can you utilize their style or ability to model proficiency in your storytelling?

_____

_____

_____

_____

_____

_____

_____

Uses of Storytelling

ENTERTAINMENT: This is a primary goal for most storytellers. Children love to hear stories and the more that these are dramatized the more they enjoy them. Children are never very far from the world of make-believe, and a skilled storyteller can allow them to explore this realm and be entertained by a story. Facilitators with five or six stories known by memory can entertain a group of children, and these can also be used strategically at times when there is a danger that idle time may not be used constructively.

BUILDING RAPPORT: Storytelling entertains and thus promotes positive feelings between the storyteller and the audience. They share the experience of the story and, in this sharing, rapport is developed and strengthened. Children feel more at ease because of the less threatening aspect of this type of communication. When children are feeling anxious or unsure of the storyteller or the situation that they are in, a well-chosen story can relieve some of the anxiety and can strengthen the relationship between storyteller and audience.

CREATING INTIMACY: The entertaining and rapport-building qualities of storytelling often create an intimacy between the narrator and the audience. The combination of the adventure, the emotion, and the life of the characters creates a bond between the storyteller and audience. This union can develop into a sense of closeness or intimacy, which strengthens the relationships between the storyteller and the children.

CHANGING MOODS: The magic created by the storyteller and the story line has the power to change the gloom of a group of teenagers into laughter or relaxation. It can motivate an apprehensive classroom to try harder, or it can calm down a room full of boisterous 10-year-olds. When the facilitator selects the appropriate story, he/she has the opportunity to creatively change the prevailing mood and to enhance the situation by creating more opportunities for success.

DESENSITIZING: When children are introduced to, or confronted with, their fears, anxieties, and apprehensions by way of identifying with a character or characters in a story, they are able to distance themselves from the stress and look at the problem with more objectivity. Bruno Bettelheim in his book, The Uses of Enchantment, stresses the quality of storytelling that allows the child to experience these uncomfortable emotions in a safe setting, and so become more comfortable with them (Bettelheim, 1976).

EMOTIONAL RELEASE: Stories told that concern death and dying could provide the grieving child with a vehicle with which to express emotions. Scary stories give ventilation to many of a child's unexpressed fears. Stories of pain and destruction often open up these feelings in their listeners, allowing them to identify and release their feelings within the context of the story. Storytellers can utilize the cathartic effect that stories have on their listeners in order to give children an appropriate way to express their emotions.

TEACHING: Stories can be used to explain and to communicate any one or a variety of skills, ideas, concepts, morals, and points specific to learning. They can be used to introduce new material or to review topics already discussed. Stories can provide step-by-step instructions on how to acquire new skills. Child and youth care professionals, in their role as educators, can make use of storytelling to enhance the learning process for the children in their care.

COMMUNICATING INDIRECTLY: Inherent in storytelling is the ability to communicate indirectly to the listener. The fact that the storyteller is, in most cases, telling a story about something that happened to someone or something else, distances the audience enough so that listeners are able to decide, both consciously and unconsciously, how certain aspects of the story relate to their life situation. Therefore, a child can listen to the story and decide that that character is exactly like me, that that part of the character's experience is similar to mine, or that the story is about someone else, and it does not apply to me at all.

This ambiguous aspect of the story allows the storyteller to communicate with the child about a topic or an event that is difficult for the child to talk about in a direct conversation. There are many situations where it is important to discuss topics indirectly in order to not embarrass or cause the child to lose face, or confuse the child. Stories that speak metaphorically to the child are often more successful in inviting change than more direct forms of communication. As a rule, children are far less resistant to the language of metaphor than they are to direct conversation. Stories can be used most effectively in situations where other strategies have proven unsuccessful (Erickson & Rossi, 1979; Rosen, 1982).

REDEFINING PROBLEMS: When children are communicated to by means of a story, they will often project their problems on to the characters in the story. This not only allows them to distance themselves, it redefines the problem for them in the eyes, ears, and emotions of the story's characters. This provides children with the opportunity to see their problems in a new way and to appreciate that others share the same struggles.

PROVIDING ALTERNATIVES/SOLUTIONS: When children are presented with solutions to their problems in a metaphorical fashion, they are free to utilize the strategy that the character in the story used, or the child can adapt a strategy better suited to his/her situation. The solutions will often come through identification with one or more of the characters in the story. The more solutions presented, the more alternatives there are to solving the problem. Depending on the developmental level of the child, he/she can be presented with as many alternate solutions as he/she can appreciate in order to choose the best decision.

STIMULATING UNCONSCIOUS SEARCH: Stories that offer no solutions to the character's problems, for example, an open-ended story that the child participates in by completing, requires the child to search his/her unconscious mind/imagination for a solution. Since the child is searching for solutions for someone else, there may be more creativity in the search. The solutions that are provided for the character(s) can be a clue or a complete strategy that the child may choose to implement in his/her life. This approach to storytelling empowers the child and shows that he/she is often his/her own best resource.

Story Selection

In the beginning, it is always best to familiarize yourself with the tried and true tales and legends that have stood the test of time. Fairy tales by the Brothers Grimm, Hans Christian Andersen, and Scheherazade of the Arabian Nights are centuries old and are still very popular today (Burns, 1999). Many of these stories have been rewritten to appeal to the modern-day audience; however, in their retranslation, much of their impact and diversity is eliminated. Bruno Bettelheim (1976), in The Uses of Enchantment, points this out in relation to the removal of frightening and violent episodes or scenes in the rewriting of the Grimm Brothers' fairy tales. When these scenes are removed, children are denied the opportunity to deal with the content and the lessons provided, or to familiarize themselves with how it feels for others and themselves in these situations. They are also denied the chance to interpret the lessons for themselves in order to gain insight from the characters and their behaviours, thoughts, and feelings. It is this exposure to these scenes that allows the child to come to grips with his/her fear, dread, loneliness, anger, and so on (Bergner, 2007); therefore, it is best to learn the story in its original form or as close to the original form as possible.

Other good sources of material are in the myths, legends, and folk tales of various cultures. These stories provide endless opportunities for the facilitator to adopt or adapt their story lines and to present them to the children in a way that they can best benefit from their messages. The storyteller should be familiar with as many of these stories as possible as a beginning step to using metaphor as a way of enhancing the lives of children.

When choosing a story for children, it is always important to collect information regarding their likes and dislikes, interests, hobbies, life-situation, and any other important material that will help in selecting a story that will catch their attention (Cook, Taylor, & Silverman, 2004). Also, the context of the story is

> Storytelling reveals meaning without committing the error of defining it.
> — HANNAH ARENDT

important, for example, it could be set in a nursery rhyme, folk tale, science fiction, or animal story; the storyteller needs to investigate what type of context to their stories the children would most enjoy.

A next step towards the use of story is to learn the intent of the story line. This requires the facilitator to study and to discuss with other professionals the essential lessons communicated by a particular legend, myth, or tale. Storytellers need to be aware of the more unconscious, symbolic, and subtle meanings of the story as well, in order to be most effective in communicating their message. Some excellent sources for story meaning and interpretation are Estes (1995), *Women Who Run With the Wolves*; Mead (2006), *The Water of Life*; Bolen's (2009) *Gods in Everyman* and (2004) *Goddesses in Everywoman*; and Burns (1999), *Into the Dark Forest*.

When selecting a story, it is always useful to decide, "What message or effect do I want this to convey?" There are several good sources of children's books, too numerous to mention here. However, librarians, teachers, early childhood educators, child and youth care workers, instructors, and colleagues are all good resources for effective children's metaphors and stories. Some research and plenty of reading is required until you find one that suits your specific needs. When you have located one of special significance, memorize it, buy it, or put it in point form in your diary, because it will prove useful in many situations. The most successful storytellers will spend the bulk of their time researching and learning specific stories; the telling is usually the easiest and most enjoyable part.

Once you have chosen a suitable story that conveys the necessary message(s), and once you know the story line well, it is time to add the finishing touches to your creation. This requires the storyteller to contact their creative artist within and to exercise these abilities in order to enhance the presentation of the story. A story comes alive in the imagination of the audience when the storyteller uses his/her voice and body to breathe life into the words to create the images, sounds, and emotions that represent the experiences of the story's characters.

Personal Reflection – Storytellers from the Past

Relax yourself by using a favourite technique or one from the preceding chapter on relaxation.

Listen for the voice or voices of your favourite storytellers, narrators, and poets. What is it about their vocal style that holds your attention?

_____

_____

_____

_____

Listen to the sound of your internal voice. What is its style?

_____

_____

_____

_____

Now listen to your parents' voices in your head. Do they use inflection and tempo to get their message across? How do their voices convey emotion?

_____

_____

_____

_____

Listen to the words of a favourite song, and be aware of how the singer conveys the song's message, the song's emotion.

_____

_____

_____

_____

Allow yourself to hear other voices from the past. How does the sender use tempo and inflection in order to convey meaning?

_____

_____

_____

_____

The Voice

Inflection, changing the pitch or tone of the voice, can make the words thunder, whistle in the wind, tremble with fear, shine like the stars, or float like a feather. Intonation, the rising and falling of the voice, can mark out key words and phrases that emphasize certain lessons, morals, or ideas. Intonation can calm or it can arouse, depending on the storyteller's wishes. Tempo, the rate of speed at which you speak, also conveys meaning. It can make words drag, move slowly, dance, run quickly, or flash like lightning. Inflection, tone, and tempo can be used to enhance the calming effect of the story, or to mark out certain words or phrases. The combination of all of these qualities brings life and wonder to the story's tale.

The Body

Gestures, positioning, and movement express emotion and convey meaning just as words do. A whole story can be told nonverbally through mime. Most of the communication between communicators is nonverbal. The use of the body can enhance the story's clarity and the intended message or moral.

Gestures, the use of movement of the extremities to express meaning, are a dramatic tool that can liven up the story. The storyteller shows size, shape, re-enacts a character's gestures or exaggerates them, shows direction, and shows actions like reaching, pulling, climbing, and kicking. Movement can beckon, quiet, scold, and threaten. Gestures can also be used as an overt or covert cue for the listener to pay attention to a specific word or phrase in order to underscore its meaning. An overt gesture could be pointing with the arm and hand; a covert gesture could be a subtle stroke of the chin. These gestures hold attention and can mark out the key learning or healing elements of the story.

Facial gestures and eye contact convey a myriad of meanings and are often used unconsciously by the storyteller. A common practice for storytellers is to tell their story in front of a mirror in order to be aware of their facial expressions and as a way to improve their ability to express meaning.

The positioning of the body in space and the movement of the body through space can also have an effect on the communication process. The position of the storyteller in relation to the audience at any time during the delivery of the story has an effect on the audience's perception. Each time the storyteller changes body posture in relation to the different members of the audience (as in sitting facing the audience, beside the audience, in back of the audience, etc.), he/she changes the meaning of the story and the focal point of the experience. The changing of body posture and position can be choreographed in order to make the story more entertaining and more effective in terms of communication.

The storyteller/facilitator must experiment in order to decide how each story should be dramatized in a way that best suits the audience. Props can be used by the storyteller for added effects or can be used by the group in the presentation of a story. Puppets, flannel boards, picture books, and artwork can all be used as communicators. And there are some storytellers who use no props and very little dramatization (Erickson & Rossi, 1979; Rosen, 1982). The facilitator must experiment and decide which stories can be more effectively presented with the use of the body and nonverbal communication.

The Content and the Audience

The importance of knowing the content of the story and its various meanings has been stressed earlier in this chapter. Another useful aspect of knowing the story line from memory is that it frees the storyteller to tailor his/her delivery of the story line and its messages to the audience. The audience gives the storyteller feedback through its nonverbal response to the telling of the story. When the audience appears to be losing interest in the story, a change is necessary to get their attention. This can be accomplished in many ways, most of which are visual, auditory, or tactile cues. A visual cue might be the use of a picture, a hand gesture, a prop, or a puppet. An auditory cue can include raising, lowering or softening the voice, a snap of the fingers, a clap of the hands, the sound of music, or an increase in the speed of the voice. Tactile cues can include a touch on the shoulder, a high-five, or the joining of hands.

Some storytellers incorporate the nonverbal responses of the audience into the action of the story. They might say for example, "The crowd sat motionless as the king walked into the room," or "The audience felt fidgety as the emperor entered the palace," or "Jason sat staring with his hand under his chin," or "Just then, he rubbed his eyes and wondered about many things." This makes the story fit the actual reality of all or part of the audience. Involving the audience in this way allows for a deeper rapport between the storyteller and listeners.

Where the storyteller may be using the story to relax or to quiet the group, using the word "quiet" or "relax" or "soften" several times in the story and changing the voice tone when pronouncing or saying the word, the message becomes embedded in the experience. Similarly, when the storyteller wishes to convey a specific message or moral (e.g., treat others as you wish to be treated), the voice tone or pitch can be changed for that specific line, or the storyteller can signal it to the audience with a wave of the hand or can actually touch a member of the audience when speaking the message. This technique marks the message out of the context of the story and causes it to stand out. When using these techniques, the storyteller can deliver the message when it appears that the audience is ready. The storyteller may want to repeat a message throughout the story in order to make it more obvious.

Writing a Story

The next logical step for the facilitator who is striving to use storytelling as an effective means of communication is to write stories that are tailored to the child's individual needs and life situation or that of the group. Stories that are written specifically for a group of children will address the group's particular problem in a personal way, and these stories present specific strategies or lessons in a manner that the group can best appreciate. The writer can pay particular attention to children's ages, level of developmental functioning, particular interests, and life situations while constructing the story. These personalized stories allow the facilitator to tailor metaphorical interventions to as many aspects of the children's lives as possible.

When writing stories for children, the younger the child, the more overt the connection should be between the child's life and that of the story's character(s). Thus, a four-year-old enjoys stories that are told which parallel his/her life identically. The older the child, the more covert the connection should be. Stories told to teenagers, for example, are more effective when the moral or lesson is not communicated directly in the story and when characters only remotely parallel the teenagers' lives.

Writers who are in tune with their audience can create stories that seem to present the next step in the developmental maturity of the listener's life. Milton Erickson, a writer of such powerful stories, spent long hours creating precise metaphorical language that created profound changes in his patients (Erickson & Rossi, 1979). Dr. Erickson, towards the latter part of his career, used story alone to treat severely psychologically and emotionally damaged clients successfully. His stories were irresistible to the patient because he was able to present them in such a way that the content was tailored to the client's life experience so precisely that the client saw clearly which step to take next on the road to restoring psychological and emotional health (Rosen, 1982).

> Fantasy is hardly an escape from reality. It's a way of understanding it.
> – LLOYD ALEXANDER

Exercise 14:1

Identify a problem that you are experiencing. Give this problem a metaphorical name, for example., Pain in the Neck could be a name for a problem with an annoying co-worker; Crop Failure could refer to an unsuccessful attempt at developing a friendship with someone.

Using the template below (Gordon, 1978) and a popular myth, fairy tale, or story as a guide, construct or select a story you believe would assist you in dealing with your problem.

SIGNIFICANT CHARACTERS	STORY CHARACTERS
SIGNIFICANT EVENTS	STORY EVENTS

Brainstorm and list all possible solutions to the problem. Remember that brainstorming allows for all possible solutions. Whether they seem to make sense at the time or not, write them down. Select the most desirable outcome(s).

DESIRED OUTCOMES	STORY OUTCOMES

Using a well-known children's story as a guide, write a story that identifies your problem, that includes all important characters, and that resolves the problem in the way chosen.

Write a draft of your story here:

_____
_____
_____
_____
_____
_____
_____
_____
_____
_____
_____
_____
_____
_____
_____

Read through the story and decide which dramatic effects would be suitable in order to present your story to a group of children.

_____
_____
_____
_____
_____
_____
_____
_____
_____
_____
_____
_____
_____
_____

See also "The Remic Storytelling Technique" in the interventions section at the end of this chapter.

> Inasmuch as the use of metaphor as a means of communication has been widespread throughout recorded history, we must assume that there are distinct advantages to delivering messages in metaphorical form.
>
> — **PHILIP BARKER**

Review

- Storytelling has been used for centuries to assist children in coping with life's problems.

- Stories can have a wide variety of influences on the audience.

- Stories can be selected to send specific messages to the audience.

- The manner in which the story is told and acted out can have an effect on the interpretation and outcomes for the audience.

- Stories can be written specifically for an individual or an audience.

Therapeutic storytelling can easily be incorporated into the techniques and interventions discussed next in Chapter 15, "Art, Drama, Movement, and Music Therapy." This following chapter addresses the use of art mediums in therapeutic programming and discusses ways of using art, drama, music, and movement as therapeutic agents for children. Chapter 15 amalgamates much of the information that has been provided by the preceding chapters in this text and gives both the therapeutic programmer and facilitator important information for dealing with complex and extensive problems experienced by children.

The following are a series of therapeutic interventions and stories intended to act as resources for the student or novice practitioner who wishes to practice his/her skills in therapeutic storytelling.

Therapeutic Interventions

Storytelling Activities

STORY FOR STORY

The facilitator begins by telling a story, and in the story, the main character finds him/herself in a dilemma, but the facilitator's story does not provide a solution. Participants are asked to come up with a mutually acceptable solution to the problem and complete the story.

Variation: Mutual Storytelling Technique (Gardner, 1993) This is a story exchange—a story for a story. This variation is usually conducted in a one-to-one situation. Children's stories often symbolically represent a problem in their own lives.

The facilitator or the participant may begin by telling a story. Once the child has told his/her story, the facilitator will tell a comparable story with a solution to the problem in the child's story or with an alternative solution or resolution. As the story exchange continues, the child is provided with a variety of solutions to one or more of his/her problems.

LIFE INTERVIEWS

Recording devices are excellent tools to use for storytelling. They can be used in many novel and creative ways allowing children to tell their own unique stories. Assign someone to be the interviewer (if there is more than one recorder, there can be several interviewers). The interviewer can interview any person in the group on a designated topic, e.g., early years, primary grades, family history, war, music, the environment, and so on. The topic should give them the freedom to talk about their experiences and about what they think as individuals.

LIFE HISTORY

This exercise is a more concrete way of telling the life story. It can be drawn from birth to the present day or from birth to death, stopping off wherever the child decides. The life history can be represented by a straight line or by a circle. Children can be encouraged to remember past events by starting at their birth and working forward or start with the present and work backward to their birth.

Children often need time to collect the necessary information for this exercise from their family members; therefore, an introduction to this exercise a day or a week prior to conducting it is advisable. The children are asked to recall significant events in their lives, e.g., birth, first steps, first words, day care, primary school, vacations, camps, divorces, deaths, injuries, failures, etc., and to make a list of these events in chronological order. If dates are available, they can be included in the exercise. Provide paper large enough to allow them to mark out their lifeline or their life circle. Younger children can be encouraged to make a pictograph by drawing pictures on small cards that represent significant events.

MAKE-BELIEVE

This exercise allows children to play with a favourite nursery rhyme, story, or fairy tale, and is an early beginning for the use of metaphor.

Ask the children to write out in brief a favourite story, fairy tale, or nursery rhyme. Instruct them to exchange their names and the names of their friends or relatives for the names of the characters in the story. When completed, these stores are to be read aloud to the group.

THE REMIC STORYTELLING TECHNIQUE

Select a problem area that can be discussed openly with an individual child or a group of children, e.g., divorce, stealing, fighting, etc. Discuss this problem with the group, and write down their responses word for word to these questions:

• What were the sensations/emotions you felt while the problem was occurring?

• What words would describe what it looked like?

• What were some of the sounds you associate with the problem?

• What was said to you about this problem?

• What did you say to yourself while the problem was occurring?

• Are their any tastes or smells that come to mind when you think about the problem?

Here are more explicit examples of typical questions to ask the children using stealing behaviour as an example:

• What did you feel just before you stole the item?

• How did you feel afterwards?

• What did you see when you entered the store?

• What were you saying to yourself before, after, and during the time you stole?

• Were there any sounds or people talking when you stole the item?

• Did you say anything out loud before, after, or during the theft?

• Was there any part of your body that felt sore, tense or just different before, during, or after the theft?

Be sure to write down verbatim what the child has said and make note of any mispronunciation or of the particular way it was said so that when the story is told, the storyteller can replicate the child's language and manner of speaking as closely as possible.

Ask the child or group of children to come up with possible solutions or outcomes to the problem using a brainstorming technique.

Once all of the information has been gathered, it's time to write your story. Select a context or type of story (e.g., animal story, science fiction, fable, etc.). Write the story using as many of the statements collected as possible. Include the most desirable solutions or outcomes generated by the group or the child, and include them as part of the story. Read the story and write in the margins the possible dramatic and visual effects that can be used to enhance the story. Read the story out loud to the group.

Therapeutic Stories

The following is a compellation of short stories taken from Stories in Child Care (Burns, 1982). They are examples of stories written for a specific child, a specific problem, or a specific group of children and can be adapted by the reader to suit his/her audience. The brief introduction at the beginning of each story is meant to orient the reader to the particular situation that inspired the story.

THE NORSEMAN

Some children have much fear and anxiety around leaving their parents or family. Such fear can be expressed through school phobias, psychosomatic illness, and acts of aggression, regression or other difficulties. The underlying fear is often the fear of loss or death. The Norseman, a Viking, a man of that seafaring race, still fears the sea he travels on. It is suggested, however, that the Norseman uses his feelings, as a vehicle for change, and by recognizing his fears, he comes to understand his good fortune.

This is a story about a Norseman, a Viking who was very brave and very kind.

This Norseman was about to set sail on a long and dangerous voyage. It was a time of great activity, packing up the ship with food and clothing to last for months, dreaming of the wonderful adventures he was soon to take part in. The day came when the sails were raised; the Norseman heard the wind slapping the sails about and knew his time to depart had finally arrived. He was very excited.

However, when he ran home to say goodbye to his family, he was suddenly sad. He hated leaving his family, and he felt maybe he would never see them all again. He loved them so much, and this time, saying goodbye seemed to be more difficult than usual.

All the way out to sea and for many days after, he continued to feel sad and lonely. His heart ached every time he thought of his family and friends, and he was so afraid that something would happen, and he'd never get to see them again. The more he thought about this, the worse he felt. After many unhappy days, he was standing at the rail, smelling the sea air, hearing the waves lap gently at the side of the ship, when he pictured his wife with her blonde, shining hair, laughing happily and smiling up at him. He realized that he could think about and remember whomever he wanted to. Suddenly, pictures and sounds and feelings flooded into his brain and all through his body.

His whole body was awash with wonderful pictures, scenes of happiness and celebration, good sounds, and the smells of his mother's wonderful feasts, his father's big red bristly beard, and his children's laughter. And then he realized that he was feeling good—these happy memories and pictures actually made him feel alive and calm.

This calmness allowed him to become more involved in the challenges of the sea, and just in time. The sky was darkening rapidly, great blue-black storm clouds were rolling in fast, and the captain was shouting orders to the crew. Everyone was rushing about preparing for the storm. The waves were crashing on all sides, and the ship was being buffeted about. With each new wave, the ship would rise up, up, up, and then rapidly fall down, down, down. The Norseman held fast and rode the storm as it carried him up, up, up again and down, down, down in a never-ending motion. With each new wave that buffeted the small ship about, the Norseman remembered his family and all the love he felt for them. As the boat sank into the troughs of the wave, he was reminded of all the fun and excitement they'd had together. Rather than feel afraid, the roller coaster movements of the boat reminded him of who and where he was, and he felt proud and brave and happy to be where he was and doing what he was doing.

The storm subsided as all storms do, and the Norseman felt so glad to be alive.

SNAKE AND THE LITTLE GIRL

This story was written for a little First Nations child who was living in a very stressful situation, and it seemed hopeless to her at the time. Her father had married a very abusive woman, and the child's mother had been placed in jail. She was, however, involved with her grandmother and aunts who looked after her on weekends.

Long ago, in a time before our own, there lived a little girl who dwelt with her father along a great river. Her father was a hunter, and she had lost her mother so long ago that she could not remember her. When her father was out hunting, she would walk through the forest. She loved the freedom and would swim in the river when it was hot, collect roots when it rained, and catch fish when it was windy. This little girl was a friend with all the animals on the land, the birds in the air, and the fish under the water.

One day Snake came to the hut of her father disguised as a beautiful woman. Immediately her father, the hunter, fell in love with the woman. Over time, Snake turned the hunter against his daughter. And one night, when the little girl's father was sleeping, Snake came into her room and carried her far off into the forest. Snake stopped at the base of a tall pine tree and took the little girl all the way to the very top. He then took a rope and slithered around the tree tying the girl to the trunk with such a clever knot that no one could ever untie it. And then Snake left.

In the morning, the little girl's friends from under the water gave the ones on the earth a special herb. Her friends from the air flew to the top of the tree and placed the medicine in the little girl's mouth. She felt nurtured by this. Then each one from the land, beginning with Bear, tried to untie the knot. But no animal could undo it and no bird or fish could either. She stayed up in the tree for many seasons, and still the knot held her fast.

One day she saw an old woman bent over with the weight of her years, walking towards the tree. As she came closer, the little girl recognized her as a grandmother who lived in her father's village. When she was close to the tree, the little girl called out, "Grandmother! Hey, up here." And the old crone looked up and saw the little girl. "Do you know how to untie Snake's knot?"

"Oh yes," she replied. "They are easy when you get to be my age. I can untie them in my sleep." Suddenly, at that very moment, the little girl fell into a deep sleep.

In her sleep she dreamed that the old grandmother climbed up the tree and untied Snake's knot. When she woke, she noticed that she was on the path to her village. "This is the way to my father's hut," she said to herself. The little girl ran all the way home to find her father sitting outside the hut waiting for her return. They both hugged each other and the little girl told him of her adventure.

THE BEAR FAMILY

This story was written for a group of children experiencing divorce or separation within their families. Characters in the story reflect the Satir "stances" (Satir, 1972). Father is a blamer, mother a placater, and the children act both irrelevant and the computer. The wise old owl, the therapist, teaches the family a technique or style called "leveling" (Satir, 1972). The ending offers hope but not false hope.

Once upon a time there was a family of three bears—the mama bear, the papa bear, and the baby bear. Do you remember the story of the three bears and Goldilocks? Well, at that time, the bears were just newly married with one little cub, and life seemed very good and trouble-free. As time went on, the baby, who was a boy bear, grew up, and a little baby girl bear was born into the family. This family of four lived very comfortably for a long time.

However, after a time, some very difficult problems arose. For one thing, food was becoming scarce, which meant papa bear had to travel far from his family. Sometimes papa bear would come home feeling terribly tired, and if he were rubbed the wrong way, he would become very upset. Mama bear would often put the blame on herself, saying that it was "all my fault" and then would begin to cry. The sight of the tears running down their mama's cheeks made the bear cubs feel very sad and scared, although they tried hard to pretend everything was all right. They tried to shut out their feelings, and sometimes they would try to trick their parents out of fighting. This way of be-

haviour became a real habit for the bear family, and the fighting got worse and worse till one night there was a terrible argument which ended with papa bear yelling, "I hate it here; I'm leaving." And out he walked, slamming the door hard behind him.

Mama bear and the children were very upset, and they cried and cried for many days, but papa bear did not return. Now, the responsibility to feed the family fell on mom's shoulders. Mama bear felt alone, tired, and very sad and blamed herself for everything. The children sometimes blamed dad, sometimes mom, and sometimes themselves. Most of the time, they tried to pretend that it never happened. All the blaming led to more fights among the family, and the pretending kept their feelings apart from each other.

This went on for a long time and probably could have gone on forever if mom had not heard about the Wise Old Owl. The Wise Old Owl, mama was told, had a way of talking to people and listening to people that seemed to help, even when things sounded like they would never get better.

Mama bear went to visit the Wise Old Owl and explained the whole situation. She was instructed to come the next day and to bring her two children. On that day and for weeks to come, the bears met in the quiet of the forest with this wise and peaceful old bird. The owl taught them a new way to talk to one other, a way that didn't blame or cause guilty feelings, and a way that dealt directly with the problem. The owl taught them new ways to find food and nourishment. He taught them many other things as well, some of them they understood right away, while others took them a long time to really understand.

One day the little girl bear asked, "Mr. Owl, do you think Papa will come back to live with us now that we have learned a new way?"

The Wise Old Owl replied, "There have been many animal families just like yours and others too that have broken apart. Some of these families have come to me to learn a new way. Sometimes the papa bear came back, learned a new way of behaving, and was able to live once again with his family. Other times, a new dad came and joined the family. But, all the animals that have used this new way have grown and lived much happier lives than the animals who continue to blame themselves and others."

The little girl sighed, wiped the tear from the corner of her eye, and smiled.

THE OLD WOMAN AND THE CAT

At the height of her desperation, the old woman finds something that gives her new life. Her hopes are later dashed when this precious gift is taken as quickly as it was given. She again falls into a deep depression. The cycles of life and death, gain and loss, joy and misery are ones that are very close to and very meaningful to children.

There was once an old woman who lived alone in a small wooden cottage. All her family and friends had grown old or moved away to live in the large modern homes of the city. No longer did she hear the gay sounds of children's laughter or the gentle buzz of friendly conversation. She was alone and getting ready to die.

One bleak and windy day, the old woman heard a faint sound coming from her door. She opened the door slowly and at her feet stood a small, orange kitten. She smiled and looked around for any sign of the owner or a mother who might claim this small treasure. Seeing no one, she gently picked up the small ball of orange fluff and brought him into the cottage. Every part of this small animal, even its eyes, was orange, and so the kitten was named Pumpkin. The old woman cuddled and brushed, fed and pampered her new prize until it grew into a huge, proud, and somewhat venturesome tomcat. She felt so much life in her since her little orange kitten arrived. And as she sat one evening listening to its gentle purr, she thought back to how useless she had felt before Pumpkin's arrival. She looked upon life now as a spring song announcing the end of a cold and bitter winter. She began to realize that she still possessed enough nourishment, love, and affection to be given out to whomever she came in contact with.

Pumpkin, like most tomcats, began to venture further and further from the cottage and would not return for days at a time. Finally, there came a time when he no longer needed the old woman. He had found a colourful and affectionate mate whose purr sounded very musical along with his own. The old woman wept and wailed when she realized her Pumpkin was gone for good, gone as quickly as he had arrived, leaving her life once again empty and hopeless. She was heartbroken for weeks.

When her tears had dried up, she began to rethink her time with Pumpkin. Had not Pumpkin given her a very precious gift—the knowledge that she is capable of caring for others and a new desire to make her life more meaningful, more fun? The old woman smiled within herself as she planned to venture out, as Pumpkin had, to see what sounds the world had prepared for her ears. For she knew now that there would always be an orange glow in her heart.

UP IN A TREE

Children often feel trapped with nowhere to go. "Up in a Tree" empathizes with this situation and offers some suggestions as to how to remedy it. This is an appropriate story for use with impulsive or resistant children and can be used as an aside during confrontation.

When I was a young child, I loved to climb trees. I would climb as high as I dared and looked way down at the ground below. I loved the feeling of the wind gently blowing over my face, the smell of leaves and outdoor freshness, and the rustling sounds of the wind as it shook the leaves.

One day I decided to climb the big oak tree that stood in the back yard next to my aunt's apartment. I had watched the tree's branches blowing to and fro for many years but had not dared to venture over and test my skills on its huge limbs. On that famous day as I climbed atop my bicycle so I could reach its bottom-most limb, my heart was beating quickly. My foot gripped each branch soundly; my arms stretched and pulled my body slowly up the tree. At first, the bark was rough and scratchy, scraping my knees, but as I climbed higher, the texture became very different—now it was almost satiny smooth. The higher I climbed, the louder and crisper the sound of the leaves rustling in the wind became. Soon I could feel the whole tree sway and stretch in the breeze, and I was part of this moving mass. I had climbed higher than I had ever been before. Stopping, I looked around to enjoy the sight of the rusty freight cars and miles of train track stretching out before me.

When it came time for me to go back down however, a much different feeling came over me. I had climbed very high and the ground looked miles down from where I sat perched on my branch. My body became paralyzed with fear. I was certain I was going to fall. My palms became wet, and my racing heart was pounding so loudly I could hear it in my ears. I began to call frantically for help, each call louder and closer to tears than the one before it. Then I began to cry, and my whole body shook, which started the trees branches shaking as well. The harder I cried, the more the tree shook, and the more afraid I became.

A woman came out of the neighbouring house and yelled up to me to find out what was the matter. Eventually I managed to hold my sobs long enough to explain my trouble to her. I begged her to come up and help me down from the tree. She replied that she was far too old to be climbing trees and promised she would bring her husband. When she left, fearing she would not return and feeling quite alone and forgotten, I cried even harder, clinging tightly to the branch I was on. My arms were aching, and my hands were red from holding on. After what seemed like hours, an old grey-haired man walked up to the tree and smiled kindly up at me. I caught my breath and begged him to help me down. He calmly told me I would have to come down myself, but only when I felt ready. This was too much for me at such a young age, and I began to sob once more. I was certain I would never make it down alive. The old man called up for me to hold on and cry till I was completely cried out. I wept and sobbed to the soothing sounds coming from the old couple below. When I had gained some control over myself, I looked down to see their smiling and encouraging faces.

Slowly I slipped my toe to the branch below and tested it to see if it would hold my weight. It did and slowly, very slowly, I began to lower myself down the tree. The further I climbed down the tree, the more even my heartbeat became. My breathing began to slow down. My feet gripped each limb firmly, and my arms carefully lowered me to where the bark of the tree began to feel rough and coarse again. The old couple's voices were very clear now and gave me a feeling of safety and trust. I jumped from the bottom branch to the ground and into the arms of that loving couple. I felt extremely safe, warm and very relieved.

I have climbed many trees since then but none have changed my life and my view of myself as much as that one.

WEATHERING THE STORM

This story was written specifically for a family experiencing a separation. It is a good example of the way in which a story can explain and reframe a negative experience. The conflict is seen as a storm, an act of nature, which places the blame on no one. The ending offers hope and suggests that satisfaction or re-union might not be achieved quietly or without pain.

This is a story about a family: a man, a woman, a boy, and a girl. These people loved each other very much. They enjoyed each other's company so much that they played together, worked together, slept together, and ate together.

This family loved to travel to the city to see all the wonders there. For as much as they liked to be together in their home, they were strongly attracted by the new ideas and excitement that the city offered. Now it was a long journey from where they lived to the city, but they would sing along the way, which seemed to make the trip much shorter.

When travelling to the city on one particular day, the weather took a drastic turn. Grey water-laden storm clouds rolled in suddenly, and the skies began to darken. The wind started blowing strongly, knocking branches off trees and tiles off roofs. Loud clashes of thunder made the earth tremble and streaks of silver lightening lit the skies continuously. Just as the family reached the city gates, the great storm broke out. The storm divided the family and scattered each member in a different direction. The wind blew and the rain pounded, trapping each family member, leaving them lonely and afraid for themselves and each other. They had not planned on a storm this great. However, the weather, as you know, is very hard to predict. Each family member was now alone, divided from each other and very frightened.

The storm was a very unusual one and lasted for days. The thunder and lightening never ceased, and the torrents of water falling from the skies turned the city into chaos.

Sometimes the rain-laden clouds darkened the sky in the middle of the day as though it were nighttime. The family wandered, homeless and frightened, in the pitch dark, unable to see or recognize familiar places. As the storm raged, each family member wandered further and further from each other. Four days passed until the storm cleared, giving way to calmer weather, sunshine, and a certain amount of peace for the family. However, the storm had left them scattered, frightened, and alone. Each member decided to return to home and hope that the other members would return as well.

There was so much destruction from the storm that returning home became a huge problem. All the familiar landmarks and scenery were knocked down or changed, so much that they were hard to recognize. Each family member had to rely on what they had with them in order to find their way back to safety—their eyes to help find the right road, their ears to listen for helpful sounds and words, and their feelings to guide them. The road was very dangerous because the storm had destroyed everything in its path. The one thing that was in their favour was the people around them. Each person they met helped in a special way and made the trip much easier. It was the little things that seemed to be the most important.

It was a long time before the first family member found the way back to the homestead. And for some, the return trip took much longer. However, when the last family member returned home there was much celebration and joy. The family had survived the storm that had torn them apart, and each member had grown and become a stronger, happier, and more independent person.

Other storms have come and gone, though not ones that have been as strong or as scary as the one remembered here.

OLD JOE

Old Joe, seemingly helpless, feels like many children who will not take responsibility for themselves. Joe meets someone even older than he who is living a happy life. He soon learns the secret and acts for himself. Preschoolers greatly enjoy this story, especially when the issues of helplessness and dependency are emphasized.

There was once a very old and tired man. He was so old and so tired that he needed a younger person to help him cross the street, wash his face, make his supper and even to take him home to bed. The tired old man felt sad and useless, as though he was not any good for anything any longer. He grumbled and complained a lot and often wore a mean face. The people called him Old Joe because no one knew his real name.

One day, as Old Joe was weakly lying out in his chair, resting in the noonday sun, he saw a much older man jogging down the street carrying a brown bag over his shoulder. Joe yelled from his chair, "Stop! Please come here." As the man came closer, Joe realized that this man, who looked older than he did, appeared to be very happy. "Why are you carrying that bag, and where do you get all your energy?"

"This is a bag of special apples," the man replied. "It is these apples, among other things, that keep me healthy and give me energy. I have one for you if you would like."

"Oh yes, please, I would like one," Old Joe replied. The man reached into his bag and gave a shiny red apple to Joe. Joe examined it, turning it all around very carefully, and then bit into it. Mmm, it was delicious, so juicy that the liquid ran down his chin, the most deliciously sweet and aromatic apple that he'd ever tasted. For a minute, Joe was speechless. He did not feel sad anymore; it was as though he had found out about a big secret. He took another bite of the apple and then asked, "These are so delicious. Where can I get more of them?"

"About two miles down the road," the man pointed, "there is a fruit stand run by some very special people. Go to them and tell them you would like some of their special apples."

"Two miles," Old Joe groaned, "I'll never be able to walk that far. And my young helper is not here now. Oh, I'm too old!" Joe complained.

"The energy from that apple I have given you," the old man replied, "will help you along the way. However, you do need to trust and have confidence in yourself."

Old Joe smiled, took another bite of the apple, and headed off down the road towards the special fruit stand.

THE WILD HORSES

This story was written to introduce summer counsellors to a group of children. The wild horses represent the counsellors: young, full of energy, yet experienced in the ways of childhood. In the story these wild horses meet and spend a short time with the other band of horses. During this time the small band learns much from the wild horses. They later take some of the wild horses' experience with them when they part company.

In a land not far from here there lived a small band of horses. There were horses of many different sizes, shapes and colours. There were roans, dapples, greys, pintos, appaloosas, both mares and stallions. For many years they had heard their fathers and grandfathers tell of a special meadow that existed far across the sandy desert. Slowly, one by one, the members of the small band began to experience a need to visit this special place. And so the band began to prepare itself for this long and difficult journey. Difficult, because as you know, a desert can seem like a very unfriendly place to those not used to the hardships imposed by the lack of water and food. The time eventually came, and the small band of horses set out across the desert.

As they travelled, the thick green prairie grass that grew on the fringes of the desert became thin and brown and more difficult to find. The weather became hotter, and the air became dry and dusty. Many of the water holes they passed were now dried up, and the herd of horses started to feel very hot and tired and hungry. As their thirst deepened and their mouths dried up, their tempers flared. Many quarrels broke out among them. They began to kick and bite and argue with one another. These uncomfortable and unhappy times went on and on. No one in the herd could see a solution as the sounds of fighting and desperation continued. Every one of the small band was feeling frightened and alone.

As I said, these bad times lasted a long time and would probably have caused a lot of hardships for the band had they not met up with a herd of wild horses. These wild horses appeared to be quite happy and comfortable with the desert's hardships. In fact, when the small band first caught sight of them, the wild horses were neighing wildly and jumping over small bushes as if playing some sort of game. As they got closer to these wild horses, they began to feel hopeful inside. "Maybe things will get better," they said to themselves. The small herd, in unison, whinnied a greeting to this wild and somewhat strange herd of animals. The small band and the wild horses approached one another in a friendly air of caution.

After much sniffing and careful looking, touching and neighing, the wild horses invited the small band to travel with them for a way, since they were both travelling in a similar direction. The small band of horses most thankfully accepted the invitation, and both groups travelled together as one.

Each morning, as was the custom of the wild horses, the whole herd assembled for food, conversation and play. It was during these times that the prairie horses learned and experienced much. These wild and sometimes crazy horses were able to find food and water in places where there seemed to be nothing at all. Dried-up water holes and strange-looking cacti were now seen as a source of food and liquid nourishment. These horses could hear the winds and the sand moving which told them whether storms or calm weather could be expected. They would use their nostrils, tongues, ears, and the very fibres of their beings to understand the ways of the desert. They delighted in play and loved to teach their games to others. The small band had many questions for the wild horses, and each one was answered very carefully. The small band enjoyed and benefitted from every minute spent with these wise and playful creatures.

Time passed by very quickly as it often does when things go well, and soon the small band were saying their final farewells to the group of horses they had become very close to. Each horse stroked and sniffed one another and then parted in different directions. But somehow, even as they turned away, it was as if some part of them was still together.

The small band travelled on. The water was still very scarce. The grass was still brownish and sparse, the weather hot and dry. The small band still quarrelled from time to time; but, somehow, something was very different. Was it the way things looked? Was it that everything sounded better? Was it a feeling? No one was absolutely sure, but they all could agree on one thing—the time together was much more comfortable and a lot more fun.

Then one day, as if by magic, it happened. All that their fathers had prophesied appeared on the horizon. They heard the sound of water splashing down a sparkling stream, birds twittering, and they saw myriads of yellow-gold butterflies filling the air. They could taste it, smell it, and feel it. They had arrived at the glorious meadow they had set out to find. There before them stood the cool, green, and peaceful meadow, that special place of their heart's desire.

The small band lived in that meadow for a long, long, time. And at times, they would drift back in their memories to the time they spent crossing the desert. They could even picture their old friends, the wild horses, neighing their special hellos. And they felt good, safe and content.

THE BONSAI

This story tells of the amazing possibilities in breathing, thinking and relaxing. The Bonsai is a story that can be effectively used in calming children. It can be utilized as a relaxation exercise through voice tone and tempo. Bonsai is also an ancient and cherished art as is child-rearing. It speaks of small treasured plants being passed from family to family.

When I was a child, I used to enjoy sitting on my grandmother's lap listening to stories of her sister who lived in Japan. Her sister, Grand Aunt Iris, would write to her of men and women who could do amazing things. She would write of people who could breathe, move, and think in a certain way so that they were able control their bodies, and, to a great extent, the world they lived in.

My grandmother would relate each of Iris' amazing letters to me, and what a wonderful storyteller she was! My grandmother had a way of telling stories that made you feel as though you were right there, living and breathing them.

Grand Aunt Iris wrote of many beautiful and wonderful things, and Grandma would make them into stories. My favourite story, the one that left me feeling good about myself, was the Bonsai Tree. I can still hear her voice telling me of this wondrous plant.

"The bonsai, my son," she would begin, "is a very beautiful and elegant plant that has a special place in the hearts of many Japanese. It is a small tree, usually no more than 12 inches high. But they are oh so graceful and flowing, like a dancer. The people of Japan take very special care of these trees. Often they are cared for and passed on through generations by the same family. Some of these trees have lived for hundreds of years. Their branches are pruned and shaped to form beautifully graceful works of art."

"The art of the bonsai," she continued, "is one requiring patience and tender care. The peaceful energy of the tree is given to the gardener and, in turn, given back to the tree. The gardener and tree patiently nurture one another and become as one object together. This miniature tree has a special root system that allows it to grow in a very small pot. Its roots are

like tiny fingers reaching into the soil and holding tight, gently taking their strength and nourishment. The roots have innate knowledge of the perfect amounts of food that are required, and slowly, carefully, they absorb it into themselves. The strength and character of the tree lies within its roots. And so, you too my grandchild can be strong and firm in your own soil."

Every time I heard that story, I felt so firmly grounded that my grandmother would often remark, "You look as solid and as strong as my John." This would make me feel warm and special inside, for John was my grandfather.

So whenever I want to feel calm and relaxed, yet firmly planted into the ground, I remember the bonsai, my grandmother, Grand Aunt Iris, and the people of Japan.

GRANDFATHER'S FISH

This story was written for children who are working on their relationships. It deals with shared responsibility for the good of the group. It can also be expanded into a relaxation exercise wherein "the waves roll in and the waves roll out and they flow one into the other". Like the Bonsai, this story distances the subject from the source, as it is a story told to me by my grandfather as told to him by his grandfather.

When I was a little boy, I spent a lot of time sitting on my grandparents' big front porch. Grandma and Grandpa lived close enough for me to walk down to their house and spend the warm summer evenings listening to Grandpa and his friends spin yarns.

My granddad and practically all his friends were fishermen, rod and reel fishermen—sportsmen. He loved to fish but never kept one fish that he caught. Once he reeled the fish in, he would very carefully remove the hook. Then he would hold up his prize proudly to show all his fishing buddies. And these fish did not have to worry, because after they had been weighed and measured, Grandpa would hold the fish over the water, where they would squirm and thrash about with the sunlight glinting off their silver grey scales. Grandpa would then gently drop them into the water, returning them to the cool waters they knew so well.

My grandfather's father was a fisherman as well as his father before him, so Grandfather had a large collection of fish stories. And what I liked best about Grandpa's stories was that parts of them were true and parts of them were imaginary.

"Well, there was this big school of fish, …" Grandpa would begin, "these were big fish, small fish, young fish, old fish, fish of all ages, men fish, women fish, girl fish and boy fish, all together like a large family."

"They travelled together and relied on each other for safety and friendship. Each fish seemed to encourage, protect, and inspire the other. When the school was tired or hungry, nothing else would be done until the fish were feeling relaxed and well again. When you travel together, you must be patient. So the fast-moving fish kept the pace but also moved slowly to allow the others to catch up. The slower ones, who were often the older wiser fish, would point out the ways of the waters to the others."

"'The mystery of the waters,' the wise ones would teach, 'is in the way it flows in complete unison, each wave into each wave, never ending, never beginning, each separate drop of water part of the larger body, each splash and ripple, each warm spring and cold ocean floor, all flowing, weaving, and dancing together. Each single part is as important as the whole lake. Without the tiny droplets of water, no ocean can exist. For the way of the waters,' the wise fish would sing, 'is also the way of the fish.'"

Grandpa would always smile at this part, and sometimes he would just finish here, which would leave me waiting and wondering what would come next.

> It's like everyone tells a story about themselves inside their own head. Always. All the time. The story makes you what you are. We build ourselves out of that story.
> – PATRICK ROTHFUSS

CHAPTER 15

Art, Drama, Movement, and Music Therapy

When Leroy walked through the doorway, he stopped and waited until his eyes became accustomed to the dimly lit, smoke-filled room. As his vision cleared, he saw musicians huddled in the far corner of the room. A flood of sound and emotion waved through his body; he groped for a place to sit so that he could give witness to this strange experience. Leroy's senses were bombarded as the stage lights exploded into reds, blues, and yellows. The musicians, in a frenzied attempt to express all that they held within, filled the room with a sound so rich that its blending with the atmosphere created shock waves through Leroy. The theme of their music was unintelligible, and as Leroy tried to collect himself, he searched for some meaning to tag onto his experience.

The music was communicating, the crowd was responding, but he was unable to make sense of it. Nothing in his experience could relate to the strangeness of the moment. He stopped questioning, closed his eyes, and let go of conventionality; he decided to let the experience direct him, instead of him trying to direct it. He listened intently and focussed his attention on the three forms in front of him. They began to speak to him, to move him emotionally through the force of their music, their movements, and their use of colour and light. Leroy got up and began to move to the experience, joining the dancers and the others. Pain and joy, his and every human's, was celebrated that night. Leroy stayed on the dance floor all night and marvelled at the colours, sights, sounds, and emotions that he allowed himself to experience. He gave up controlling and let the artist inside take the lead. Leroy has never been the same since that night at the club.

> Art enables us to find ourselves and lose ourselves at the same time.
>
> – THOMAS MERTON

This chapter on art, drama, movement, and music therapy is intended as an introduction to these forms of therapy. It points out the value of each art form and the usefulness of various combinations of the four when working with children. It suggests a variety of interventions to allow children to become comfortable and familiar with experimenting and creating using the various mediums. The chapter highlights art as a means of self-expression, drama as a way of providing insight, music as a form of self-expression or as a mood-setting device, and movement as a way to stimulate and express sensory and emotional experience. The later part of the chapter provides the facilitator with activities that will assist in the introduction of these art forms to groups of children.

Understanding, appreciating, and expressing the Self through the arts requires a shift from the logical, analytical frame of reference to one that is more creative and unorthodox. Leroy made this shift by opening himself up to the musicians' experience and by allowing his heart and soul to influence his intellectual interpretation of his experience. In simplistic terms, this shift allows the logical linear mind (left hemisphere) to integrate with the creative imaginative mind (right hemisphere) (Sperry, 1961 & 1980). Chiron, Jambaque, Nabbout, Lounes, Syrota and Dulac (1997) point out that the right hemisphere is more highly developed in children and develops more quickly in childhood than the left hemisphere. This makes the arts, which are primarily right hemisphere activities, excellent mediums for the expression of feelings, which are also primarily right brain functions. When discussions and presentations, primarily a left-brain activity, of children's art are incorporated into the children's art experience, this supports and underscores this integration of the two hemispheres. Trauma, cognitive deficits, mental illness, brain injury, and extreme stress may hamper, and in some cases arrest, this flow of information between the two hemispheres (van der Kolk, McFarlane, & Weisaeth, 1996). Assisting children to stimulate this flow of energy and information allows them to function more effectively when under stress (Levine & Kline. 2007).

Most children are able to make this shift quite easily, allowing them more integrated experiences and ways of being—logic dwells side by side with creativity. This integrated Self has great potential for the programmer and facilitator of therapeutic activities because it provides children a wider frame of reference with which to experience, understand, and appreciate their worlds. This integration is a move towards homeostasis or balance within the organism. This integration of Self is often called being centred (see Chapter 13, "Relaxation, Imagery, and Guided Fantasy"). The use of art, drama, movement, and music in the programming of activities for children provides them with opportunities to exercise and utilize this ability to integrate their experiences and to heal their minds (Campbell, 1997; Levine & Kline, 2007; Malchiodi, 2007; Rubin, 2010; Steele 2003).

The arts also have the ability to allow children to let go of repressive, constrictive thoughts and linear thinking, opening up a world of creative expression that need not make sense or appear to have any concrete purpose. They can express themselves, their feelings, thoughts, and behaviours, without a need to explain or define them (Rubin, 2005, 2010).

The usefulness of the techniques discussed will rely upon facilitators who are able to make their own shift to the integrated Self and who are able to foster this ability in others. It also is reliant on an environment that allows children sufficient freedom and structure to express themselves.

Personal Reflection – Drawing Emotions

Collect some art materials that you have at your disposal. Find a comfortable spot where you will not have any disturbances. Relax yourself using a favourite relaxation technique.

When you are relaxed, concentrate on a feeling: sorrow, fear, jealousy, or anger. Try to allow your thoughts to flow in whatever way is comfortable. Symbols such as human figures, colours, motions, shapes, and words will come into your mind and cause your physical Self to feel this emotion. When you feel the emotion, try to intensify it as much as possible.

Now pick up the art materials and create. Do not erase or plan your picture, but allow the symbols and images to take shape on the paper.

When you have completed your composition, give it a title. Stand back and view your creation as a stranger would.

What does the picture appear to say to you?

What is this piece of art telling you about how you experience this emotion? Write down some of the more important aspects of this experience and discuss them with a friend.

_____

_____

_____

_____

_____

_____

_____

Facilitation of the Expressive Arts

Children's need to create, to fantasize, to use their intuition, is a drive and a natural form of self-expression (Jung, 1971) and is a major source of learning and personal discovery for the child. When a child is allowed to satisfy the drive to create in a way that best suits his/her individual needs, self-esteem and self-concept will be enhanced. The relationship between artist and facilitator is critical to the self-expressive experience (Rubin, 2005, 2010; Steele & Malchiodi, 2012; Warren, 2008).

The role of facilitator has been discussed several times in preceding chapters of this text and involves the basic skills of relationship-building, pacing, and the awareness of when to intervene and when to disengage. The facilitator's style in art-based activities is that of a laissez-faire leader (see Chapter 5, "Facilitating Therapeutic Programs"), allowing children more latitude in behaviour and response to programming. The program is more of a self-directed experience than one where the facilitator takes control and directs play. The role of facilitator in the arts also requires the facilitator to learn and to demonstrate techniques in the arts, not necessarily to the point of mastery but of sufficient skill to provide examples and choice for the artist. Facilitators who take an active role in the art experience through their own creations can provide leadership in experimentation, styles, and appropriate behaviour. The role of resource person requires the facilitator to be able to readily access materials and to provide avenues for the child to access information and styles in order to enrich the art experience.

Minimizing restrictions on children's artistic expression and art production allows the child to freely express him/herself. The most destructive restriction placed on children's art today is that of standards. The art is said to be good or bad, age-appropriate or not age-appropriate, worthy of the bulletin board or not worthy, correct form or incorrect form, on topic or not on topic, and so on. These judgments, based on someone's idea of what is acceptable, have no place in the promotion of children's expression of Self through art media. They are useful in formal art instruction but not when art is being used as a vehicle of self-expression. In many cases, the adult's standards are unrealistic and counterproductive to creativity. They can be very inhibiting, especially in the early stages of experimentation and discovery for the child. If the goal were to produce competent artists, then perhaps criticism and value statements would be of some merit.

The goal and philosophy behind creative expression of Self through art mediums is to provide an atmosphere of acceptance and respect in which the child can be expressive and create something truly individual and, in this creation, find value and self-regard. This philosophy gives sufficient license to allow the child to explore and create in whatever way best suits his/her needs. It also allows the child to make use of areas of the brain that are seldom exercised. Intuition and resourcefulness are often not given the emphasis they warrant. In his book Development Through Drama, Brian Way (1967) states, "Intuition might well be considered the most important single factor in the development of inner resourcefulness, and full enrichment depends on this inner resourcefulness" (p. 5). Within this philosophy of free expression, the child relates to the facilitator as an equal. The adult becomes the resource person, the facilitator, and part of the art experience. This role complements the activity and the goal behind the activity. Once again, the least intrusive role provides optimum opportunity for personal and interpersonal growth.

Nevertheless, some limits and structure are important in the provision of activities in the arts. They provide safety, predictability, and order to the experience. Children need to feel safe in their environment in order to feel free to express themselves. Rules that limit invasion of personal space, ridicule, and destruction of materials are necessary in order to provide safety and order. Predictability that materials and boundaries will always be there also allows the child to feel safe and free. Order insures that the materials will be in the same place, that space will be free of obstacles, that sequencing of activities when necessary will be implemented, and that there will be a way to begin and end each activity.

The free expression of art, whether it is dance, drama, mime, music, or any of the graphic arts, is most often a metaphor for children's life situations; therefore, it can provide insight for them into who they are and possibly why they and others behave in the way that they do. Children communicate through art, and their expressions are statements about themselves. In most cases, these statements are obvious and need not be responded to directly at a conscious level. However, the facilitator may wish to use a portion of the art experience to ask children to talk about or translate their creations into their own words and meanings.

Facilitators trained in creative art therapies can provide the child with an opportunity to become more aware of what is being expressed. This must be done with great sensitivity to the artist, and with the understanding that what adults see in children's art is sometimes influenced by their own unconscious. Interpretations need to take the form of questions to the artist and not as statements of fact. These questions are meant to stimulate the child to become more self-aware and not to interrogate, interpret, or force disclosure. Self-disclosure sometimes happens as children become aware of their emotions and experiences as they are depicted in their art. These moments need to be handled with sensitivity and respect for the child.

Facilitators without formal training should question the artist out of a sense of curiosity rather than as an authority. Occasionally children will wish to interpret a dance, drawing, or creation on their own, and this should be encouraged. Children's creations should never be judged or analyzed by the untrained facilitator or the other children in the group. Most interpretations, and thus insights, come best from the artist, and in these cases the untrained facilitator can only patiently wait until they are realized.

A useful technique is to provide time at the end of the art period, or throughout the period, for children to tell the story or theme behind their creations. Questions from the facilitator or group members for clarification or to make an observation are appropriate provided that these are respectfully presented and that the artist feels comfortable with this form of dialogue. An open-ended, positively oriented discussion of what the art creation communicates is a very effective way of using art as an enjoyable and therapeutic exercise. These observations and clarifications can be useful contributors to the growth and development of the child's self-esteem.

Resistance to trying something new in the creative arts, like resistance to change, is a perfectly healthy response. Children need time to become comfortable with certain mediums and situations; therefore, time and patience have no equal. Art forms can be incorporated in other more familiar activities such as a favourite game, or can be done in conjunction with other activities such as drawing a picture in a discussion group. Drama can be introduced slowly with games and activities that require children to act or take centre stage but only for a short time. This gives them the opportunity to ease into such interventions that require more skill such as role-plays. Music and movement can be easily incorporated into many games and activities. This slow introduction of the art form gives the child more exposure to the medium or technique, providing for a wider variety of response with less stress.

Sometimes children decide not to become involved in the process and this is also a valid response. Inactivity can be a very productive state, and often a very necessary stage of development to the overall expression of Self. It, too, should be encouraged and fostered. This assures children that a wide variety of responses are acceptable and that they are free within the confines of their imaginations to do what is most important for them at that given moment. The creative art activities provided at the end of this chapter are presented from the simplest and least threatening activity to the more complex and demanding activities.

Personal Reflection – Images in Childhood

Take out paper and markers, crayons, etc. Find a quiet and comfortable spot. Quiet yourself until you feel fully relaxed. Think back through your childhood to your early years, 5 years old to 10 years old. What pictures, symbols, and colours come to mind? Allow as much time as you need, thinking about your early years and remembering.

Now sketch the most important symbols, pictures, shapes, etc., on the paper, and add words if you like, to better communicate their meaning.

Step back and look at your picture as if you were a stranger. What do you see?

_____

_____

_____

_____

_____

_____

Share your drawing with a friend, and tell them the story of your drawing.

> To create one's world in any of the arts takes courage.
>
> – GEORGIA O'KEEFFE

The Creative Milieu

Essential to the success of any expressive art project is the environment (Burns, 2006; Malchiodi, 2007; Rubin, 2005, 2010; Wright, 2003). The environment must allow for uninhibited expression. The ideal art environment would be one that allows the child to experiment in all the major art forms: art, music, movement, and drama.

Two work areas are needed: one, an area large enough for each child to have space to work individually but with very little open space; and two, a space large enough for all the children to move freely without fear of collision. Furniture can be rearranged in a classroom; tents and shelters can be erected on playgrounds and camping areas; or, a room with free access to a play area—all can be converted into excellent art environments.

Adequate lighting, heating, and a source of water are next on the list of essentials. Once the "housing" needs are met, an adequate source of materials and equipment will complete the physical needs of the environment. Here is a list of possible materials for the therapeutic milieu.

ART MATERIALS: Materials can include sand, mud, clay, plasticene, play dough, finger paint, oil paint, acrylic paint, poster paint, water colours, pastels, chalk, charcoal, crayons, markers, pencil crayons, felt pens, pen and ink, pencil, glue, paper of various sizes, colours, and textures, knives, sticks, rolling pins, and brushes. Other useful materials are natural substances such as bark, small stones, or dried flowers to glue or attach to paper or be used alone. Easels, boards, tables, chairs or cushions, drop sheets for clay and finger paint, and paint shirts for all can also be provided.

DRAMA SUPPLIES: Some examples are costumes, old clothes, hats, shoes, glasses, canes, makeup, jewelry, body paint, puppets, marionettes, and a puppet stage. Various props for improvisation can be hoops, sticks, rope, scarves, sheets, blankets, etc.

MUSIC ACCESSORIES: You can use various percussion instruments like blocks of wood, metal bars, glass bottles, triangles, drums, maracas, tambourines, bells, etc. Other instruments can include the ukulele, harmonica, guitar, piano, banjo, trumpet, recorder, etc. A sound system along with various musical selections is an important addition.

The arrangement of equipment and materials depends upon the types of programs provided and upon the physical layout of the room. Equipment and materials should be arranged to provide for easy transition from one activity to another. For example, clay, finger paint, painting, and related activities should be situated close to a water supply for easy access and clean up. The sound system should be easily transferred from one area to the next and be equipped with headphones to allow for quiet listening.

The more portable and versatile the materials and equipment in a creative arts milieu are, the more adaptable and fluid the environment is, allowing for a wide variety of artistic expressions. Simplicity in wall design and room furniture should provide a sense of order and openness for creative thought and maximum use of space. Decor should reflect a balance in terms of providing a variety of visual experiences for the artist without over-stimulating and confusing the child.

Personal Reflection – The Ideal Milieu

Find a comfortable spot and relax your physical Self and your intellectual Self. Summon up your knowledge of milieu and design, and imagine the perfect room for the expression of the arts. Take all the time you need to create this ideal space in your mind.

Draw the floor plan of this room, complete with details of the equipment.

List of equipment

_____

_____

_____

_____

_____

_____

_____

_____

_____

_____

Art: As a Medium of Self-Expression

The manipulation of art materials to express feelings, thoughts, and behaviours is a powerful form of communication and, in some instances, the most effective way for children to bring understanding, insight, and clarity into their lives. Children who have experienced trauma, abuse, loss and separation, physical or mental illness, social isolation, or other painful experiences often internalize these experiences, and artwork can assist them in dealing with these experiences either implicitly or explicitly (Levine & Kline, 2007; Naumburg, 1973; Rubin, 2005, 2010; Steele, 2009; Steele & Malchiodi, 2012).

Many times children have told someone how they feel but were ignored or misunderstood. Other times they may have been too ashamed or fearful of the consequences of sharing these experiences. And still other times they may have no conscious memory of the experience(s). Art therapy can assist children to express feelings, thoughts, and behaviours from both their conscious and unconscious mind in a way that is less threatening and more natural.

Regardless of the sophistication of the artwork, whether a scribble drawing or a detailed mural, artists express a part of themselves and their interpretation of their experience. The expression of feelings and thoughts through the use of art can result in a purging of these feelings, a release from them, or an expression of them in order to gain insight and understanding—all therapeutic outcomes for the artist. Children's natural closeness to their feelings and the fact that they are not always able to understand or effectively deal with them, makes art programming very beneficial. The style of expression and type of communication depends upon the child and the art medium selected.

The most fundamental art medium is a pointed stick and the earth. Children write their names in the sand; they draw plans of action and boundaries for games in the earth; and they create three-dimensional objects (like sand castles) out of the earth itself. Finger paint, plasticene, clay, and sand sculptures are more primitive, earthy, and base mediums. These basic art

> Painting is poetry that is seen rather than felt, and poetry is painting that is felt rather than seen.
>
> **– LEONARDO DA VINCI**

agents often provide a vehicle for the expression of basic urges and desires as well as a means of regressing to an earlier and more primal time of life.

Art materials vary from lead pencils to felt pens, from poster paints to oil paints, and from small pieces of white paper to large rolls of newsprint for making murals. The mediums used and the size of paper or physical boundaries of the artwork varies considerably. Children can be given the opportunity and encouragement to explore as many mediums of expression as are possible within the limitations of the environment. Play dough, clay, paper mache, wood, metal, and so on allow a three-dimensional approach to the art experience.

Pounding, pinching, and squeezing clay, and splattering paint can also be a way of releasing tension and anxiety. Drawing and colouring an abstract or a scene can offer the child a novel way to communicate. Craft mediums such as bark, paper tubes, magazine photographs, feathers, and string are useful in collages and three-dimensional art projects. The most effective art program provides a wide range of mediums and the opportunity to use them freely and spontaneously.

Drama: As a Way of Providing Insight

Drama allows children to express their feelings and thoughts and to recount their experiences and behaviours and those of others; it provides insight into their view of the world and how others view it (Landy, Weber, & Haen, 2004; Maier, 1991; Pinciotti, 1993; Warren, 2008). Drama in this context includes mime, plays, skits, acting out stories, puppet play, role-play, and improvisation. In most cases, actors are not given scripts or much direction from the facilitator and should be free to ad lib, diverge from the story line or plot, or provide their own script to other actors (Butler, 2000; Maier, 1991)

Drama can provide insight for the child in two ways: one, in the role as performer; and two, in the role of observer of the action. The child, as performer, can gain insight by experiencing through acting, how different characters view the world and how they relate to it. Children can also gain insight by playing themselves or by playing a significant character in their lives. Further insight can be obtained through discussing the thoughts and feelings that arise in the course of the acting. Children, in their role as observers, can discover how different characters think, behave, and relate. They can choose to use these characters as models of desirable and undesirable behaviour, of effective and ineffective ways of thinking, and of acceptable and unacceptable ways of relating to others. When observing their own behaviour as it relates to a character in a play or as someone playing them in a short skit, children get a chance to remove themselves emotionally from the situation and view their behaviour and that of others. This objectifying of experience often allows them to gain a lasting insight into how their behaviour affects others and, in turn, themselves.

Life skills can be taught through role-playing social situations such as travelling on the bus, getting help, asking a friend to dance, handling issues with parents, or speaking in public. Preschoolers often take on various roles in their play in order to learn and to practice social skills. The dramatic play area and housekeeping area are very busy and well-used spaces in the daycare centre. Those in middle childhood enjoy skits, mime, and short plays that have simple plots and little dialogue to remember. Preadolescents and adolescents enjoy a variety of styles of drama such as humorous skits, air guitar, rock musicals, improvisation, and for some, epic dramas, classical plays, and Broadway shows.

The activity section of this chapter has various warm-up exercises and dramatic activities that will assist in the use of drama with children. Chapter 13, "Relaxation, Imagery, and Guided Fantasy" has exercises that are excellent ways to set the stage for the child to utilize drama as a teaching, learning, and fulfilling activity.

Drama is also movement and nonverbal communication. The movement activities in this chapter will assist children to learn how to manipulate their bodies in order to better express themselves. Mime and improvisation are excellent ways to increase the child's dramatic skills and talents. Drama is a form of the arts that allows children to strengthen not only their ability to communicate, but also their ability to understand better the communication of others (Aguilar, Bedau, & Anthony, 2009). Life is a drama and, for many children, this drama is a struggle. The child and youth care professional, through the use of drama, can offer insight and new strategies to assist children in coping with life's struggles and can provide opportunities for them to realize their abilities and strengths.

Personal Reflection – Relationship Drama

Find a comfortable spot and relax. Concentrate on a relationship problem you are experiencing currently or have had in the past and one that is unresolved.

List the key persons involved and any other characters that are partially or indirectly involved.

_____

_____

_____

_____

_____

_____

_____

Replay a scenario in your mind that clearly represents the problem you are having. Take on the role of one or more of the significant characters, and play the scenario back in your mind taking this character's perspective. List any insights into this character.

_____

_____

_____

_____

_____

_____

_____

Replay the scenario from other characters' perspectives, and list any insights into any of these characters.

_____

_____

_____

_____

_____

_____

_____

_____

Finally, play yourself again, and be aware of key emotions, thoughts, and behaviours. List them here.

_____
_____
_____
_____
_____
_____
_____
_____

When all the characters are played, slow down your breathing and relax. Clear your mind, slow your pulse rate, and allow your thoughts to take you to a favourite peaceful place where your information can be assimilated.

Relax for five minutes. Write down any new awareness of the problem.

_____
_____
_____
_____
_____
_____
_____
_____

Movement: As a Vehicle of Expression

Movement is the expression of being alive; it is natural, necessary and, in many ways, life-giving. Movement, as a means of self-expression and communication, can be a positive and healthy vehicle for children to understand and feel comfortable with their feelings (Loman, 2006; Warren & Coaten, 2008). Movement expresses time, space, weight, force, locomotion, cooperation, isolation, and mood. When children are provided with opportunities to express themselves, nonverbal communication is often the most valid. Movement in the programming of activities for children, like art and music, provides a vehicle in which children can express what they cannot put into words. The diversity with which the physical Self can clearly express the unconscious Self makes movement activities excellent additions in all programming. There is self-expression in the way a toddler moves across the nursery floor, in the way a preschooler climbs, in the games of tag with school-age children, in the way an adolescent walks, and in all this common movement, a certain individuality exists. Activities such as art, drama, yoga, gymnastics, sports, dance, music, and play itself are a coordination of movements that express who I am and how I feel about myself.

Creative movement is unstructured movement and is focussed on the way a child moves in time and space. It can be expressed using music as an inspiration, or the child can create his/her own stimulation. The activity can purge emotions from the past; it can create emotions in the present; it can foster fantasies about how it will be in the future. This nonverbal expression of the Self allows the child to reveal feelings without the fear of reprimand, questioning from others, consequences, justification, explanation, embarrassment, and at times, conscious awareness. Creative movement is an excellent activity for children who are nonverbal, who are resistant to talking about their feelings, who have experienced trauma, and who are unaware of their feelings.

The other positive aspect of creative movement is its effect on the physical development of the child. The unstructured aspect of creative movement eliminates failure and thus frees the child to move in whatever way is desired. Movement to music pro-

> After silence, that which comes nearest to expressing the inexpressible is music.
>
> – ALDOUS HUXLEY

vides the child with an opportunity to practice motion skills with a beat that will enhance coordination. Body awareness is another aspect of creative movement that can be utilized in programming. Specific parts of the body can be emphasized and used in creative movement to enhance awareness and coordination of these parts. Creative movement, like centring, can assist in the integration of mind and body. The child who expresses emotion and thoughts nonverbally integrates the physical Self with the intellectual and emotional parts of the Self.

Creative movement activities can be done seated, lying, standing, and moving the whole body or specific parts. The amount of space necessary depends upon the activity and the number of participants. The milieu should conform to the conditions pointed out in the section on the creative milieu in this chapter. Also, the selection of music and props can be useful as it allows for the integration with the other performing arts outlined in this chapter.

Music: As Expression of Self

Music is a powerful medium. It is a strong emotional communicator, and it has the ability to change the emotional experiences of its listeners. Music has a number of therapeutic uses: it can be used to relax the child and as background for a relaxation exercise; it can be used in conjunction with an art experience as inspiration or as background; it can be used in drama exercises and productions in a variety of ways; it can be used as an impetus in movement exercises to allow children to express themselves and to interpret the music through their bodies; it can be used as dance music in much the same way as it is used in movement therapy; it can be used as a vehicle of emotional expression; and it can be used as a form of self-expression.

Music as an expression of the Self (Jones, 2000) and as a therapeutic agent (Campbell, 1997) is the primary focus in this chapter. Therapeutic programmers and facilitators can use music as a vehicle for children to express themselves at a feeling level, emotionally by relating emotional experiences from playing, singing, and listening to music, and at a sensory level by the physical sensations and messages music sends to the child through the body. Humans can actually hear music through the skin (Norden, 2007), so feeling the music is very real at a sensory level.

Classical music by the various composers provides a wide range of uses for the programmer such as background music or music to inspire feelings: Mozart, Beethoven, Chopin, Korsakoff, Strauss, Bach, Vivaldi, Wagner, Pachelbel, Handel, Mendelsohn and Satie are excellent sources. New age music by composers such as Ray Lynch, Michael Jones, Andreas Vollenweider, and many others provides good background and expressive music. Children's music by Sharon, Lois and Bram, Raffi, Bob Schneider, Pete Seeger, Peter, Paul and Mary, Sesame Street, Hap Palmer, and others are excellent sources for games, listening pleasure, dance, and background music. Popular, folk, and country music are also useful sources for all types of situations. The wider the variety of exposure to music, the more varied the experiences for the children.

There is no real shortcut to finding the right piece of music for the specific situation. A good strategy is for programmers and facilitators to listen to a particular piece of music, then experiment with the group and ask for feedback. Sometimes children will want to bring in their own favourite pieces, or they can make suggestions to the facilitator. When music is utilized, it has a way of adding a special element to the group experience that can promote cohesion and a sense of belonging. Music can add a sense of personal autonomy and positive self-esteem to the individual child.

Exercise 15:1

Research and locate tapes, discs, and records that are available to you. Try to select a wide range of musical types and styles. Listen to these selections as a programmer and facilitator of therapeutic experiences, and select music that you feel will be most useful to groups of children, listing them in the following categories and the following age ranges. Record the title of the composition, its author or performer, and where this piece of music is available.

RELAXATION: soft, quiet music that will slow down the activity level, reduce the amount of verbalization, and relax or deeply relax a group of children.

Ages 4 to 6

_____

_____

_____

Ages 7-9

_____

_____

_____

Ages 10-12

_____

_____

_____

Ages 13-15

_____

_____

_____

Ages 16-19

_____

_____

_____

Ages 20-25

_____

_____

_____

EMOTIONAL EXPRESSION: all types of music that will inspire anger, fear, joy, pride, sorrow, courage, and so on.

Ages 4 to 6

_____

_____

_____

Ages 7-9

_____

_____

_____

Ages 10-12

_____

_____

_____

Ages 13-15

_____

_____

_____

Ages 16-19

_____

_____

_____

Ages 20-25

_____

_____

_____

INSPIRATIONAL: all types of music that will inspire self-expression, through dance, movement, or art.

Ages 4 to 6

_____

_____

_____

Ages 7-9

_____

_____

_____

Ages 10-12

_____

_____

_____

Ages 13-15

_____

_____

_____

Ages 16-19

_____

_____

_____

Ages 20-25

_____

_____

_____

NARRATIVE: musical compositions that tell a story.

Ages 4 to 6

Ages 7-9

Ages 10-12

Ages 13-15

Ages 16-19

Ages 20-25

PLAY: music (all types of compositions) for games, to enhance enjoyment of the activity.

Ages 4 to 6

_____

_____

_____

Ages 7-9

_____

_____

_____

Ages 10-12

_____

_____

_____

Ages 13-15

_____

_____

_____

Ages 16-19

_____

_____

_____

Ages 20-25

_____

_____

_____

Now you have the beginning of a list of music that you will find useful for your work with children. As you use music with children, ask them for feedback and suggestions so that your list can be most effective. Update and revise your list periodically to keep it current.

Review

- Art forms such as drawing, sculpting, acting, and moving provide emotional outlets for children.

- The creative arts can be a form of self-expression, a means of providing insight, or can be used to set a mood.

- The expressive arts milieu needs to be designed for safety, comfort, and free expression.

- Facilitators of creative arts experiences usually take on a laissez-faire role.

- It is important for facilitators to honour the child's expression of Self though the various art mediums and not to judge or interpret it.

- Art mediums can assist children in integrating left and right hemispheric activity.

The following and concluding chapter in this text Chapter 16, "Special Programs," provides the learner with four detailed and successive therapeutic activity programs for children. These programs form a basis for further group development in therapeutic activities.

The following are a series of therapeutic interventions intended to act as resources for the student or novice practitioner who wishes to practice his/her skills in facilitating activities in the arts with children and youth.

> "The aim of art is to represent not the outward appearance of things, but their inward significance."
> – ARISTOTLE

Therapeutic Interventions

Music

DANCE TO THE MUSIC

This is a non-threatening activity that works well with all groups as long as you get the music right. Put on a musical selection that has an upbeat tempo. You may want to choose a selection that is popular with the group or ask for suggestions.

Ask group members to move, run, or dance freely in time to the music. Inform the group that when you stop the music they must freeze in that position. Stop the music suddenly, and ask members to hold that position for about 10 seconds, check into how they are feeling both at a sensory level and an emotional level, and then resume play.

NAME THAT TUNE

This activity is a good icebreaker and group favourite. The facilitator will need to choose a series of musical selections that are familiar to the group.

Divide the group into teams of 2–3 players each. Play the musical selections one at a time; the team players are asked to shout out the name of the song and/or artist as soon as they recognize it.

Variation: Ask the children to sit in a circle. As a demonstration, the facilitator will clap out the rhythm of a song familiar to the group members. The group will be asked to then name the song. Then go around the circle giving each participant a chance to clap out a rhythm for the group to guess.

GROUP FAVOURITE

Ask the participants to think of a song that is known to all the group members. Inform them that the object of the game is to try to get as many group members to stop singing their own song and sing your song along with you. Play begins with participants singing their favourite song. Group members are allowed to switch songs at any time. Allow two minutes for play. When you stop, see who has managed to get the biggest group together.

MY TYPE OF MUSIC

This activity is a favourite with group members as well as facilitators. Some preparation is needed ahead of time. Ask group members to bring in 1-3 selections of their favourite songs. Ask members to play one of their selections and to comment on why this song is a favourite. The facilitator may wish to ask for comments from group members as well.

Members can be encouraged to write out the lyrics and discuss them with the group.

The group facilitator will now have a selection of music to use with the group.

WHAT I SEE WITH MY EARS

Select a composition of music that is well known to the group, perhaps a popular song, holiday tune, song from a specific genre, or classical or instrumental music that you feel would inspire children to visualize. Hand out the art materials to the group members, and be sure to have extra paper available for this activity. A relaxation exercise works well with this activity (see Chapter 13, "Relaxation, Imagery, and Guided Fantasy").

Instruct the group that you will play a piece of music or a series of musical selections, and then group members will be encouraged to draw the images that the music produces in their minds or imagination. Assure them that they may begin by making random shapes or lines on the paper and that they can use several sheets of paper if they wish.

WHAT I HEAR IN MY HEART

Ask group members to bring in a musical selection that causes them to feel one or more emotions. Participants in turn play their selection, or a portion, to the group, and the group is asked to determine which of the emotions it inspires in them.

IMPROVISATION

This series of activities moves the group step by step towards musical performance and does not require any musical training.

AIR GUITAR

This activity requires some music and lots of imagination. It can be done solo or in groups. It can also be air drums, sax, keyboard, bass, or voice. A musical selection is decided upon by the performer(s). The activity begins with playing the musical selection while the participant(s) mime the performance of the musician(s).

LIP SYNC

Group members put on a musical selection of their choice and mouth or mime the words to the song over the artists' voices. Dramatization of the performance, as in Air Guitar, is also an option.

KARAOKE

This is a little more sophisticated than Air Guitar and Lip Sync and requires a karaoke machine, which re-creates a popular performance of a song without the vocals. The Karaoke player(s) provide the vocal(s).

DRUMMING

Drumming can be an excellent form of nonverbal expression and is usually a favourite with most group members. If there are not enough drums for each member, they can be shared. Plastic pails, waste baskets, and flower pots make good improvised drums.

Drumming with novice drummers begins with the facilitator playing a series of simple beats for the group to imitate. After a time, group members can take turns playing out a beat and the group repeating it (this is termed "call and response").

Drumming can also be improvisational and/or chaotic. Facilitators can suggest themes for the drummers to drum to such as, death, loss, freedom, anger, or pride.

Movement

ONE HAND AND ANOTHER

Ask group members to sit in a circle. Slowly demonstrate a movement with your right hand (snapping fingers, waving, circling, wiggling fingers, etc.). Now ask the group to imitate your movement. Make another movement, and ask the players to join in and repeat the movement as accurately as possible. Now make 2-3 movements and ask the group to follow. Then, switch hands and demonstrate the same movements with your left hand, and ask the players once again to join in and repeat the movement several times.

Variation: Use both hands and move them together in the same way and in the same direction. Have the players copy the movements. Introduce a new movement and have the players follow. Gradually make the movements more difficult. If you see that everyone can follow the pattern easily, change from large gestures to small gestures, or vice versa.

MY NAME, YOUR MOVE

Ask group members to stand in a circle and to call out their names one by one. The next time around the circle, the first player calls out his/her name and adds a movement. The rest of the circle must then call out the player's name and imitate, as best they can, the first player's move. Each player then takes a turn to call out his/her name and add a movement. The group in turn repeats the players name and his/her movement

SEVEN MOVEMENTS

This activity works well with music and can be modified to three moves for younger children. Select a series of the group's favourite musical selections that contain a variety of tempos and beats.

Ask the group to spread out around the room, and inform them that you will be calling out seven different movements—gallop, jump, hop, walk, shuffle, crawl, and slither. Then call out the movement words one by one and give the group enough time to enjoy each movement.

Now ask them to select their favourite movement, of the seven just performed, and repeat it over and over as you play the various selections of music.

When this is accomplished, ask the group members to form sub-groups based on each member's favourite move. Ask the groups to face one another and perform their favourite move together when they hear the music.

Now ask members in each group to decide together on what other move they want to add to their favourite move. Once all have decided, request groups to perform their favourite move along with this new move. And then, request that they add another and so on until group members are all doing their own series of the seven movements.

BE A BIRD, BEE, OR TREE
Ask the children to close their eyes and to imagine what the music is saying to them.

Select appropriate musical selections and ask the children to move to the music as if they were:

• an eagle or other bird soaring among the clouds

• a seed growing into a beautiful flower

• a member of a marching band in a parade

• a honey bee flying from flower to flower

• clowns performing at a circus or carnival

• mountain climbers going up a steep mountain

• tiptoeing across the room so as not to wake your pet mouse

Variation: These exercises can be combined with the mime exercises. Props can be added to enhance arm movement such as scarves, brightly coloured strips of cloth or ribbons, or balloons on small pieces of cord.

STRIKE A POSE

Ask the group to form a circle and stand in one spot. Instruct them that you are going to ask them to try on a number of poses. The facilitator may need to demonstrate to begin. Here are some ideas:

• Making yourself very, very small

• Puffing yourself up into a huge person

• Jumping up as high as you can

• Bouncing around like a spring

• Standing fixed to one spot in terror

• Trembling and shaking with rage/anger

• Shuddering with fear

• Bursting into laughter

• Screaming and yelling for help

• Skulking and creeping away in fear

• Standing fearless against the enemy

LET THE BODY LEAD

This is an activity that can be conducted with music. Some children may have difficulty leading with internal body parts.

Ask the group to stroll or move around the play space in a natural and relaxed way. Instruct them not to look at others but to try to focus their attention inward on their bodies. Allow them to move until they appear comfortable.

Now ask the group to continue to move at that comfortable pace and to focus their attention on a specific body part such as an arm, foot, elbow, or ear. Instruct players to stop moving once they have decided on a body part.

Once everyone has stopped, instruct the group members to move around the room again but this time to lead with the body part chosen. They can move at any speed they like provided they do not run into one another. Continue the activity by periodically asking the players to lead with a different body part.

Now ask the group to go back to moving around the play space in the slow natural walk that began the activity. Once they get back into that rhythm, ask them to imagine an internal body part such as the heart, brain, stomach, or even a blood cell. Instruct players to stop moving once they have decided on an internal body part.

Once everyone has stopped, instruct the group members to move around the room again but this time to lead with the internal body part. They can move at any speed they wish provided they do not collide with one another. Continue the activity by periodically asking the players to lead with a different internal body part.

FEELING THE MOTION

Ask the group members to stand and form a circle. They must stay in one spot for this exercise, but they can move their feet up and down. Instruct the group that you will be calling out a variety of names for physical sensations and emotions (hot, cold, anger, sadness) and they are to move their bodies as if they are experiencing that feeling. Continue this until each feeling has been enacted.

Now this time, tell group members that they can move around the room in order to express the feeling. Call out the same group of feelings or another series, and ask the group members to express their feelings with their whole body.

WATCH ME NOW

This is a favourite for teens and pre-teens to show off their moves.

Ask the group to form a circle giving themselves lots of room to move. Instruct the group that you are going to call out each member one at a time to come into the centre and show off their favourite dance moves.

This is also a good activity to have group members teach one another dance moves.

KARATE – HI YAW

This is another activity in which players can show off their moves. This time it is their karate moves.

Ask the group to stand and form a circle leaving about 60 centimetres between each player. Inform the group that this is an activity in which they are required to tag the player beside them, either the one on their left or their right. Tagging can only be done hand on hand. Instruct the group that, when you call out the word "Karate," they are required to freeze into their favourite karate pose. And when you call out "Hi Yaw," they can make only one move to tag their frozen teammate, and he/she can make only one move to avoid being tagged.

Drama

MIME

Mime is the oldest and most universal art form; it is both drama and expressive movement. It is also an easier and less threatening way to begin to use drama as a therapeutic tool. There are endless possibilities for mime, and a few are given below. All of these can be accompanied by suitable musical selections.

Popcorn - Instruct the group to find a space in the environment where they have room to move. Ask them to squat down and make themselves a kernel of popcorn. Suggest to them that the heat has been turned on and that they are getting warm, which is making them expand until suddenly they pop. Now try the same exercise with the whole group close together, as if in a popcorn popper.

Flower - Instruct the group to find a comfortable space. Ask them to squat down and make themselves as small as possible. Suggest to them that they are a seed of their favourite flower. Tell them that it is beginning to rain gently, which is causing them to germinate and to grow into a beautiful flower. Caution them to grow slowly.

Pass the Object - Ask the group to form a circle. Suggest that you have an imaginary object in your hand. Begin with hand-miming a balloon and progress to a ball, medicine ball, worm, snake, flaming torch, etc. Pass the imaginary object around the circle.

Variation: Ask the group to shape different objects out of imaginary clay. The first person hand-mimes an imaginary ball, then claps his/her hands together as if to flatten it, then passes the flattened ball to the player on the left. The second player begins then to hand-mime the formation of another object that, once completed, will be handed to the next person in the circle who will handle it as though he/she knows what it is. This same player then flattens the object and passes it on to the player on the left who in turn shapes a new object. This continues until the imaginary clay has been passed around the circle.

Pick an Action - Write out a series of actions (e.g., starting an automobile, moving a piano, carrying out the garbage, skiing down a hill, eating dinner, painting a house, etc.). Put each action on a slip of paper and into a bowl. Instruct each member to come up one at a time and pick an action. They have 30 seconds to act it out for the group. The group is to guess what the action is.

FAVOURITE CHARACTER

Ask the participants to think of their favourite fairy or folk tale or comic-book character. Then have them concentrate on a unique trait that makes their favourite character different from other characters.

When they are ready, ask them to imagine that they are all at a party and must interact with each other in character. Explain that the object of the exercise is to see if the players can guess what character is being portrayed.

Give the group ample time to act out their characters, and then stop the play and ask members to guess who each participant was acting out.

ACT A STORY, FOLK TALE, OR MYTH

This activity allows children to live out a story in dramatic form. Taking a part in the myth or tale can make it more meaningful.

Choose a favourite tale or myth, and read it out to the participants. Allow children to audition for any or as many parts as they wish. Do not limit characters to humans or animals; children can sometimes derive more meaning or direction from playing a plant or inanimate object. The audition requires that they act out a small section of the character's part in the story. The facilitator chooses who is best for what part (each part can be played by more than one person). Once the auditioning is over, the group acts out the story.

ROLE-PLAY

Role-play can be an excellent way for children to gain insights into their own behaviour and that of others. This activity should be presented after the group has had some time to do the mime exercises and some of the other less demanding drama activities. Begin by asking volunteers to act out the scenarios listed below:

• a teacher trying to control a room of unruly students

• a child and youth care worker trying to motivate a group of bored teenagers

• the classroom bully trying to get what he/she wants from a group of peers

• a police officer among a group of gangsters trying to convince them to go straight

• a group of teenagers trying to get a friend to try drugs, smoking, or drinking

• a room full of babies at lunchtime in the daycare centre

• a pregnant woman stuck on an elevator who is about to give birth

• a group of unwilling preschoolers asked to share their toys at nursery school

Variations: Other possibilities might be acting out scenarios that require the participants to act out creatures from another planet, various wild and domestic animals, robots, or machines.

PERSONAL ROLE-PLAY

Once the group members appear to be comfortable acting and have reached a level of trust among one another, ask them to come up with difficult scenarios in their lives that they did not handle well or ones that they wish to rehearse to insure that they handle them in a way that pleases them.

Children can act as directors to their personal role-play, take on other characters' roles, or act out their part in the scene. They can ask the group for ideas about how they might handle the situation or for feedback to get insight into the characters in the scene.

SOCIO-POLITICAL PLAYS

This activity is used as a tool for youth to develop and increase their awareness about a social or political issue. The group decides on an issue or topic that is affecting them either locally or globally. This is an excellent activity to utilize the artistic talents of the group.

Members develop a skit, mime, vignette, or reenactment of a story to focus their awareness, and that of those around them, on the issue. Participants decide on script, staging, audience participation, music, scenery, and all other elements of the performance.

Art

SCRIBBLE DRAWING

Sometimes with art activities it is difficult to get started, and children need a structure to help them to begin to create. The scribble drawing provides such structure.

Instruct the children to choose a colour of the art medium provided and a sheet of paper. They should then find a spot in the room where they feel comfortable and alone with their thoughts (this exercise can also be done to music). Once they feel comfortable, they are to take the colour and scribble over the sheet of paper. Allow them to scribble for approximately one minute. When they have finished, they are to look at their page from all different angles in order to locate familiar shapes, figures, or objects that are within the scribbling, similar to the way we see shapes in the clouds on a cloudy day. The group is then instructed to outline one of these shapes in a different colour. They will get this different colour by trading with a group member. When the outline is completed, they are to give their drawing a title.

THE BLOB

This is another technique useful when the artist is stuck or does not know where to start. This activity is used with paints, clay, or play dough. See the recipes for paint mixture and play dough at the end of this chapter.

When the art materials are passed out, the children are instructed to dab or drag the paintbrush over the paper, or take a piece of clay and shape it with their eyes closed. Next, they are to create a drawing using the dab, drag, or clump as the focal point.

CRAYON TAG

Using a large sheet of paper for each pair of children and one crayon each, instruct them to draw a racetrack onto the sheet of paper. When their track is complete, they are to take turns chasing each other's crayon along the track. One player will go first and start drawing his crayon down the track; the other player is to chase him and try to reach the end of the track first.

A game of tag can develop when one player chases the other player's crayon, using the paper as the playing area. When the chaser tags the opponent's crayon, then they switch roles.

COLLAGES

There is some preparation needed prior to facilitating this activity. Collect old magazines that are age- and gender-appropriate. The activity also requires a pair of scissors for each participant and a piece of heavy paper or cardboard to act as a canvas for the collage.

Instruct the group that this is an art exercise that requires them to find magazine pictures that represent their likes, dislikes, heroes, villains, or anything that would make a statement about who they are as a person.

Distribute the materials and give the group plenty of time to create.

Variation: Arrange the group in pairs and provide a theme such as Friendship, Pain, Anger, Wishes, etc. Partners will select pictures that represent the theme and create a collage together.

SELF-PORTRAIT

This is an art exercise that provides an avenue for children to share their feelings of how they view themselves. These portraits can reveal aspects of the child that may not have surfaced or been discussed.

Instruct the group members to create a self-portrait. It can be a silhouette, a figure drawing, or an abstract. The portrait should reveal information about the artist such as likes and dislikes, strengths and weaknesses, tastes in music and clothes, etc.

When the group members have completed their self-portraits, participants will be asked to display their pictures and, one at a time, introduce themselves by describing their portrait to the group.

Variation: This exercise can be accomplished by using clay or finger-paints as a medium. Group members construct an abstract or symbolic representation of themselves.

MASKS

Masks are very self-revealing and make an excellent activity in which to explore self-esteem.

Distribute pie plates, crayons or paints, construction paper, and assorted materials (e.g., bark, feathers, shells, beads, etc.). Instruct the children to use the material provided and create a mask.

Masks can be made from paper mache using a frame of chicken wire as a mold. They can also be made from rolls of plaster used in the making of casts. These rolls can be obtained through a medical supplier. See the end of this chapter for a recipe for making paper mache.

For this mask, the group is paired up, and the masks are made using the human face as the mold. The pair is instructed to choose who will go first. This person is to cover their face with petroleum jelly. The plaster rolls are moistened and laid across the face to form a mask. The person can choose to have holes made for the eyes, nose, or mouth. They must have at least the nostrils or the mouth clear in order to breathe. The mask will dry in approximately 15 minutes. As it dries, it will begin to pull from the face, and when it is dry, it will easily pull off the face. These masks can dry for a day and then be painted.

FAMILY PORTRAIT

Family portraits are as revealing as self-portraits in that they show a number of aspects about the family that may not have been revealed through conversations with the child.

Distribute art materials and instruct the group to draw a picture of their family doing something together. When the participants have completed their drawings, they are asked to display their picture, introduce their family to the group, and tell three things about their family.

Variation: Pass out a large piece of clay or play dough (see recipe for play dough at the end of this chapter).

Ask group members to divide their clay into pieces, one for each family member, and make sure they have one piece for themselves. Once they have the required number of pieces, instruct them to close their eyes at first, think about that family member, and mold the clay as they are concentrating on the family member. Once they feel ready, ask them to open their eyes and complete the shape in any way they wish.

DRAW ME A LIFE STORY

This activity opens the door to a wide variety of responses and possibilities for both artist and facilitator. Children have the option of exploring any experience, either positive or negative in content.

Participants are asked to draw a picture that would tell a story about them—a life story—and one that they are comfortable sharing with the group.

Once completed the participants are asked to introduce their artwork and tell the story behind the picture. Group members are able to ask the artist questions for clarification or interest.

AN UNHAPPY MOMENT

This activity, like the previous one, gives the artist a spectrum of possible responses. The medium here is clay, play dough, finger paint, or splatter paint (see recipes for these at the end of this chapter). It could merely be a moment of unhappiness, or it may be much more than that.

Group members are asked to recreate a moment in their lives that was an unhappy experience and one they are comfortable sharing with the group.

Once completed, the participants are asked to introduce their artwork and tell the story behind the creation. Group members are able to ask the artist questions for clarification or out of interest.

THREE SELVES

This is an excellent activity to provide opportunities for children, and in particular teens, to develop or increase their self-awareness. It should be conducted in a well-established group as it may make some children feel vulnerable.

Begin with a discussion with the group on the concept of: a Personal Self—the parts of us that are private or that we show only to our family and close friends; the Social Self—the parts of our Self that we allow the world to see—our outward personality; and the Ideal Self—the Self we want to develop into in the future.

This activity can be enhanced by adding a relaxation exercise along with a guided fantasy focussed on meeting each one of the three Selves.

Distribute the art materials along with three sheets of paper for each participant and ask them to draw their three Selves.

RECIPES FOR ART MATERIALS

Paint Mixture: This type of paint washes out of clothes and is an excellent medium for all ages. It can have a thick consistency, which is good for easel drawing. It can be mixed as thick as an oil paint or as thin as a watercolour.

In a saucepan, add one cup (1C) of dry laundry starch OR one and one half cups (1 1/2C) of liquid laundry starch. Slowly add four cups (4C) of water to dry mixture OR three cups (3C) to the liquid starch and put on a low heat. Stir the mixture until it thickens into a paste.

Remove the mixture from the heat source and add one tablespoon (1 tbs) of glycerin or mineral oil. Mix well.

Add one cup (1C) of soap flakes or laundry detergent and mix thoroughly.

Store this mixture in the refrigerator or in an airtight container.

This mixture is then mixed with dry tempera or poster paint, adding enough water to get the desired consistency.

Finger Paint: In a saucepan, add five cups (5C) of water to one cup (1C) of cornstarch and heat on a low heat until the mixture thickens and is a clear colour. Allow the mixture to cool and then add one cup (1C) of soap flakes or laundry detergent and mix thoroughly. Powdered tempera or poster paint can be added to produce the various colours. Talcum powder can also be added to improve consistency.

Play Dough: Mix two cups (2C) of flour and one cup (1C) of salt together in a mixing bowl. In a separate bowl, mix one cup (1C) of lukewarm water, one tablespoon (1tbs) of salad oil, and two to four drops of food colouring.

Gradually add the liquid to the dry mixture of salt and flour and mix as you blend. Mix and knead well. Repeat the procedure until you have all the different colours desired.

Store the play dough in a plastic bag or container and refrigerate or keep in a cool place.

Paper Mache: Buy premixed wallpaper paste or buy the powered paste and mix according to directions.

Cut or tear various sizes of strips of paper.

In a plastic tub or basin, soak the newspaper in the paste mixture.

There are various methods of using paper mache. It can be layered over a frame usually made of wire, especially for larger projects. It can be molded with the hands into various shapes when the paper is thoroughly soaked.

CHAPTER 16

Special Programs

Maurice, ex-gang leader of the Scorpions, who had lived a life of crime, was now making his last turn on to the final leg of a 26-mile foot race. In a way, he had trained for this race all his life, and today he was fulfilling a life-long dream. He smiled as a wheelchair competitor raced past him and in a faint whisper said, "You can make it."

"Man, can those guys fly!" he thought. "Handicaps are in the eyes of the beholder." Upon thinking this, he was reminded of the handicaps he had to deal with in his lifetime—the poverty, the drugs, the violence, and worst of all, the desperate awareness that no one cared. "I have overcome all that," he said to himself. "Thanks to God and my friends, and now another milestone in my recovery." The last mile of the race was now before him, and Maurice knew that this was a very critical part of his conquest. It is at this point that many runners lose their concentration, injure themselves, or drop from exhaustion. He stayed focussed by reciting his affirmations, "I am lovable and capable. Nothing is out of my grasp."

As he chanted these lines, his thoughts drifted to the one person who had been the most influential in his personal growth, Jack. A youth worker, Jack had met him on the street one day and struck up a conversation with him. This encounter changed his entire life. It was a slow and painful journey with many hard times. Five years ago he had been on the streets in New York, and now, he was about to complete the Boston Marathon. He smiled as the finish line came into view and silently thanked himself for giving what only he could give—the gift of Self.

> The seeds
> of great
> discoveries
> are constantly
> floating
> around, but
> they only take
> root in the
> minds well-
> prepared to
> receive them.

– JOSEPH HENRY

This final chapter takes into account all that has been discussed in the previous chapters and presents a series of therapeutic activity programs that provide group members with special training in the area of personal and interpersonal life-skills. Initially this series addresses how to understand, appreciate, and learn from feelings, thoughts, and behaviours. This basic information allows children to benefit in their present situation and sets the stage for the continuing group development provided in the rest of the special programs. The second topic shifts from feelings, thoughts, and behaviours to the Self and helps children to begin or continue the journey of self-discovery. The ability to learn from the Self and to incorporate this learning into self-development and healthy living, as with the first topic, benefits children in the present and also provides them with the knowledge and experience to further benefit from the topics to follow. Developing social relationships, which is perhaps the most vital of all life-skills, is presented next to the group. The focus here is on assisting children in developing, improving, and integrating social skills into their daily lives. The final topic is about the most devastating loss, apart from the loss of Self, a child can experience—the loss of family. This last topic in the special programs assists the child in recovering from the trauma of separation and divorce. The previous topics and sessions have been orchestrated to this point to best prepare the child for dealing with this incredible and often devastating loss.

Special programs helped a special person like Maurice to fulfill a life-long dream. They were instrumental in changing a troubled adolescent into a healthy, disciplined, young adult. The student or novice facilitator can conduct special programs as long as they have a seasoned staff member as a co-facilitator. A support staff of psychiatrists, psychologists, social workers, or other experienced personnel is necessary for the safety and effectiveness of the programs. The following program guides are intended to act as parameters for the facilitator's individual program needs. They cover the basic issues in each program area and provide a variety of ways in which to stimulate discussions. The facilitator may wish to add, subtract, or rearrange the program structure to suit a specific group's needs. Stories that pertain to the topic are an excellent way to begin and end the program. Warm-up and cool-down activities that allow children to express themselves in all areas of development round out the effectiveness and the overall enjoyment of the program.

Each topic, following an initial warm-up, begins with a discussion. This discussion should start with a review of what was discussed in the previous session. Encourage all members to assist in the review. Also, prior to beginning the current group discussion, it is useful to outline the session, giving group members a good idea of what the upcoming group discussion will be like. And finally, a recap or summary of the session prior to the cool-down activity assists in determining how the group is functioning following the discussion and gives the children a final opportunity to discuss the topic.

Safety and comfort levels are always a consideration when facilitating group process (see Chapter 4, "The Therapeutic Group"). It is always helpful to remind group members periodically that they may not want to discuss or divulge painful or recent events with the group. It is essential to assure them that they do not have to share all their thoughts or experiences with the group, only those that they are comfortable sharing. During the relationship-building process (see Chapter 6, "Developing Therapeutic Relationships"), the facilitator may wish to set up an agreement with each child should he/she wish to share his/her experience in private. This reassurance provides the child with the necessary protection to enable him/her to discuss and deal with whatever surfaces during the group experience.

Another safety feature in managing therapeutic groups is a group "check-in" and "check-out." The check-in entails going around the group and asking each member how they are feeling and asking them to briefly highlight their time away from the group. The check-out comes at the end of the discussion period and is a time to ask each group member how he/she is feeling at that point. These "checks" can be very helpful, especially for children living under stressful circumstances. Finally, facilitators may wish to assign homework to further support the children in the change and development process.

These programs are developed for groups who have moved into the second or third stage of group development (see Chapter 4, "The Therapeutic Group"), and in most cases, participants should be at least seven years old. The program is cognitive and behavioural in orientation, however the warm-up and cooldown activities (see Chapter 3, "Designing Therapeutic Programs) should be focussed more on sensory and emotion-based experiences. The programs are divided into six sessions which can be adapted to fit a six, ten, or twelve week/session time period.

Topic 1:
Feelings, Thoughts, and Behaviours

This topic is an excellent way to begin most group programs as it sets a standard for discussing feelings, thoughts, and behaviours. It assists the group members in appreciating the connections between the three and begins to teach participants how to manage and learn from them. This group is also recommended as a prerequisite for all the groups outlined in this chapter.

Session 1

The focus of this session is on thoughts, probably the least threatening of the three, as most children are not criticized as readily for their thoughts as they are for their behaviours and their feelings. It is important for the participants to begin to appreciate their thoughts and not judge them as good or bad but as products of who they are and their experiences in the world. Thoughts can be pleasant and unpleasant, and they are an important part of each individual.

This group will require some preparation: art materials and paper.

WARM-UP ACTIVITIES

Discussion: Pleasant and Unpleasant Thoughts

Ask the group to sit down and form a circle. Begin by providing the group with examples of pleasant thoughts. Ask them to think of two examples of their own pleasant thoughts—thoughts that make them feel good. Using the examples provided by the participants, formulate a discussion that will clarify for them what constitutes a pleasant thought and what effect that thought has on them.

Now give examples and explain to the group what an unpleasant thought is. Ask the group members to recall one or two thoughts that they found unpleasant. Conduct a discussion around the examples given by the group.

Ask group members to draw a picture of what a pleasant thought would look like and what an unpleasant thought would look like.

When they are finished, ask group members to share with the group, if they are comfortable doing so, their artwork depicting their pleasant and unpleasant thoughts.

COOL-DOWN ACTIVITIES

Session 2

The intention of this session is to discuss feelings in a similar manner as thoughts. Feelings can be comfortable or uncomfortable but they should not be judged as good or bad. Feelings just are, and we often have little control over how we feel, only how we respond to our feelings.

WARM-UP ACTIVITIES

Discussion: Comfortable and Uncomfortable Feelings

Ask the group to sit down and form a circle. Begin by discussing with the group the difference between sensations and emotions (see Chapter 12, "Dealing with Feelings" for an explanation and examples), both of which make up our feelings.

Ask the group to select two comfortable sensations and two comfortable emotions. Instruct group members to focus their attention on one of these comfortable feelings (either sensations or emotions) and recall a time when they felt that way.

Organize a discussion around the examples given by the group participants. When each group member has given both their examples of comfortable feelings, ask them to recall their uncomfortable ones and the situations when they felt that way. Continue the discussion focussing on their specific examples of uncomfortable feelings.

When the group has completed this part, ask for a volunteer to role-play their example of an uncomfortable feeling, or provide an example for the group to act out. Conduct a role-play session and ask the group for comments and feedback.

COOL-DOWN ACTIVITIES

Session 3

This session is directed at assisting children to appreciate that behaviours are inappropriate in some situations and appropriate in others. One behaviour (running) can be acceptable in one social situation (recess) and unacceptable in another (classroom).

This group will require some preparation; you will need art materials and a large sheet or roll of paper suitable for a group mural. Divide the mural paper in two sections with a vertical line down the middle, and tape up the mural paper before the group arrives.

WARM-UP ACTIVITIES

Discussion: Appropriate and Inappropriate Behaviours

Explain to the group that behaviour is appropriate and inappropriate based on the context in which the behaviour is exhibited. Ask group members to recall either a situation when they felt that their behaviour was inappropriate or a situation where an adult or peer judged their behaviour as being inappropriate. When each group member has an example of an inappropriate behaviour, begin the discussion about inappropriate behaviour using the group's examples. Ask group members to identify their feelings and thoughts prior to their inappropriate behaviours.

Now ask the group to recall a time when they felt that their behaviour was appropriate or a time when an adult or a peer judged their behaviour as appropriate. When each group member has an example, continue the discussion on behaviour using the group's examples.

Ask the group to gather up some art materials and find a spot on the left hand side of the mural. Instruct members to draw an example of an appropriate behaviour on the paper. Once completed, they may now go over to the right hand side and draw an example of an inappropriate behaviour. Discuss the mural contents with the group.

COOL-DOWN ACTIVITIES

Session 4

Session 4 focusses on the variety of connections within the feelings-thoughts-behaviours triad. It assists children to appreciate that there are these connections and that one can cause the other. This session also attempts to prepare children to learn to act on this information.

WARM-UP ACTIVITIES

Discussion: Linking Feelings, Thoughts, and Behaviours

Ask the group to find a comfortable position anywhere in the play space. Play some music that will set the mood for relaxation, and conduct a relaxation exercise (see Chapter 13, "Relaxation, Imagery, and Guided Fantasy" for relaxation exercises). When the group appears to be relaxing, ask them to focus their attention on an unpleasant situation. Ask them to become aware of how they were feeling both physically and emotionally before, during, and after the situation. Ask them to recall some of their thoughts before, during, and after the situation. Ask them to observe and to listen carefully as they recall this situation from the past. Give them all the time that they need to complete this process.

Ask group members to share their examples. As each member recounts his/her situation, point out how thoughts and feelings affect the behavioural outcome. Suggest to the group that sometimes people blame others for their feelings and behaviours, but these are often a result of how the individual thinks about the situation. Often when individuals change their thoughts or feelings, their behaviour changes as a result. Explain how changing one or two of the three elements can result in a change in the third.

Here are three examples that may be helpful when explaining this concept to the group.

Changing Feelings and Thoughts to Alter Behaviour: Every time Tom's teacher calls out, "It's time for math," he gets agitated, starts to act-up, and thinks, "I hate math!" With practice Tom learns to take a deep breath after he hears the word "math" and change his thought to, "I don't like math, but I am going to do my best at it, and then we have recess." This has helped him to avoid acting-out in class.

Changing Behaviour and Thoughts to Alter Feelings: Every time Janis goes by Rick's old house she feels depressed that he has left the neighbourhood and that she has lost her best friend. In time, Janis has decided to walk home a different way, and when she thinks of Rick, she remembers their good times and sometimes sends him a note to say "Hi!" Now she is less depressed with the loss of her friend.

Changing Feelings and Behaviours to Alter Thoughts: Ramar keeps thinking that he will never make the baseball team. He feels nervous at practice and often makes simple mistakes on the playing field. With time and practice, Ramar has learned to settle his nervous feelings and stay a little bit longer after practice to work on basic playing skills. Now Ramar thinks that he has a good chance of making the team.

COOL-DOWN ACTIVITIES

Session 5

The next two sessions are intended to assist children to take the initiative to learn to regulate their feelings, thoughts, and behaviours. This session focusses on feelings (sensory and emotional experiences) and attempts to give the children ways in which they can channel and regulate these experiences. The information and interventions in Chapter 12, "Dealing with Feelings," provide a more detailed account of self-regulation. This session requires art materials and paper and can be conducted with clay, paint and other art mediums.

WARM-UP ACTIVITIES

Discussion: Regulating Feelings, Thoughts, and Behaviours.

Ask the group to find a comfortable position anywhere in the play space. Begin with a relaxation exercise (see Chapter 13, Relaxation, Imagery, and Guided Fantasy" for relaxation and guided fantasy exercises). When the group appears to be relaxed, ask them to focus their attention on a recent unpleasant experience they had at home. Conduct a guided fantasy experience for the group requiring them to re-experience this situation. When the guided fantasy is complete, ask group members to draw the situation.

When the children have completed their artwork, ask for a volunteer to explain his/her artwork and the details of the unpleasant experience at home. During this part of the session, discuss the experience with the children in terms of feelings, thoughts, and behaviours. When the group member has explained his/her artwork, discuss with the artist, and encourage input from the group, ways in which he/she could have altered feelings, thoughts, and/or behaviours to possibly bring about a different outcome. Continue until all group members have discussed their unpleasant experience.

COOL-DOWN ACTIVITIES

Session 6

This session completes the topic of feelings, thoughts, and behaviours and attempts to assist the children to practice self-regulation in a controlled setting.

WARM-UP ACTIVITIES

Discussion: Regulating Feelings, Thoughts, and Behaviours

Ask the group to sit down and form a circle, and conduct a review with them of the last session. Suggest to them that this time you want them to recall an unpleasant experience that happened outside the home and did not have anything directly to do with home life. Conduct a brief relaxation and guided fantasy to assist them to recall the details.

When it appears that the group is ready, explain to them that this time they will have an opportunity to act out their unpleasant experience. Ask for a volunteer to go first and to begin by briefly explaining his/her experience. Once the child is finished and key players have been identified, ask the group for volunteers, or the group member may wish to ask specific members, to play the characters in the unpleasant experience. Conduct Act One of the role-play with the child as the director and have him or her direct the players on how to act out the scene. In Act Two of the role-play, the director takes on his role in the scenario. When Act Two is completed, the child may wish to play one or two other characters in the scene to get a sense of their perspective. If so, continue to complete these vignettes until the child feels he/she clearly understands what happened. Once complete, discuss with the child how he/she may have altered feelings, thoughts, and/or behaviours to produce a more favourable outcome. The child may wish to ask the group for their input too. Act Three consists of the child, along with group volunteers, reenacting the same scenario, or one like it, including the child's new strategies. Continue until all group members have had the opportunity to act out their unpleasant experience.

COOL-DOWN ACTIVITIES

Topic 2: Self-Awareness

The topic of self-awareness is critical in working with children. So often the focus in various therapies is on self-esteem, however the building of the Self is based on how well an individual knows who they are as a person. Self-esteem takes a very long time to develop and change in children who have a negative view of who they are. Self-awareness however can be taught more easily and used effectively to assist the individual to appreciate who they are in relation to the person they wish to become. Self-awareness begins in infancy and develops over the life span (Demetriou & Kazi, 2001). It is an important factor in making meaning out of experience, whereas self-esteem is a highly cognitive and abstract concept, which is difficult for most young children and even for many young adults to understand and appreciate. Self-awareness can be explained and defined more easily than self-esteem and can be defined in more concrete terms at a sensory and behavioural level as well as at a cognitive level.

Children (Piaget 1962) and young adolescents (Elkind, 1967) are egocentric at various stages of development, and the facilitator needs to take this into account when discussing the Self. Self-awareness is often easier at these stages, but the group members may have difficulty appreciating differences amongst one another.

Session 1

This first session is used as a way to orient the children to the concepts and methods of attaining self-awareness. The discussion on awareness generally varies in complexity depending on the cognitive and developmental level of the group. This session will be geared to the young child, allowing the facilitator to use it as a base and to alter its level of complexity depending on the audience. This session requires art materials for a self-image drawing.

WARM-UP ACTIVITIES

Discussion: Awareness of Self

Present to the group the concept of self-awareness. "Self-awareness is getting to know your Self better and comparing that idea or picture of your Self with the type of person you want to be. Learning more about who you are as a person involves discovering how you feel (sensations and emotions), what you think, and how you behave." If this group completed the group on feelings, thoughts, and behaviours presented earlier, the facilitator can use some of the information and examples from that group to support the concept of getting to know your Self better.

Ask the group to collect some art materials and a sheet of paper. Instruct them to begin by drawing a self-portrait. When they have completed their drawings, ask the participants to write down some of their feelings, thoughts, and behaviours on the front or the back of their self-portrait.

When the group members have completed this, ask them to form a circle and sit down. Instruct the group that each member will have an opportunity to present their drawing and share with the group some of their feelings, thoughts, and behaviours.

Once this discussion is completed, ask the group to return to the art materials, collect another sheet of paper, and this time draw a picture of how they imagine they will look in high school. When they have completed their drawings, ask them to write down on the front or back of this drawing how they imagine they will feel, think, and behave in high school.

When the group members have completed this, ask them to form a circle and sit down. Inform the group that each member will have an opportunity to present their drawing and share with the group some of their feelings, thoughts, and behaviours.

When this is completed, ask group members to compare their two drawings and discuss what will need to change or what changes would make this new way of feeling, thinking, and behaving possible.

COOL-DOWN ACTIVITIES

Session 2

Understanding the difference between wants and needs and the learning strategies required to get needs met is essential to developing self-awareness. This session is intended to introduce to the group members the concept of wants and needs and begins to address the importance of needs. This activity requires pencils and paper for the participants.

WARM-UP ACTIVITIES

Discussion: Determining Wants and Needs

Begin the discussion with the group about the concept of wants and needs by reading aloud the following statement (you may wish to post this statement somewhere in the room). "A need is a desire for someone or something essential to the individual's physical, mental, emotional, social, or spiritual health. Everything else is a want." Ask for the group members to give examples of their wants and needs. The facilitator at this point in the discussion should not give an opinion as to whether he/she feels those suggested by group members are wants or needs.

Pass out paper and pencils and ask the group to compile a list of their needs then write beside that need the name of the person who most often fulfills that need for them. When the lists are complete, have them share their lists. Discuss with the group their findings. Typically, the younger the person, the more reliance there is on others to meet their various needs. Ask the group to comment on how they feel about depending upon others to meet their needs.

Ask the group to form a circle, and instruct them to silently mouth the words, "I want!" Have them join hands and mouth the words, "I want!" as if they are shouting it. Now ask them to say it out loud and say it like they are whining. Instruct them to say it again, only now like they are taking responsibility for their wants. Now ask them to shout it out, "I want!" Discuss with the group their thoughts and feelings about the exercise.

COOL-DOWN ACTIVITIES

Session 3

Children often get stuck in determining need fulfillment. Some do not feel worthy of having their needs met, others present as incapable of meeting their needs, others do not know how to ask for assistance to fulfill their needs, and still others seem to be full of need. This session assists the child to appreciate individual needs and find ways to have them fulfilled.

WARM-UP ACTIVITIES

Discussion: Need Fulfillment

Ask the group members to form a circle and be seated. Have them recall a time when their needs were not met or they were only partially met. Have group members share their situations with the group.

Now ask group members to recall their example and decide if there was anything they could have done to have their needs met. Go around the circle and ask members to share their evaluations but do not critique them.

Model for the group ways to ask for assistance in getting a need met.

• Getting help with homework

• Being allowed to play in a certain area

• Dealing with a friend who is not playing fairly

• Having a group that does not want to play with you today

Now explain to the group that people sometimes use a passive or indirect way of asking for what they want or need. Sometimes they expect people to anticipate or always know what they want or need, to be like a mind-reader. For example, Tom is hungry but expects his mother to know this and have a snack prepared. When she does not have anything prepared for him, he begins to pout and whine. Using the examples above, model for the group these types of passive requests.

Once this task is completed, divide the group into smaller groups of 4-6. Instruct the groups that the point of this exercise is to learn to ask directly in order to get wants and needs met.

Instruct each group to think of something that they can ask each member for, something which that person has the capability of giving. They will need to be specific about what it is that they want and to ask the person directly. They may ask the person to do something for them (e.g., bring your stamp collection to group); they may want someone to change his/her behaviour (e.g., "Stop calling me names," or "Call for me after school."); or they may want to do something for or with the other person (e.g., "Can I come over to watch you practice soccer?").

When each member has thought of something for each member of the group, the group members take turns asking each other for something. The group members are instructed to answer honestly and to be responsible for following through with it with the other person. They are encouraged to say no if they really do not wish to do it or if they are unable to do it. When a member says no to a request, the group members are instructed to negotiate with one another until they reach a mutually satisfying solution.

COOL-DOWN ACTIVITIES

Session 4

This session is intended to give the group some insight into, and strategies for, taking responsibility for their negative self-talk. The intervention "Owning Emotions" in Chapter 12, "Dealing with Feelings," is a useful prelude to this session.

This activity requires pencils and paper for the participants.

WARM-UP ACTIVITIES

Discussion: Negative Self-Talk

Discuss with the group the concept that individuals are responsible for what they think, feel, do, and say. For example, if a person thinks unpleasant thoughts, he/she is the only one who can change that way of thinking. Others can assist him/her to stop thinking unpleasant thoughts, but it is ultimately up to the individual.

Pass out paper and pencils or markers to the group members, and have them write down all of the negative thoughts or statements that they have said to themselves (e.g., "I'm never going to make that team," "I can't do math," "No one wants to be with me," "I suck at baseball."). Ask them to list as many statements as possible.

When the group is finished, discuss the effects these thoughts have on them.

Now ask the group to write down on a second sheet of paper as many positive thoughts or statements as they can think of to say that counter the negative statement, for example: "I am really excited about trying out for the team," "I like math even though I have to work at it," "I am a good person and I need a friend," "I need to practice my baseball skills more often."

When they appear finished, ask them to invent some other positive thoughts they could say about themselves. Discuss the effects that these thoughts have on them.

COOL-DOWN ACTIVITIES

Session 5

This session continues the focus on negative self-talk and points out how discounting can negatively affect feelings, thoughts, and behaviours. This activity requires pencils and paper for the participants.

WARM-UP ACTIVITIES

Discussion: Discounting

Discounting is a process where the individual does not accept a compliment given to them by someone or makes statements to minimize its positive intent. Here are some scenarios to assist the group in understanding the term discounting.

Statement: "I really like your hair!"
Response: "Oh, I hate the colour though."

Statement: "That was a good game you played last night."
Response: "Yeah, well, you didn't see all my mistakes."

Statement: "You are really good at math."
Response: "But I suck at reading."

Ask the group to divide up into pairs, and role-play the three scenarios above, giving each partner a chance to play both roles. When complete, ask members to role-play the scenarios again, but this time they must accept the compliment.

Discuss with the group their feelings and reactions to the role-play.

Pass out paper and pencils and ask the group to write down any negative thoughts or statements that they use to discount themselves while with friends or family. Discuss the effect that these statements have upon the speaker and on the listener(s).

COOL-DOWN ACTIVITIES

Session 6

This session attempts to link what has been discussed over the past five sessions and to assist the participants to integrate all aspects of the Self. This activity requires a large sheet of mural paper, push-pins or tacks, art materials, and several sheets of paper for each participant.

WARM-UP ACTIVITIES

Discussion: Integration of the Selves

This activity works well with a relaxation and guided fantasy exercise to complement the learning experience. Once the group is relaxed, ask them to imagine an image of themselves that would represent their Physical Self (that part of them that others are able to see). Give them all the time they need to complete that image in their minds. For younger children you may want to ask them to complete that drawing now and to discuss it with them while it is fresh in their minds. With older children you can proceed and ask them now to create an image in their minds that would represent their Emotional Self (one that depicts how they feel most of the time). Continue along these lines asking for images of the Social Self (that part that they show to their friends) and their Intellectual Self (that part of them that is smart and knows things). Hand out paper giving each participant four sheets of paper, and request that they select their own art materials. Instruct the group to proceed to draw their four images, one on each sheet of paper. Once competed, ask group members to briefly explain their drawings to the group.

Now pass out a final sheet of paper, and ask group members to complete another self-portrait that includes aspects or elements of all four drawings. Once completed, ask group members to pin up their portraits anywhere on the large sheet of mural paper.

COOL-DOWN ACTIVITIES

Topic 3:
Developing Peer Relationships

This next focus, relationships, is designed to follow the two preceding topics. The children should by now have a solid understanding of feelings, thoughts, and behaviours and will have begun to integrate some of this knowledge in their daily lives. Many children will have had negative experiences in their peer relationships and may still have difficulty functioning in their peer groupings. This sequence, "Developing Peer Relationships," allows them to practice a formula that will increase their likelihood of success and address any problems they are having presently with their peer groups inside and outside of the group program.

This activity requires paper, art materials, and a black/whiteboard or flip chart with markers.

Session 1

This initial session gives the group members a chance to recall friendships from the past and begin to appreciate what qualities and behaviours make a good friend.

WARM-UP ACTIVITIES

Discussion: Past Relationships

Begin this session with a relaxation exercise and conduct a guided fantasy (see Chapter 13, "Relaxation, Imagery, and Guided Fantasy"). The guided fantasy should begin by regressing the child to age four or five or recalling their earliest social experiences. Slowly guide them through the years up to the present, suggesting that they will be able to remember many of their friends and the times they had together. When the fantasy is completed, pass out the paper and art materials to the group. Ask the group members to draw pictures of the friends they recalled during the guided fantasy.

When the group has completed their drawings, ask them to form a circle and, one at a time, present their drawings to the group.

Once this is completed, instruct them to go back to their drawings and, with a pen or pencil, write down beside each friend, one quality each person had that made him/her fun to be with or a good friend. The younger child may need some assistance understanding this task, and examples can be shared among the group members. When this task is complete, ask the group to share the words that they have written. Write the key words down on a flip chart, and when each member has had a turn, discuss with the group these qualities and behaviours. Suggest to the group members that the words they have on their drawings may be a list of the qualities they look for in a friend.

COOL-DOWN ACTIVITIES

Session 2

Children who have difficulty socializing often lack solid strategies to contact other children in order to make friends. They often choose one another because they feel the more socially skilled children will not accept them. They have often been raised in families with the same lack of social skills. Often their parents are socially isolated and do not have the appropriate skills themselves to teach their children. This session gives them a formula to apply outside and inside the group.

The best strategy for making a friend is a sensory-based strategy, which begins with the visual sense. This involves observing a group of children or an individual child and determining if they look friendly. This period of observation discourages the impulsive child from moving in too quickly and also suggests that group members should use their senses before deciding to approach the individual—"Does this person seem like a good candidate?" The second step requires the child to get physically close to the person and get a sense of how it feels to be around this person. If their senses say go ahead, then the next step is to verbally communicate with the candidate to initiate a connection. Here is the formula:

Step 1: Look and feel.
Step 2: Get closer and feel.
Step 3: Make verbal contact and feel.

This activity requires art materials, paper, and a black/whiteboard or flip chart with markers. Write the formula on the flip chart before the group convenes.

WARM-UP ACTIVITIES

Discussion: Strategies for Making a Friend

Discuss the formula in detail with the group and ask for their feedback.

Hand out the art materials and paper and ask the group to draw a picture of someone their age who they feel looks like a friendly person.

Discuss with each member his/her drawing and ask that they describe what it is about this person that makes them friendly.

Conduct a brief relaxation exercise, and ask the children to imagine that they can experience the feelings they would have around someone who is friendly. You may want to use a guided fantasy to assist the group members in experiencing these feelings. When this is completed, ask the children to sit down and form a circle. Request that each member describe the feelings that they experienced.

Ask the group to suggest opening lines or strategies to engage a new friend. Write down each of their suggestions, and, as a group, decide on which opening lines would be the most effective.

Now ask the group members to pair up; one player is designated as A and the other as B. As and Bs are asked to face one another and stand back about 2 metres. When the pairs are ready, ask A to approach B and use one of the opening lines or strategies. Instruct the group to take turns until all members have used at least three of the opening lines in their dyads.

Once completed, discuss the experience with the group members.

COOL-DOWN ACTIVITIES

Session 3

Open and honest communication is a sure way to maintain healthy friendships. So often, children do not communicate their thoughts and feelings towards one another, and this can lead to relationship problems. This session highlights Thomas Gordon's (2000) technique, the "I" statement. This is a difficult strategy to master, and only one session will not prove effective unless it is continually reinforced throughout this topic and the next. This session needs to have the steps posted so the group can refer to them throughout the discussion and group exercise. It also requires pencils and paper.

Step 1: Identify feeling and approach the individual.
Step 2: State "I feel (state the feeling) …
Step 3: "when you (state the behaviour), …
Step 4: "because it (consequences of behaviour)."

WARM-UP ACTIVITIES

Discussion: Direct Communication

Instruct the group on the proper use of an "I" statement (Gordon, 2000). The "I" statement goes like this: "I feel (feeling) when you (behaviour) because (consequence of behaviour)." Give group members several examples of "I" statements.

Now pass out paper and pencils, and ask the group members to construct an "I" statement of their own, based on any one of the three scenarios below.

A friend borrowed and lost your favourite movie.

A friend is teasing you because of your clothing.

A friend has not picked you up like he/she promised.

When the group is finished, ask them to pair up and deliver their "I" statements to each other in a role-play situation. Emphasize with the group that in order for the "I" statement to be effective, their body language must be congruent with their verbal language. Children often forget to include the last part of the "I" statement, the "consequences of behaviour," and this should be drawn to their attention.

Once completed, discuss with the group their experiences.

Now ask group members to recall a time in their past when they were upset with someone but could not find the right language to say so. The group will need some time for this piece, and they may need to lie down or to sit back and relax quietly until they can come up with an example.

When all group members have an example, ask them to pick a different partner. The pairs are instructed to take turns delivering their "I" statements. The person giving the "I" statement must give the person receiving it the background information with regards to the context of the scenario. When the "I" statement is delivered, the person receiving the message can give the sender feedback on how he/she felt and what he/she was thinking during the role-play.

Once completed, ask the group members to share their experiences with the group.

COOL-DOWN ACTIVITIES

Session 4

Often the "I" statement is a prelude to problem-solving or conflict resolution. Now that the individuals in the friendship know how the other person feels, they may wish to problem-solve their situation to see if they can come up with ideas to make their friendship stronger. The first and most important part of problem-solving and conflict resolution is dealing with the emotions of the people who are involved.

Conflict resolution, like the "I" statement, is not mastered in one session, and the group will need to be given more opportunities to practice and discuss the outcomes in the group setting.

This activity requires a black/white board or flip chart with markers as well as pencils, paper, and art materials.

Scenario One: Two friends are playing cards, and the one friend (A) has won all the games so far. The other friend (B) decides to cheat so that he/she can win. A catches B cheating and delivers an "I" statement.

Scenario Two: Two friends are walking to school, and another friend approaches them. A runs off to school with the friend leaving B alone. Later on that day A attempts to connect with B, and B ignores A. A gives B an "I" statement based on the ignoring behaviour.

Scenario Three: Two friends are skateboarding. A is a much better skateboarder than B and often laughs or comments when B does not complete a stunt or manoeuvre properly. A attempts a difficult jump and falls, scraping his knee. B starts laughing and calling A names. A gives B an "I" statement.

Steps to Problem-Solving

Step 1: Deal with feelings by using "I" statements.
Step 2: Decide on the problem
Step 3: Generate at least three solutions that all can agree on.
Step 4: Engage in a solution for a period of time.
Step 5: Check in with each other to see if the solution is working

WARM-UP ACTIVITIES

Discussion: Conflict Resolution

Post the above scenarios in the room and discuss each situation. State to the group that in the three scenarios it is obvious that B also has strong feelings about the situation as well. Emphasize with the group that this is not a battle of "I" statements but a technique to reduce conflict in the relationship. B will need to respond appropriately to A's "I" statement before delivering his/her own. B then sends his/her own "I" statement, expressing his/her feelings about the scenario.

Ask the group to pair up and try out two of the three above scenarios.

Once completed, ask the group to come together and discuss their experiences with the whole group.

Post the steps to problem-solving and discuss with the group. Hand out pencils and paper.

Ask the group to form the same dyads as before and select the one scenario they did not act out in the first part of this session. Instruct them to act out the scenario, and when they have completed their "I" statements, to attempt to complete the steps to problem-solving. They may wish to write down their suggestions for step three.

When the pairs have finished, ask them to return to the group and share their experiences.

COOL-DOWN ACTIVITIES

Session 5

One of the most dysfunctional roles that affect interpersonal relationships is the role of the rescuer. What appears on the surface to be a role that is of great value and prestige turns out to be a role played by someone who is exercising his/her superiority over the other. The rescuer appears to be a well-meaning person who feels that the other person is unable to solve his/her own problem. The person being rescued is, in most cases, capable of solving his/her own problem and may be acting helplessly. The rescuer prevents the rescued from standing up for him/herself and from learning to solve problems on his/her own.

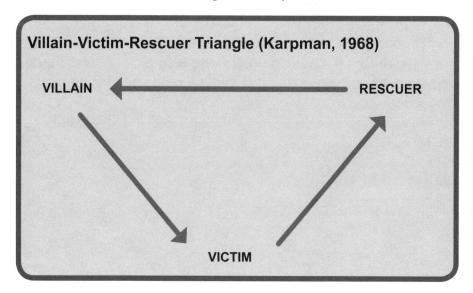

Villain-Victim-Rescuer Triangle (Karpman, 1968)

VILLAIN

RESCUER

VICTIM

The dialogue used to describe the triangulation experience reads: Villain says, "I'm going to get you!" Victim says, "Help, somebody save me (I'm helpless)!" Rescuer says, "I will save you (you are helpless)! Villain, get lost; I am the most powerful!"

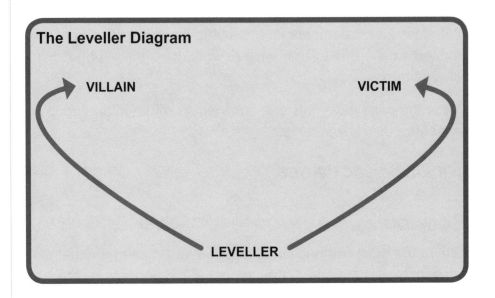

The Leveller Diagram

VILLAIN

VICTIM

LEVELLER

The levelling response (Satir, 1972) is a resolution to the rescuer's dilemma and suggests that he/she act responsibly in these situations by responding in a supportive manner. The leveller takes responsibility for his/her own behaviour and does not remain passive when confronted with victimization. He/she approaches the Villain, Victim, or both together and asks if they are in need of any support. This is not an attempt to rescue but only to provide oneself as a resource to either or both parties. If one or both ask for assistance, the leveller does not take over the situation like the rescuer but attempts to provide assistance in resolving the conflict.

This activity requires a black/white board or a flip chart with markers

WARM-UP ACTIVITIES

Discussion: Rescuing and Levelling

Begin the group by briefly giving them an example of a villain-victim-rescuer situation (perhaps a personal example). Ask the group to recall the last time they rescued someone or a time when someone else rescued them. Once completed, ask them to share their situation with the group. Write down a brief sketch of the situation on the flip chart or use a word or two to identify it.

Now post Karpman's Triangle in the room, and read out the brief descriptive dialogue provided. Discuss this concept with the group, giving each member an opportunity to comment or ask for clarification.

Return to the scenarios collected earlier and discuss them, applying the villain-victim-rescuer concept. Ask each member as they review their scenario, "What could you have done to avoid being rescued?" Write down their suggestions or any others provided by the group.

Now post the Leveller Diagram and read out the brief explanation provided. Discuss this concept with the group, giving each member an opportunity to make a comment or ask for clarification.

Return once again to the scenarios and discuss how all three players could act like a leveller.

COOL-DOWN ACTIVITIES

Session 6

Children need to learn assertiveness (levelling) rather than aggressiveness or passive-aggressiveness when dealing with others in order to develop and maintain happy and healthy relationships. In order to be assertive, children need the proper guidance and vocabulary as well as a solid sense of Self. Assertiveness in interpersonal relationships requires the individual to be aware of, and to take responsibility for, feelings, thoughts, and behaviours. Assertiveness comes from a position of strength and is not intended to overpower or control the other individual(s). It is a way of stating clearly and without guilt or blame how the individual is feeling and thinking. Here are four steps to assertiveness:

Step 1: Think Before You Act.
Step 2: Say How You Feel
Step 3: Take Care of Yourself and Your Needs
Step 4: Support Others

Scenario 1
Someone (A) has stepped in front of you in a long line waiting for the movie theatre. You (B) and your date have been in line for the past 30 minutes. You decide to assert yourself.

Scenario 2
You (A) have your final exams coming up, and you need to study. A family member (B) continues to make noise even after you have asked them to be quiet. You decide you must assert yourself.

Scenario 3
Your teacher (A) has accused you of not doing your homework. You (B) did your homework but forgot it at home. She is threatening to take you to the principal. You decide to assert yourself.

Scenario 4
a.) A friend of yours has told your brother a secret that you had confided in her. Your brother (A) is threatening to tell your parents. You (B) decide to assert yourself.

b.) Role-play how you (A) would assert yourself with your friend (B) in this scenario.

Scenario 5

You (A) feel your friend (B) is cheating on her exams, and you are afraid that she will get caught. You decide to assert yourself.

WARM-UP ACTIVITIES

Discussion: Assertiveness/Levelling

Post the four steps to assertiveness and discuss. Ask the group to pair up and decide who will play A and who will play B. Present the five scenarios and ask the dyads to pick two of the five to role-play. Suggest that they be mindful of the four steps and make use of all the training they have had to date in order to act responsibly and resolve the scenario to both A's and B's satisfaction.

When the group has played out their role-plays, ask them to discuss their experiences. The ones who had difficulty can be encouraged to role-play their scenario for the group and then to ask for feedback.

COOL-DOWN ACTIVITIES

Topic 4: Separation and Divorce

Separation and divorce can be a traumatic experience. It is often the single most devastating event in a child's life (Wallerstein, 1991). Children are a product of both parents and carry their combined genetic make-up; it is difficult to impossible, especially before the age of abstract thought, for children to separate themselves psychologically from either parent—"You criticize my mother, you criticize me; you hurt my father's feelings, you hurt mine." The worst predicament of all for young children in situations where there is marital conflict is when one parent criticizes the other parent. It is like being attacked from both sides, and it sets up an internal conflict in the child's mind.

Separation and divorce, the last topic in this series, requires a great deal of healing and repairing of the child's world. The topics in this series have been leading up to assisting children with some of their greatest and most devastating problems. The children in the group at this point would have an extensive knowledge of feelings, thoughts, and behaviours and how they relate. They would be making conscious adjustments to these three to assist them to function more effectively. They will have begun to look into their own personal make-up and are beginning to appreciate their strengths. And most recently, they are learning to communicate in a way that reduces tension and conflict as well as improves peer interactions. They will need all these skills and more in order to heal from the wounding of the loss of family.

Session 1

One of the most difficult problems for children from separated families to resolve is understanding and appreciating their roles and the roles of their parents and other family members in relation to the break up of the family. Children have great difficulty understanding adult behaviour and, more specifically, adult thinking. As a result, children almost always carry a portion of the guilt and resentment about the separation. Often they are unable to separate themselves from the problem; they often feel responsible in some way for their parents' pain. The concept that they did not cause the break-up is often difficult or impossible for young children to appreciate. However, the discussion is still an important beginning in healing from the effects of loss. The younger children will still have a memory of the discussion to draw upon when they are older and better able to process this information.

A review of Topic 3, "Developing Peer Relationships," and in particular "Session 6," the role of the leveller, is most effective prior to conducting the discussion below.

This group will require art materials and paper.

WARM-UP ACTIVITIES

Discussion: Who's Responsible?

Ask the group members to recall a conflict they had recently with a good friend. Once they have remembered one such conflict (a relaxation and guided fantasy will assist them), instruct them to draw a picture depicting the conflict.

Once the pictures are completed, ask group members to present their drawings. At the conclusion of their presentations, ask the group members the following questions, and discuss their answers among the group.

Who do you feel caused the fight?

Did you have a part in the argument?

Did your friend blame you for the fight?

Did either of you blame someone else for your fight?

When friends fight with each other, which one is responsible for the fight?

What can happen if friends cannot settle their argument on their own?

Now ask the group to draw a picture of their parents having an argument—an incident that they feel comfortable sharing with the group (often parental disputes become violent, and it is important for facilitators to be prepared).

Once the pictures are completed, ask group members to present their drawings. At the conclusion of their presentation, ask the children who they feel was the cause of the disagreement —who is to blame for it?

Ask the group members the following questions, and discuss their answers among the group.

When your parents had conflict with each other, did you feel you were to blame for their fight/argument?

Was there ever a time when they blamed you for their conflict?

Was there ever a time when they blamed others (brother, sister, grandparents) for their conflict?

Was there ever a time when you blamed yourself for your parents' separation/divorce?

Was there ever a time when they blamed you for their separation?

When good friends or parents fight, who is responsible for the fight?

What can happen if parents cannot settle their arguments on their own?

COOL-DOWN ACTIVITIES

Session 2

This next session begins to explore the children's feelings and experiences with their mothers. Introduce the topic of the session by defining mothers in their various forms (e.g., biological mother, step-mother, male-mother, grandmother, foster mother, nanny, or caregiver). This relationship is of primary importance when discussing and healing from the wounding caused by separation and divorce. This session can reveal a great deal of information and give children an opportunity to discuss their feelings and experiences.

This group will require art materials, paper, pencils, some background music, a black/whiteboard, or flip chart and markers.

WARM-UP ACTIVITIES

Discussion: Mothers

Ask the group to find a comfortable spot, to close their eyes, and to relax. Play relaxing music and ask the group members to recall both positive and negative experiences with their mothers. Allow them ample time to recall several experiences, and periodically restate the instructions. When the group appears to be finished, ask them to slowly wake themselves up and then to form a circle quietly. Pass out paper and markers, and ask the group to draw a picture of themselves with their mothers doing something. When they have completed their drawings, ask each member to share their experience and their drawing with the group.

Write the word Mother at the top of the board or flip chart. Ask the group to brainstorm all the things that they enjoy doing with their mothers. When the list is exhaustive, ask the group to look over the list and to select one or two things that they have not done with their mothers for a long time. Suggest to the group that the next time they want to do something special with Mom, they can discuss with her the possibility of doing one of the activities on the list.

Pass out paper and pencils and ask the group members to complete the following statements.

MY MOM

One thing I like about my mom is ………...……………………………

One thing I do not like about my mom is …………..………………

I wish my mom would …....……………………………………………..

It is a difficult job being a mother because …………………...………

One way that I am the same as my mom is ……………….………

When my mom gets angry she ………………………………………

When my mom feels happy she ……………………………..……

One thing my mom does not know about is ………………...…..

I saw my mom sad when…………………………………………

My mom taught me to ……………………………………………

One way that I am different than my mom is ……………...……..…

One more thing about my mom is …………………………………

Once completed, ask the group members to share their answers.

COOL-DOWN ACTIVITIES

Session 3

This next session begins to explore the children's feelings and experiences with their fathers. Introduce the topic of the session by defining fathers in their various forms (e.g., biological father, step-father, female father, grandfather, foster father, or caregiver). As with mothers, this relationship is also of key importance when discussing and healing from the wounds caused by separation and divorce. This session can reveal a great deal of information and give children an opportunity to discuss their feelings and experiences.

This group will require art materials, paper, pencils, some background music, a black/whiteboard, or flip chart and markers.

WARM-UP ACTIVITIES

Discussion: Fathers

Ask the group to find a comfortable spot, to close their eyes, and to relax. Play relaxing music and ask the group members to recall both positive and negative experiences with their fathers. Allow them ample time to recall several experiences, and periodically restate the instructions. When the group appears to be finished, ask them to slowly wake themselves up and then to form a circle quietly. Pass out paper and markers, and ask the group to draw a picture of themselves doing something with their fathers. When they have completed their drawings, ask each member to share their experience and their drawing with the group.

Write the word Father at the top of the board or flip chart. Ask the group to brainstorm about all the things that they enjoy doing with their fathers. When the list is complete, ask the group to look it over and to select one or two things that they have not done with their fathers for a long time. Suggest to the group that the next time they want to do something special with Dad, they can discuss with him the possibility of doing one of the activities on the list.

Pass out paper and pencils and ask the group members to complete the following statements.

MY DAD

One thing I like about my dad is ………………….....…..……………

One thing I do not like about my dad is ………………….....…….…

I wish my dad would ……………………………………………...……

It is a difficult job being a father because …………………….……..

One way that I am the same as my dad is ………………….....….…

When my dad gets angry he ……………………………………….…

When my dad feels happy he ……………………………………..…

One thing my dad does not know about is …………………...………

I saw my dad sad when ………………………………………..…..…

My dad taught me to ………………………………………………..…

One way that I am different than my dad is ……....………….....……

One more thing about my dad is ………………….....………...…..…

Once completed, ask the group members to share their answers.

COOL-DOWN ACTIVITIES

Session 4

When children experience separation and divorce in their lives, they experience severe loss. These losses can have serious effects on later development. Children need to be encouraged to grieve the loss of what was, in order to be able to fully embrace that which is new and, in many cases, healthier.

This activity requires art materials, pencils, and paper.

WARM-UP ACTIVITIES

Discussion: Healing the Loss

Ask the group to recall the time their parents' decided to separate, and ask them to share their experience with the group and cover the following questions:

Where were you when you found out?

How did you feel (sensory and emotional experience)?

What thoughts were going through your mind?

What did you do—what was your behavioural reaction?

Once completed, conduct a relaxation exercise in order to relieve some of the tension in the group and to help them refocus their thoughts. When the children appear to be relaxed, ask them to remember some of the things they lost when their parents separated. When the group has finished, pass out the art materials, pencils, and paper. Instruct the group to draw some of the most important things they lost and to list the other losses in pencil somewhere on their paper. Allow each member to explain his/her losses to the group.

COOL-DOWN ACTIVITIES

Session 5

Awareness and acknowledgment of the pain, and a better appreciation of its effect on the Self, is a very useful and necessary step towards healing. The next step in the process is honouring what was and moving forward.

This activity requires art materials, pencils, and paper.

WARM-UP ACTIVITIES

Discussion: Healing the Loss (continued)

Ask group members to think back to the painful experiences that were recalled in the last session.

Ask the group to find a comfortable spot, and use a simple relaxation exercise to quiet the group. Once they are relaxed, conduct a guided fantasy asking them to visualize themselves and how they looked when they were experiencing the pain of the family's breakup. Suggest to the group that they can remember some of these situations now, without experiencing as much fear or pain. Explain that they can now understand the situation a little better and that they can realize that they have survived—they are here today, getting healthier.

In visualizing the break-up, instruct them to be aware of the following: facial expression, body posture, type and colour of clothing; who else is with them; what is their environment like; are they saying anything to themselves; is anyone else speaking, and if so, how does their voice sound (e.g., sad, angry); is there a kind of feeling or emotion in the room. When their past experience has been remembered, ask them to focus their attention on themselves. Request that they be aware of their right-now sensory and emotional experiences. Suggest they be aware of anything they might be thinking or saying to themselves and of any images that come to mind. When the group appears to be finished, pass out paper and markers, and ask them to draw a picture only of themselves and how they looked in their guided fantasy.

When their pictures are complete, ask the group to find a comfortable and quiet spot in the room and to focus their attention on their own drawings. Suggest to the group that they imagine that they are sending loving and healing messages to the character of themselves in their drawing. Some messages might be "I love you." "You are a good boy/girl." "You have survived." "You are special." Ask them to reassure this character that they will always be there for them.

When this is completed, ask them to silently ask the character in the picture what they need in order to feel safe again. Instruct them to write down the words or messages they feel that the character in the drawing needs in order to be fully healed.

Now have each of them display their drawings and explain to the group what they feel they need now in order to fully heal themselves. Help each member to be specific about what their wants and needs are, how they can be met, and by whom.

Complete this discussion with the story in Chapter 14, "Therapeutic Storytelling," The Bear Family.

COOL-DOWN ACTIVITIES

Session 6

Many children experience some form of new relationship in their family constellation shortly after the separation. It might be with Mom's new boyfriend, or Dad's new wife's children, or Grandma moving in to help out; but, whatever the situation, it often causes more stress, more emotional upsets, and further questions in the child's already unstable state. There will be a few children in the group who have not experienced this directly but have likely thought about it, or are likely to experience this situation in their future.

This activity requires art materials, pencils, and paper.

WARM-UP ACTIVITIES

Discussion: Families

Instruct the group to form a circle and to quietly relax themselves. Explain the concept of blended families and ask the group to suggest possible family compositions (mother, son, and mother's boyfriend; grandma, grandpa, and grandchild, etc.). Once the possibilities are exhausted, pass out two to three sheets of paper and art materials.

Instruct group members to find a quiet and comfortable part of the room and to prepare themselves to draw their families. Ask the group members to draw their new family or families and to be sure to include themselves and all of the members that belong to each family grouping.

When this phase has been completed, ask the group to return to the circle and to present their new family or families to the group. For this part of the session, it is useful for the group to merely state the characters' names and their relationship with the artist.

Once this has been completed, instruct the group to return to their quiet and comfortable spot with their drawing(s). Request that they place their drawings in front of them and that they focus their attention on one family at a time.

Ask them to think about the following:

"What problems do this family have?"

"What do I dislike about the members?"

"What problems might this family have in the future?"

"How do I feel being in this family?"

Instruct the group to write the answers to these questions somewhere on their drawing. It is useful to have the questions posted somewhere where the group can easily read them. Request that they go through this exercise with all of the families that they are involved with.

When this phase is completed, ask the group to return to the circle with their drawings. Give each child an opportunity to discuss their drawings with the group. Ask each member to present one drawing on the first turn and then another drawing each turn afterward until all have been discussed. While the child is presenting the problems within the family, ask the group to refrain from problem-solving for the child. They may ask questions for clarification of the problem, but the problem-solving will come later.

When each member has presented his/her family and its problems, instruct the group to return to a quiet and comfortable space in the room and bring their drawings with them. Instruct the group members to focus their attention on one of their drawings and ask: "What strengths or assets does this family have?"; "What do I like about each member?"; "How can I use the positive parts of this family to help me solve my problems within this family?"; "How do I want to feel in this family?"; "What needs to happen before I can feel this way in the family?" Instruct the group to write the answers to these questions somewhere on their drawings or on another piece of paper that they can attach to the drawing. Request that they go through this exercise with each of their drawings.

> "We are told that talent creates its own opportunities. But it sometimes seems that intense desire creates not only its own opportunities, but its own talents."
>
> — ERIC HOFFER

When this is completed, ask the group members to return to the circle again. Provide each child with the opportunity to discuss one of his/her drawings. This time the group can also provide problem-solving feedback to the artist if the child requests feedback. After each turn, encourage the child to write down any new awareness or solutions that come as a result of discussion with the group. Continue this process with the group until all of the members have presented all of their drawings.

Finally, ask the group members to return to their quiet and comfortable spaces once again. Instruct them to focus their attention on each drawing and to send positive messages to each member that they feel good about. They may send requests or demands silently to other members. When they feel finished with their first drawing, ask them to complete the process with any other drawings.

COOL-DOWN ACTIVITIES

The programs presented in this chapter can be adapted, extended, and modified to meet the individual needs of group members. These programs can build a foundation of knowledge and experience, which children can utilize and act upon well into adulthood.

CONCLUSION

Play, over the course of human history has managed to transcend social, political, linguistic, cultural, ideological, environmental, and interpersonal barriers. The world has now reached a stage in its development where the power of play can be our strongest medicine in healing the planet and its inhabitants. The material in this text emphasizes the necessity of play in healthy childhood, adolescent, and young adult development. It highlights cooperative group activities and spontaneous creative group exercises as ways to make play time more beneficial and enjoyable. Within its pages lie countless strategies to improve the social climate and environment so that children, adolescents, and young adults have the necessary play experiences to help them to progress into healthy adulthood, free of mind-body dysfunctions.

Childhood is a magical time; it is a time when the human experience is unlimited in its capacity to live in the present. This living in the present allows children to experience their vitality. When people in the child's world assist the child in cherishing this capacity, self-appreciation, self-love, and reverence for the other are easily attainable. Children who live in the present are participators in life; they feel confident that they have the ability to access the resources and people around them in order to solve life's challenges. They move with boldness and see their world as being a wonderful place in which to live. A child who is forced by her memories to live in the past or the future becomes a spectator and more of a victim of life, feeling powerless because of past experiences and filled with anxiety about the future. When this child can be encouraged to experience life in the form of a game, an art activity, a role-play, or a spontaneous play experience, the fears and anxieties of the past and the future disappear. The therapeutic activity programmer and facilitator have a duty to make the activity interesting and attractive enough so that the child prefers to live in the present. The natural healing power of play and positive group interaction will, in time, heal the wounds of the past and lessen the anxieties of the future.

This text, I hope, is an ever-present reminder that child and youth care professionals are responsible for their mind-body health and are required to model self-responsibility and self-love so as to motivate the child to continually strive for this goal. Self-reverence is an essential ingredient in life, for without this, the individual lives lost in a world that is not fulfilling. When programmers and facilitators model and promote this self-responsible way of feeling and relating, children have a living example of their task in life. If children are unable to be filled with this sense of self-love by the significant adults in their life, they are doomed to a life of trying to prove their worth. When they reach maturity, they now must rely on themselves to generate this feeling of self-worth. This is extremely difficult to accomplish if the individual has limited experiences of this feeling of Self-Full-Ness and an abundance of feelings of Self-Less-Ness or Self-Ish-Ness. This reverence for the Self is not a narcissistic love that excludes all others; nor is it a self-less love that includes everyone else at the expense of the Self. It is a sense of total commitment to the Self in connection with the Other—a state of mutual acceptance.

Group interaction as a way towards self-awareness, self-exploration, and self-responsibility represents the moving force behind this text. It is in relationship to the other that we appreciate ourselves and find meaning in our lives. This cannot be taught; it must be experienced. Group experiences provide the child with the opportunity to practice relationship development. Healthy facilitation with an emphasis on a healthy group environment increases the chances for the child to be successful. Hundreds of thousands of our children and youth long for this type of opportunity, and with it, they can, no matter how difficult the past, learn to respond to love again and to live life in a loving way.

Play has been the overall focus of this text and has been presented as the expression of the life force—vitality. The models of play experiences for our modern-day children are ones that are highly competitive, and at times they border on ruthlessness. The society has replaced the "play for play's sake" attitude with a "win at all costs" attitude. This rings true from the highly sophisticated sports programs to the excessive use of structured learning in the education systems. The playground has been replaced by the recreation room and the monkey bars by the joysticks. Play times are relegated to fifteen minutes at recess and to the time it takes for the ride or walk home from school. Once at home, television, computers, and other electronics take on the role of parents.

Play has been formalized to the point that when children act in a spontaneous way, they are accused of cheating or not playing by the rules. The play toys of the past few decades lack imagination and are picture perfect in every detail. No longer does imagination turn the branch of a tree into the queen's sceptre or the knight's sword. Today, each child can have an authentic replica of a MAC-l0 machine pistol, one that makes the real sound, and one that later is often adopted by those forced onto the streets. Homework, excessive TV and video viewing, and passive involvement or over-involvement in formalized athletics is using up time for spontaneous play—for the child to be him/herself. The expectations of parents and other adults in many children's lives stress a race towards maturity. "Grow up!" "Act your age!" "Graduate!" "Get a job!" Children and youth are being asked to act with adult maturity without being given the time to reach that level of maturity. Worse still are those children who, through violence, poverty, addiction, abuse, neglect, loss, or other trauma, can not play, have forgotten how to play, or have never had the chance to learn play—these children are in the greatest need.

Child and youth care professionals can challenge and often replace these conditions with imaginative, creative, cooperative, challenging activities, and spontaneous play experiences. This type of programming will allow children to begin to, or once again, experience life in their own bodies and express this vitality through their emotions. Children are naturally adept at experiencing life in this way. All they need is a supportive adult and the opportunity to do so.

My greatest wish, as I complete the 20th anniversary of this text, is that it will continue to be used, expanded upon, and surpassed by the professionals who teach college and university students to work with, and care for, our earth's most precious resource—the children and youth of today.

"
At its core, ours is a service occupation; we have taken on nothing less than the future of the world. "

— JEROME BEKER

BIBLIOGRAPHY

Aguilar, J., Bedau, D., & Anthony, C. (2009). Growing emotional intelligence through community-based arts. *Reclaiming Youth*, 18(1), 3-7.

Anglin, J. (2003). *Pain, normality, and the struggle for congruence: Reinterpreting residential care for children and youth*. New York: Routledge.

Artz, S. (1993). Feeling as a way of knowing. *Journal of Child and Youth Care*, 8(4), 1-11.

Ateah, A., Kail, R. & Cavanaugh, J. (2009). *Human development: A life-span view*. Toronto, ON: Nelson Education Ltd.

Bandler, R. (2008). *Richard Bandler's guide to trans-formation: How to harness the power of hypnosis*. Deerfield Beach, FL: Health Communications Inc.

Bandler, R. & Grinder, J. (1976). *The structure of magic II*. Palo Alto, CA: Science and Behavior Books.

Barbe, W. (June, 1982). *What we know about modality*. Paper given at the 25th Council for Exceptional Children, Chicago.

Baumrind, D. (1978). Parental disciplinary patterns and social competence in children. *Youth and Society*, 9, 239-276.

Benson, H. (2000). *The relaxation response*. New York: HarperCollins.

Bergner, R. (2007). Therapeutic storytelling revisited. *American Journal of Psychotherapy*, 6(2), 149-162.

Bettelheim, B. (1976). *The uses of enchantment: The meaning and importance of fairy tales*. New York: Vintage Books.

Bolen, J. (2004). *Goddesses in everywoman: Powerful archetypes in women's lives*. New York: HarperCollins.

Bolen, J. (2009). *Gods in everyman: Archetypes that shape men's lives*. New York: HarperCollins.

Boyle, G. & Joss-Reid, J. (2004). Relationship of humour to health: A psychometric investigation. *British Journal of Health and Psychology*, 9(1), 51-66.

Brascoupe, S. (2009). Cultural safety: Exploring the applicability of the concept of cultural safety to aboriginal health and community wellness. *Journal of Aboriginal Health*, November, National Aboriginal Health Organization.

Brendtro, L. (1969). Establishing relationship beachheads. In A. Trieschman, J. Whittaker, & L. Brendtro. *The other twenty-three hours: Child care work with emotionally disturbed children in a therapeutic milieu*, 51-99. Chicago: Aldine.

Brendtro, L. (1969). Avoiding some of the roadblocks to therapeutic management. In A. Trieschman, J. Whittaker, & L. Brendtro. *The other twenty-three hours: Child care work with emotionally disturbed children in a therapeutic milieu*, 219-235. Chicago: Aldine.

Brendtro, L. & Mitchell, M. (2010). The profound power of groups. *Reclaiming Youth*, 19(3), 5-10.

Burns, M. (1982). *Stories in child care: A metaphorical approach to change*. Sarnia, ON: Child Care Press.

Burns, M. (1984). Rapport and relationships: The basis of child care. *Journal of Child Care*, 2(2), 47-56.

Burns, M. (1999). *Into the dark forest: Therapeutic Storytelling*. Sarnia, ON: Child Care Press.

Burns, M. (2006). *Healing spaces: The therapeutic milieu in child and youth work*, Kingston, ON: Child Care Press.

Burns, M. (2012). *The self in child and youth care, A celebration.* Kingston, ON: Child Care Press.

Butler, J. (2000). Using dramatherapy with teens. *Journal of Child and Youth Care*, 13(4), 67-76.

Campbell, D. (1997). *The Mozart experience: Tapping the power of music to heal the body, strengthen the mind, and unlock the creative spirit.* New York: Avon Books.

Chapman, A. (1976). *Humor and laughter: Theory, research, and applications.* New York: John Wiley & Sons Ltd.

Chiron, C., Jambaque, I., Nabbout, R., Lounes, R., Syrota, A., & Dulac, O. (1997). The right brain hemisphere is dominant in human infants. *Brain*, 120(6), 1057-1065.

Cook, J., Taylor, L., & Silverman, P. (2004). The application of therapeutic storytelling techniques with preadolescent children. *Cognitive and Behavioural Practice*, 11, 243-248.

Corey, G. (2012). *Theory and practice of counselling and psychotherapy.* Belmont, CA: Thomson Higher Education.

Demetriou, A. & Kazi, S. (2001). *Unity and modularity in the mind and self: Studies on the relationships between self-awareness, personality, and intellectual development from childhood to adolescence.* New York: Routledge.

Dilts, R., Bandler, R., Cameron-Bandler, L., DeLozier, J., & Grinder, J. (1980). *Neuro-linguistic programming: Volume 1,* Cupertino, CA: Meta Publications.

Dowling, J., Hockenberry, M., & Gregory, R. (2003). Sense of humour, childhood cancer stressors, and outcomes of psychosocial adjustment, immune function, and infection. *Journal of Pediatric Oncology Nursing.* 20, 271-292.

Elkind, D. (1967). Egocentrisim in adolescence. *Child Development* 38(4), 1025-1034.

Elkind, D. (2006). *The hurried child: Growing up too fast too soon.* Cambridge, MA: Da Capo Press.

Erickson, M. & Rossi, E. (1979). *Hypnotherapy: An exploratory casebook.* New York: John Wiley & Sons Inc.

Erikson, E., (1950). *Childhood and society.* New York: Norton.

Estes, C. (1995). *Women who run with the wolves: Stories of the wild woman archetype.* New York: Random House.

Evans. G. (2006) Child development in the physical environment. *Annual Review of Psychology*, 57, 423-451.

Fewster, G. (1987). The paradoxical journey: Some thoughts on relating to children. *Journal of Child and Care*, 3(3), 1-7.

Fewster, G. (1990). *Being in child care: A journey into self.* New York: Haworth Press.

Fewster, G. (2001). Turning myself inside out: My personal theory of me. *Journal of Child and Youth Care,* 15(4), 89-108.

Freud, A. (1922). *Beyond the pleasure principle,* London, England: The International Psychoanalytic Press.

Gardner, R. (1993). *Storytelling in psychotherapy with children.* Lanham, MD: Jason Aronson.

Garfat, T. (2008). The interpersonal inbetween: An explanation of child and youth care practice. In G. Bellefeuille & F. Ricks (Eds.), *Standing on the precipice: Inquiry into the potential of child and youth care practice,* 7-34. Edmonton, AB: Grant MacEwan Press.

Garfat T., McElwee, N. & Charles, G. (2005). Self in social care practice. In N. McElwee & P. Share (Eds.), *An Irish Social Care Text.* Dublin, Ireland.

Gibson, B, (2011). *The complete guide to using and understanding nlp: Neuro-linguistic programming explained simply.* Ocala, FL: Atlantic Publishing Group, Inc.

Ginsberg, K. (2007). The importance of play in promoting healthy child development and maintaining strong parent-child bonds. *Pediatrics,* 19(1), 182-191.

Gladding, S. (2011). Counselling: A comprehensive profession. Toronto, ON: Pearson Education Canada.

Gordon, D. (1978). *Therapeutic metaphors: Helping others through the looking glass.* Cupertino, CA: Meta Publications.

Gordon, T. (2000). *Parent effectiveness training: The proven program for raising responsible children.* New York: Three Rivers Press.

Greenman, J. (1988). *Caring spaces and learning places,* Redman, WA: Exchange Press.

Hanley, J. (1999). Beyond the tip of the iceberg: Five stages towards cultural competence. *Reaching Today's Youth,* 3(2), 9-12.

Hendricks, G. & Willis, R. (1975). *The centering book: Awareness activities for children, parents, and teachers.* Englewood Cliffs, NJ: Prentice-Hall.

Hendricks, G. & Roberts, T. (1977). *The second centering book: More awareness activities for children, parents, and teachers*. Englewood Cliffs, NJ: Prentice-Hall.

Hillman, C., Castelli, D., & Buck, S. (2005). Aerobic fitness and neurocognitive function in healthy preadolescent children. *Medicine & Science in Sports & Exercise*, 37, 1967-1974.

Huges, F. (2003). Spontaneous play in the 21st century. In O. Saracho & B. Spodek (Eds.), *Contemporary perspectives on play in early childhood education*, 21-40. Greenwich, CT: Information Age Publishing.

Isenberg, N., & Quisenberry, N. (2002). Play: Essential for all children. *Childhood Education*, 79, 33-39.

Isenberg, J. & Jalongo, M. (2006). *Creative thinking and arts-based learning preschool through fourth grade*. Upper Saddle River, NJ: Prentice-Hall.

Jacobs, E., Masson, R., & Harvil, R. (2009). *Group counseling: Strategies and skills*. Belmont, CA: Thomson Higher Education.

Jones, J. (2000). The voice of music in child and youth care practice. *Journal of Child and Youth Care*, 14(3). 49-57.

Jung, C. (1971). *Collected works of Carl Jung, Volume 6: Psychological types*. Princeton Township, NJ: Princeton University.

Karpman, S. (1968). Fairy tales and script drama analysis. *Transactional Analysis Bulletin*, 7(26), 39-43.

Klein, M. (1932). *The psychoanalysis of children*. London: Hogarth.

Knight, S. (2011). *Risk and adventure in early years outdoor play: Learning from forest schools*. Thousand Oaks, CA: Sage Books.

Krueger, M. (1995). *Nexus: A book about youth work*. Washington, DC: CWLA Press.

Krueger, M. (1999). Presence as dance in work with youth. *Journal of Child and Youth Care*, 13(2), pp. 59-72.

Krueger, M. (2007). *Sketching youth, self, and youth work*. Rotterdam/Taipei, Sense Publishers.

Lambourne, K. & Donnelly, J. (2011). The role of physical activity in pediatric obesity. *Pediatric Clinics of North America*, 51, 1481-1491.

Landy, R., Weber, A., & Haen, C. (2004). *Clinical applications of drama in child and adolescent treatment*. New York: Routledge.

Levine, P. (1991). Revisioning anxiety and trauma. In M. Sheets (Ed.), *Giving the body its due*. Albany, NY: SUNY Press.

Levine, P. (1997). *Waking the tiger; Healing trauma*. Berkley, CA: North Atlantic Books.

Levine, P. (2010). *In an unspoken voice*. Berkley, CA: North Atlantic Books.

Levine, P. & Kline, M. (2007). *Trauma through a child's eyes: Awakening the normal miracle of healing*. Berkley, CA: North Atlantic Books.

Loman, S. (2006). Dance/movement therapy. In C. Malchiodi (Ed.). *Expressive therapies*. New York: Guilford Press.

Maier, H. (1971). The child care worker. In R. Morris (Ed.), *Encyclopedia of social work*, 111-114. New York: National Association of Social Workers.

Maier, H. (1979). The core of care: Essential ingredients for the development of children home and away from home. *Child Care Quarterly*, 8(3), 161-173.

Maier, H. (1987). *Developing group care of children and youth: Concepts and practice*. New York: Haworth Press.

Maier, H. (1991). Role playing: Structures and educational objectives. *Journal of Child and Youth Care*, 6(4), 145-150.

Malchiodi, C. (2007). *The art therapy sourcebook*. New York: McGraw-Hill.

Mash, E. & Wolfe, D. (2013). *Abnormal child psychology*. Belmont, CA: Wadsworth.

Mead, M. (2006). *The water of life: Initiation and the tempering of the soul*. Seattle, WA: GreenFire Press.

McCain, M., Mustard, F., & Shanker, S. (2007). *Early years study 2: Putting science into action*. Toronto, ON: Council for Early Child Development.

McElwee, N., McKenna-McElwee. S. & Phelan, J. (2002). Living in the risk society: Some implications for child and youth workers in relation to the "touch and hugging" debate. *Journal of Child and Youth Care Work*, 17, 118-129.

McWhirter, J., McWhirter, B., McWhirter, A., & McWhirter, E. (2010). *At-risk youth*. Belmont, CA: Thomson Brooks/Cole Publishing Co.

Morrow, G. (1960). *Plato's Cretan City*. Princeton, NJ: Princeton University Press.

Montague, A. (1986). *Touching: The human significance of the skin*. New York: Avon.

Montessori, M. (1948). *The discovery of the child*. Madras, India: Kalakshetra Publications Press.

Moustakas, C. (1953). *Children in play therapy*. New York: McGraw-Hill.

Norden, J. (2007). *Understanding the brain* [Film]. (Available from The Great Courses, 4840 Westfields Blvd, Suite 500, Chantilly, VA: 20151-2299).

Oatley, K. (2004). *Emotions: A brief history*. Carlton, Victoria, Australia: Blackwell Publishing.

Parten, M. (1932). Social play among preschool children. *Journal of Abnormal and Social Psychology*, 27, 243-269.

Phelan, J. (1990). Child care supervision: the neglected skill of evaluation. In J. Anglin, C. Denholm, R. Ferguson, & A. Pence (Eds.), *Perspectives in professional child and youth care*, 131-143. New York: Haworth.

Phelan, J. (2008). Building developmental capabilities: A developmentally responsive approach to child and youth care intervention. In Gerald Bellefeuille & Francis Ricks (Eds.), *Standing on the precipice: Inquiry into the potential of child and youth care practice*, 73-106. Edmonton, AB: Grant MacEwan Press.

Phelan, J. (2008). Relationship beachheads: Three levels of therapeutic connection. *Reclaiming Youth*, 17(2), 39-42.

Piaget, J. (1962). *Play, dreams and imitation in childhood*. New York: Norton.

Pinciotti, P. (1993). Creative drama and young children: The dramatic learning connection. *Arts Education Policy Review*, 94(6), 24-29.

Porges, S. (2007). The polyvagal perspective. *Biological Psychology*, 74, 116-143.

Porges, S. (2011). *The polyvagal theory: Neurophysiological foundations of emotions, attachment, communication, and self-regulation*, NY: Norton.

Redl, F. (1952). *Controls from within: Techniques for treatment of the aggressive child*. New York: Free Press.

Ricks, F. (2003). Relatedness in relationships: It's about being. *Relational Child and Youth Care Practice*, 16(3), 70-77.

Rivkin, M. (1995). *The great outdoors: Restoring children's right to play outside*. Washington, DC: National Association for the Education of Young Children.

Rolls, E. T., (2005). *Emotion explained*. Oxford, Oxfordshire: Oxford University Press.

Rosen, H. (1982). *My voice will go with you*. New York: W. W. Norton.

Rothschild, B. (2000). *The body remembers: The psychophysiology of trauma and trauma treatment*. New York: W. W. Norton & Company.

Rubin, J. (2005). *Child art therapy*. Hoboken, NJ: John Wiley & Sons, Inc.

Rubin, J. (2010). *Introduction to art therapy: Sources and resources*. New York: Routledge.

Samuels, M. & Samuels, N. (1975). *Healing with the mind's eye: The history, techniques, and uses of visualization*. New York: Random House.

Satir, V. (1972). *Peoplemaking*. Palo Alto, CA: Science and Behavior Books Inc.

Simon, S. (1988). Six conditions for nurturing self-esteem. Paper presented at the American School of Counselors Association Convention, Brekenridge, CO.

Sperry, R. (1961). Cerebral organization and behaviour: The split brain behaves in many respects like two separate brains, providing new research possibilities. *Science* 133(3466), 1749-1757.

Sperry, R. (1980). Mind-brain interaction: Mentalism yes; dualism, no. *Neuroscience*, 5(2), 195-206.

Steele, W. (2003). Helping traumatized children. In S. Dugger & L. Carlson (Eds.), *Social Work and Mass Violence*. New York: Allyn & Bacon.

Steele, W. (2009). Drawing: An evidence-based intervention for trauma victims. *Reclaiming Youth*, 18(1), 20-23.

Steele, B. Malchiodi, C. (2012). *Trauma-informed practices with children and adolescents*. New York: Routledge.

Steele, W. & Raider, M. (2009). Structured sensory intervention for traumatized children, adolescents and parents (SITCAP): Evidence based interventions to alleviate trauma. New York: The Edwin Mellen Press.

Straussner, S. & Phillips, N. (2003). *Understanding Mass Violence: A Social Work Perspective*. Boston: Allyn & Bacon

Stuart, C. (2009). *Foundations of child and youth care*. Dubuque, IA: Kendall Hunt Publishing Company.

Sutton-Smith, B. (1971). Play, games, and controls. In J. Scott (Ed.), *Social Control*. Chicago: University of Chicago Press.

Tuckman, B. (1965). Stages of small group development. *Group Organization and Management*, 2(4), 419-427.

van der Kolk, B. (1994). The body keeps score. *Harvard Review of Psychiatry*, 1(5), 253-265.

van der Kolk, B., McFarlane, A., & Weisaeth, L. (1996). *Trauma stress: The effects of overwhelming experience on mind, body, and society*. New York: Guilford Press.

Warren, B. (2008). Drama: Using the imagination as a stepping stone for personal growth. In B. Warren (Ed.), *Using the creative arts in therapy*. New York: Routledge.

Warren, B. (2008). *Using the creative arts in therapy and healthcare: A practical introduction*. New York: Routledge.

Warren, B. & Coaten, R. (2008). Dance: Developing self-image and self-expression through movement. In B. Warren (Ed.), *Using the creative arts in therapy*. New York: Routledge.

Wallerstein, J. (1991). Is divorce a major trauma? *Journal of the American Academy of Child and Adolescent Psychiatry*, 30(3), 349-360.

Way, B. (1967). *Development through drama.* London: Prometheus Books.

Wright, S. (2003). *The arts, young children, and learning*. Boston, MA: Allyn and Bacon.

Yalom, I. (2005). *The theory and practice of group psychotherapy*. New York: Basic Books.

ABOUT

About the Author

Michael Burns has been practicing the discipline of child and youth care for 40 years. He has written six books and several articles in the field and has taught for over 30 years with 5 different colleges across Canada. Michael received his Child Care Worker advanced diploma from St. Clair College in Windsor, Ontario, his B.A. in Sociology from the University of Windsor, Windsor, Ontario, and his M.A. in Adult Education from St. Francis Xavier University, Antigonish, Nova Scotia. Michael is certified in child custody and access mediation and a certified trauma assessment specialist and clinician. He was awarded the Alumni of Distinction Award by his alma mater St. Clair College in 2006.

About the Editor

Dennis E. McDermott, has over 40 years experience in the CYC field, as a front-line child and youth worker (CYW) and college CYW program faculty (George Brown College, Toronto; St. Lawrence College, Kingston). In 1998 he became the first full-time Executive Director of a professional CYC association in North America, the Ontario Association of Child and Youth Counsellors (OACYC). Besides his diploma in Child Care Work from the Ontario Ministry of Health, Dennis has a BA in psychology and sociology (University of Toronto), and a Masters of Education degree in curriculum design (Queen's University, Kingston). He is a Certified CYC with the OACYC and was recently made an Honorary Lifetime Member in recognition of his 38 years as a member, and his 13 years as an executive of the Canadian Council of Child and Youth Care Associations.

About the Graphic Artist

Karin-Ann Bosma is a graphic designer, painter, illustrator, and mixed-media artist. She received her Bachelor of Fine Arts at the University of Alberta, and an Advanced Diploma in Graphic Design from St. Lawrence College in Kingston, Ontario. Karin currently designs, exhibits her art, and teaches classes for kids at the artist-run centre, VASA (Visual Arts Studio Association) in St. Albert, Alberta. She invites anyone and everyone to view examples of her other work at www.kabosma.com.

About the Design Artist

Danielle Adams is a graphic designer, illustrator, and artist. Danielle received her Advanced Diploma in Graphic Design from St. Lawrence College in Kingston, Ontario. Since graduating Danielle has worked as a freelance designer as well as an in-house designer for marketing firms. Her clientele includes a diverse array of businesses and organizations, both large and small. She enjoys the creative challenge, working directly with her clients, and pushing herself to produce the best work possible. Danielle is a member of the Association of Registered Graphic Designers of Ontario. Danielle encourages anyone to contact her at danielleadams.design@gmail.com for future project partnerships.

About the Cover Designer

Matt Garton is a graphic designer and animator. He studied Fine Art photography at Drew University in New Jersey and received his MFA in Design and Technology from Parsons The New School for Design in NYC where he specialized in Motion Graphics and Interaction Design. He has worked in a variety of environments from small advertising shops to large, national broadcast networks designing promos, opening title sequences and special effects. A collection of his motion graphics work can be viewed at www.mgfive.com.

OTHER PUBLICATIONS

Healing Spaces:
The Therapeutic Milieu in Child and Youth Work

This new text in the field of child and youth care uses the foundational theories of the field – milieu therapy and activity-based programming – and constructs a new perspective on child and youth work that addresses the expanding needs of troubled children in the new millennium. Theory and practice are interwoven to create a paradigm that students, educators, and front-line workers will find practical and efficient. Over 45 exercises invite the reader to become personally involved in the learning experience and 90 therapeutic activities create opportunities to immediately put theory into practice on the job or in the field placement practicum. Healing Spaces will ground you back into that place where it all happens – the physical, emotional, social, cultural, and ideological milieu. **Copyright 2006**

The Self in Child and Youth Care: A Celebration

This text is a self-directed learning manual for students and junior practitioners in the field of child and youth care. The text addresses the importance of the Self in the field and provides opportunities to its readers to integrate this knowledge into their practice of child and youth care. The Self is presented in a journal format and provides students with a variety of learning opportunities to further develop their awareness and effectiveness in the intrapersonal and interpersonal skills required of professionals working with children, youth, and young adults. **Copyright 2012**

Into the Dark Forest: Therapeutic Storytelling

Into the Dark Forest is a therapeutic storytelling text that presents a unique method of using relaxation and mindfulness, in combination with specially adapted versions of ancient myths and folk tales, to assist children and youth experiencing a wide variety of social, psychological, and emotional problems. These stories, when read to children using the techniques outlined, can produce powerful changes in the lives of their listeners. This storybook will make an excellent addition to any CYC library. **Copyright 1999, 2008, 2012**

ORDER ONLINE: WWW.CHILDCAREPRESS.NET